Hirsch and Ferguson share a great blend of theory and practice that will help you reenvision the way you do church. This is a must-read if you want to transition your church into the future.

—Craig Groeschel, Lead Pastor, Life Church

Alan and Dave give me hope that the church can be better in the West. Read and believe their timely words. We don't have to settle for business as usual.

—Darrin Patrick, Pastor, The Journey;
author of *For the City* and *Church Planter*

While pointing to a need for a new paradigm, Hirsch and Ferguson give a needed framework for getting from where we are to where we are heading.

—Dave Travis, Managing Director,
Leadership Network

I couldn't put this book down. A spot-on approach for the mega-churches and church-growth churches of the last decades to reframe ourselves as high-impact, exponentially reproducing missional movements.

—Mike Slaughter, Ginghamsburg Church;
author of *Change the World*

I truly believe God could use this work to usher in a whole new paradigm for pastors and ministry leaders across America. Every church leadership team in the country should be reading this together right now.

—Shawn Lovejoy, Lead Pastor,
Mountain Lake Church

With careful analysis, thoughtful theory, and real-life examples, this book paints what it looks like when pastors and leaders realize that expanding the kingdom is far more important than building a bigger church.

—Larry Osborne, author;
Pastor, North Coast Church

On the Verge not only connects you to the possibilities but gives you practitioner-based principles and stories to help you live and lead in God's gospel wave for the future.

—Hugh Halter, author of *The Tangible Kingdom*, *TK Primer*, *AND*, and *Sacrilege*

This book does more than provide solutions; it gives hope that the church's best days are yet to come.

—Greg Surratt, Lead Pastor, Seacoast Church

This book won't just make you think. It'll make you rethink the way you lead, the way you dream, and the way you do church.

—Mark Batterson, Lead Pastor,
National Community Church

This book is a challenge to established churches to follow Jesus into the real mission fields all around us rather than expect the people to come to us. My hope for the future has been elevated.

—Neil Cole, founder of Church Multiplication Associates
and author of several books

If you're ready to move your church beyond conceptual conversation toward real-world practice, then *On the Verge* is the next book you should read.

—Rob Wegner, Pastor of Life Mission,
Granger Community Church

On the Verge gives principles that will help churches of all sizes understand the missional conversation and move toward a missional understanding of who we are as the people of God. You must read it often.

—Cam Roxburgh, National Director, Forge Missional Training
Network in Canada; Pastor, Southside Community Church

A fantastic book showing different models and expressions of what "missional" looks like. I loved the variety of expressions.

—Bob Roberts Jr., author of *Transformation*
and *The Multiplying Church*

Hirsch and Ferguson point the way toward an exquisitely hopeful future for the church. They call upon it, in all of its various expressions, to rekindle and release its essential missional DNA. Brilliant.

—Linda Bergquist, church planting strategist
and coauthor of *Church Turned Inside Out*

This is not a call to new and quick fixes; it is an invitation to reflect and work hard, to question, to be open to emerging structures, and to do all of this with a prayerful confidence in the moving of the Lord. I highly recommend it.

—Dr. Kurt Fredrickson, Director of the Doctor of
Ministry Program, Fuller Theological Seminary

This is a must-read. Alan and Dave have masterfully described the path to multiplication by revealing what it means to see an orchard in every seed. This is the "both/and" approach that is desperately needed in the church.

—Tammy Dunahoo, VP Nat'l Church/General Supervisor,
The Foursquare Church

On the Verge is an outstanding resource packed full of lessons for those serious about engaging in this exciting yet challenging adventure. I highly recommend it!

—Mark Conner, CityLife Church, Australia

This book is a gift to the church and a must-read for every leader. It calls every church and Christ-follower to join God in his mission, and gives a framework and tools we all can use to start the journey.

—Egil Elling, Lead Pastor, IMI Kirken, Norway

With this book, inspiration and encouragement are given for all existing and future churches in Europe.

—ND Strupler,
ICF Movement—Church Planting for Europe

Other Books in the Exponential Series

EXPONENTIAL
series

on the verge

a journey into the apostolic future of the church

Alan Hirsch and Dave Ferguson

ZONDERVAN®   Leadership✳Network
Innovation Series

ZONDERVAN.com/
AUTHORTRACKER
follow your favorite authors

ZONDERVAN

On the Verge
Copyright © 2011 by Alan N. Hirsch and David W. Ferguson

This title is also available as a Zondervan ebook. Visit www.zondervan.com/ebooks.

This title is also available in a Zondervan audio edition. Visit www.zondervan.fm.

Requests for information should be addressed to:
Zondervan, *Grand Rapids, Michigan 49530*

Library of Congress cataloging-in-publication data data is on file with the Library of Congress.

ISBN 978-0-310-33100-1

Cover design: David Stevenson
Cover photography: Getty Images / Gary S Chapman
Interior design: Sherri L. Hoffman

Printed in the United States of America

11 12 13 14 15 /DCI/ 23 22 21 20 19 18 17 16 15 14 13 12 11 10 9 8 7 6 5 4 3 2 1

To my comrades in Forge Missional Training Network,
especially the new networks in the USA and in Canada.
It's my joy to be identified with you.

To all the fantastic churches involved in Future Travelers.
I believe you will all get to shape the future
of Western Christianity through your actions now.
—Alan

To Jon:
We shared a trundle bed growing up
and were roommates in college.
We were coworkers in the birth of a church
and the launch of a movement.
All along the way, you have been
my partner, my friend, and my brother.
Thanks.
I love you.
—Dave

Contents

Part 2—Shift

Part 3—Innovate

Part 4—Move

Foreword by Mike Breen

I love watching sports news on TV. And the kinds of sports programs I love the most are the ones with a dual anchor. The two voices provide me with interest, humor, and the right kind of depth that I am looking for in my daily sports fix. Having two voices in Dave and Alan's book has a similar effect. As you consider the issues of developing a "Verge" church, you hear with great clarity how both the attractional and the missional are needed in equal measure. If we are to build strong centers of mission-churches that resource networks of missional congregations and communities, we need the strongest attractional forces and the most vibrant missional impulses to be present.

As you read through the text of this serious and yet surprisingly readable study, I know you will be struck by the depth of what is offered. Science tells us that our depth perception comes through our binocular vision. The binocular vision of this book provides a perspective that I've not seen anywhere else.

As we move farther into the twenty-first century, the church will need to engage with the necessity of recalibrating our expectations of church. If we can maximize the potential of the twentieth-century church that found its final flower in the megachurch and multisite movements, we will offer a great service to the church of the new millennium. This will be achieved as the church shapes itself to respond to the missional impulse. Attractional churches that become missional begin to look like movements. If we can capture the heart and vitality of the reborn global missional impetus, we will see high-impact congregations transforming their wider communities.

A good friend of mine, Professor Eddie Gibbs, has said that the church in the twentieth century had achieved great things, but one of its sad legacies was the growing schism between missiology and ecclesiology. In his opinion, this led to a missionless church and a churchless mission. What Alan and Dave are offering is the possibility that the twenty-first century might be quite different: by reconnecting the forces of attraction and mission, we see something that is greater than the sum of its two parts. We see a church that is much more like the one Jesus intended. He was the most attractive man who ever walked the planet, and his life was a constant expression of God's mission to the world. His church should therefore be the visible manifestation of his life.

I would encourage you to read this book more than once. My expectation is that you will find that the two voices, like the warp and woof in any good fabric, merge into a single entity. The Lord's voice, we are told, is a voice of many waters. As you read this book, I'm sure you will find that the voices of these two great leaders become one and you hear the voice of Jesus inviting you to join his mission and love the church he is building.

Foreword by Reggie McNeal

We are living in a time when God appears to be changing the conversation he is having with the church. The dialogue revolves around the church's self-understanding of its mission in the world. *Missional church* is the buzzword for this conversation. While there are some nuances and various dialects of missional being spoken, widespread agreement exists around a core expression of what it means to be missional. The missional church engages the community with the intent of being a blessing. It looks for ways to connect with the world beyond the walls of church real estate and programming.

For many congregations, this external focus finds expression through service, not more "services." The congregation becomes the church not just *in* the community but *for* the community. Cross-domain collaboration with other sectors of the city enables the church to begin to address some of the challenging issues that threaten the welfare of the city. Typically, existing congregations are entering the missional movement across this threshold.

More recently, a new expression of missional church has captured the attention of those of us who are tracking the missional movement. It is the rise of missional communities. This development signals the arrival of a new life form in the taxonomy of church life. The emergence of missional communities is part of the Spirit's response to deploying the church in an increasingly postcongregational era. Translated into English, that means the church is figuring out a way to be present in populations that are not susceptible to becoming church people (people who align their spiritual journeys with the goals and rhythms of organized congregational church). Yet these people are spiritually inquisitive and open to relationship with Jesus and with other believers. It is just that their lifestyle or their employment or their personal interests don't intersect with the spiritual scripting of congregational church.

Missional communities take the church beyond engaging the community. These life forms are church *lived out* in the community. These missional communities are all the church that many people will ever know—or ever need. They are real church, not church lite or quasi church.

Establishing missional communities can become a key part of the missional strategy of existing congregations. In the book before you, Dave Ferguson and Alan Hirsch explore this possibility, specifically in the context of how mega-congregations can implement and fast-forward this approach to mission.

There can never be a timelier conversation than the one God wants to have! And there could never be two more qualified voices to further the dialogue. Dave and Alan embody the right approach to the discovery of new life: a sense of wonder, a spirit of curiosity, and a genuine stewardship that what they have uncovered not just belongs to them but also has been entrusted to them to be shared with others.

I am thankful they have invited you and me into the conversation.

Acknowledgments

Special thanks to:

Pat Masek for just being Pat, a tireless advocate for all things apostolic. You are amazing!

Rob Wegner for giving us fantastic feedback and suggesting ways to improve the text. Can't wait to read your book.

Jon Ferguson, Carter Moss, and Sher Sheets for designing a great set of discussion questions and making this a more practical book as a result.

David Stevenson for lending us your creative genius. We hope people judge this book by its cover.

Mike Morrel, who aided in the editing and marketing of this text.

Todd Wilson and Exponential Network for building the stage upon which we stand and never wanting the mic.

Our good friends at Leadership Network: Greg Ligon, Stephanie Plagens, Mark Sweeney, Dave Travis, and Bob Buford. Thank you for your partnership.

The great people at Zondervan: Chris Fann, Ryan Pazdur, Brian Phipps, and Paul Engle.

Chad Harrington for doing the research into the Future Travelers churches.

(Dave) My wife and best friend, Sue, for encouraging me, loving me, and working with me on this book. I love you.

Introduction

It is with a deep sense of privilege, mixed with an urgent and deep-rooted sense of obligation to God and his church, that we offer *On the Verge* to you. We would even be bold enough to claim we feel called to write this book. But we do so in fear and trembling, because we also recognize it is largely a visionary book that points to a possible future that is only beginning to be worked out as we speak.

Unfortunately, but for reasons that we hope will become clearer, there aren't many mature expressions of apostolic movements in the West, and yet it is largely to the Western church that we wish to speak. The task of this book is nothing less than to call the church to recover her most ancient, her most potent, and also her most beautiful form, that of the apostolic movement.

Both of us sense something immense happening in our day. Like a phoenix arising from the dying embers of Christendom, something essentially new and yet as ancient as the faith itself is emerging. It is the birth of apostolic movements again in the West. This, we believe, is a sign of great hope, and this book is written to help birth the paradigm shift, to compellingly describe it, and then to help churches practically implement it. We do this on the assumption that if the church fails to make the shift to apostolic movements again, Christian influence in Western culture will continue to fade, and church attendance will remain in its current trajectory of decline. All we can say in writing this book is, *not on our shift!* Not if we can help it.

We're honored to have this book set the agenda for Exponential 2011: On the Verge, the conference put on by the Exponential Network, arguably the largest gathering of church planters in the world. We believe that church planters and grassroots missionaries have always represented the productive future of the church, and we're honored to serve them in whatever way we can. Hence, a lot of our work goes toward their cause. However, this work has a much broader focus. It is to *all* expressions of church, but especially those that have been operating in the contemporary church-growth paradigm, undoubtedly the most successful and dominant ecclesial paradigm from the last forty years. Practitioners of all contemporary forms of church (missional church and church planting included) will find that *On the Verge* is very much written with them in mind.

Why We Wrote This Book

The clue to how and why this book was written lies in the people who wrote it and in how God has shaped us and our callings.

I (Alan) come to this book as an Australian who believes he is called to North America on the assumption that the future of the church in the West is somehow bound up with what happens in and through the church in this context. As distasteful as this might appear to non-American readers, we are all forced to recognize that the church in every Western context is in serious decline. If the answer was going to come from Europe (or Australia and New Zealand, for that matter), it would have done so by now, and yet biblical Christianity in these contexts continues to be increasingly marginalized, and in some places is nearing complete extinction. Paradoxically, we seem to be inhabiting a pivotal age — a time in which decisions and directions take on a strategic significance. What happens in the U.S. context, in *this* time, will in many ways determine the shape and the viability of Christianity in both the West and beyond.

My own sense of calling is to somehow call the church to recover her original — and originative — apostolic ways and to become a high-impact Jesus movement again in the West. I don't have a grandiose sense of my role in this, simply that I must play it out to the best of my ability and get out of the way. In order to do this, I have come to believe, we simply have to activate what is clearly one of the most significant church movements in the last fifty years — the megachurch in its various forms — and allow them to help negotiate a way into a new future. It won't be the only form of apostolic movement that will emerge, but it will be a very significant one. And I have little doubt many of the people and churches I'm working with in this (particularly the Future Travelers cohort and Exponential Network) are going to map a way forward for others to follow. I come to this task as a person deeply committed to grassroots, incarnational mission, and I must serve what is now called this Verge movement in whatever way I can, offering whatever insights and resources I might have gained along the way. *On the Verge* is an integrative attempt at such an offering.

Readers familiar with my work thus far will find that while there is new material added here, *On the Verge* is really a serious attempt to process and apply the Apostolic Genius paradigm, developed in *The Forgotten Ways*, to existing (largely evangelical and evangelistic) churches, as well as to other existing church systems. So while the core ideas are consistent with what I have laid out in my previous work, there is a radical reframing of these to be able to inform and engage a healthy megachurch movement. There is a lot of change management and systems processing going on here, and this is what I bring to the table.

I (Dave), on the other hand, am a church planter turned megachurch pastor with a passionate conviction that the strategy Jesus describes for accomplishing his mission is a movement of reproducing churches of all kinds. The church I lead, Community Christian Church *(www.communitychristian.org)*, is a reproducing missional community that has always dreamed, worked, and prayed to be a catalyst for a movement of reproducing churches. To that end, Community has championed reproduction at all levels (Christ followers, leaders, artists, groups, teams, sites, churches, and networks), with a dream of two hundred locations in Chicagoland. Community has also given birth to NewThing *(www.newthing.org)*, an international movement of reproducing churches that is doubling its number of churches and networks every year. My brother Jon Ferguson and I tell the story of movement making and give practical how-tos in *Exponential: How You and Your Friends Can Start a Missional Church Movement*. It is also my pleasure to serve as the president of the Exponential Conference and chairman of the board of the Exponential Network. Why tell you all this? I list this as a resume not to impress but to show you how, on a day-to-day basis, I'm trading my life to catalyze a movement of reproducing churches.

Despite our passion for movement and the perceived success of both Community and NewThing, there was within me and my team at one point a growing discontent. While we continued to reproduce sites and churches locally, nationally, and globally, it was friends like Neil Cole and exposure to Alan's teaching in *The Forgotten Ways* that helped us see there was something missing in our understanding of movement. We understood and were putting into practice the apostolic mission of reproductive church planting, but we were not mobilizing all of God's people into every sphere of life. We had too many people supporting our missional movement with prayer and finances, but not with their 24/7, everyday lives. We had become skilled at reproducing *macro* (sites and churches), and now we needed to become equally proficient in reproducing *micro* (mobilizing every person for mission in their context).

It was in conversations with other pastors of large multisite churches in Future Travelers that I discovered we were not alone. As I talked with these leaders, whose churches make up the list of the most innovative, fastest-growing, and largest churches in America, I found they were on a very similar journey. And if God had us all on this journey, our hunch was that he had many of you on this journey too.

How We Wrote This Book

Alan comes to the task as a missional strategist and apostolic theologian, offering systemic and architectural perspectives. Dave approaches the task as an apostolic practitioner, always asking these questions: How do we do this in real life? How can a church really make this happen?

As in all attempts at harmony, singular voices in their own right work to create something greater than the sum of their parts. We've penned this book similarly: instead of writing in one voice, we've kept our own voices, writing from our own perspectives, such as they are.

Alan's style is more technical and deals more with ideas as they relate to practice, while Dave brings the leader's driving need to align the systems and get them moving. Alan is therefore more systemic, objective, and design-focused, while Dave is more motivational, pragmatic, and implementation-focused. And although we have come to our conclusions via very different histories, approaches, and perspectives, we speak with the same awareness and from within the same paradigm. With this in mind, we've written the main section of the book as a dialogue — each chapter as a proposal of sorts with an accompanying response. When one of us writes a chapter, the other responds, and so on.

We have divided the material according to our relative strengths and interests, and we've each written chapters and sections, with the other responding. The book is broken into four main sections after the first chapter:

Part 1: "Imagine" (written by Alan, with Dave responding)
Part 2: "Shift" (written by Alan, with Dave responding)
Part 3: "Innovate" (written by Dave, with Alan responding)
Part 4: "Move" (written by Dave, with Alan responding)

Given our approach and our relative strengths, Alan's sections are packed with ideas and concepts derived from missional thinking and approaches. Dave's are intensely practical, derived as they are from his leadership of a budding movement based in Chicago. For those who are pragmatically inclined, we encourage you to slow down and really take in what is being laid out in the more theoretical foundations. For theorists, we suggest that you really attend to how it is being worked out in practice. It is vital that we retain the integrity of a true biblical knowledge that is based on the outworking of ideas in practice.

Also popping up throughout the text will be ideas, slogans, and the stories of the various churches trying to implement what we call Verge church thinking. We hope this approach works for you.

One final thing should be said before we launch into the book proper. With all that will be said about theology, sociology, organizational theory, leadership studies, and so on, we don't want to give the impression that reigniting apostolic movements can be simply a work of human endeavor. It must be, and is, a work of the Spirit of God. Certainly, we must do our part, but in the end the church exists by the grace, presence, and power of God himself, and to him we must constantly turn if we are going to be the kind of people he wants us to be. Forgive us if we ever give you the impression to the contrary. We prayerfully submit this work to you, and to the Holy Spirit, that he might enliven it in your hearts and in the life of your community.

We are poised at a precipice. Women and men with hungry hearts, wide-open imaginations, and hands ready to work will find much to work with in these pages. In cooperation with the sending Father, sent Son, and commissioning Holy Spirit, we join our prayer to yours: that every member contains within them a church, and every church contains within her a movement. We are standing at a pivot point of history. We are on the verge.

Chapter 1

On the Verge of the Future

ALAN AND DAVE

The dogmas of the quiet past are inadequate to the stormy present. The occasion is piled high with difficulty, and we must rise with the occasion. As our case is new, so we must think anew and act anew.

— ABRAHAM LINCOLN,
PRESIDENT OF THE UNITED STATES

In times of drastic change, it is the learners who inherit the future. The learned find themselves well equipped to live in a world that no longer exists. — ERIC HOFFER

Yet the truly great companies of the 21st century will change within the context of their core ideologies while also adhering to a few timeless fundamentals. — JIM COLLINS

The fact that this book is the defining document of the Exponential 2011: On the Verge conference, the largest gathering of church planters and pioneering church practitioners in the Western world, is very significant because for the first time, the frontier idea of missional movements as it relates to the multisite and church-planting movement is being main-staged. But when one considers that this conference is actually a fusion with Verge (one of the new, highly energetic, missionally oriented gatherings in North America),[1] it further demonstrates that something momentous is happening in our day.

But this isn't about big-staged events and theoretical writing: this book represents an effort by Alan and Dave to articulate a dynamic learning journey called Future Travelers. Future Travelers is a two-year learning cohort initially composed of twelve megachurches (representing more than eighty thousand people) committed to seriously factoring missional movements into their current equation of church. For many of these churches, this journey is not just tinkering on the side; it involves a major commitment to somehow reframe their relative churches as high-impact, exponentially reproducing, missional *movements*. In many ways, these pioneering churches represent the widespread interest, in evangelical church circles, in becoming more genuinely *missional* in approach. Because of these reasons, Future Travelers will provide a window into the future of the church in the West. In many ways, we will be weaving this book around the stories, experiments, learnings, and best practices of the innovative, frontline churches in this forum.

We feel very excited about what God is doing in the church at this time. And while we're fully aware the movement is in the early stages of the life cycle, we believe there's a certain inevitability about what is happening. According to the sociology of ideas and theory of tipping points, all that is needed for an idea to become an inevitable reality within any given population (in our case, American evangelicalism) is for significant adoption by the first 16 percent of that population.[2] This is because the first to adopt represent the innovators and early adopters and therefore represent the progressive, future-oriented, and creative side in that population sample. We believe there is now a

Introducing the Future Travelers

We will be telling the stories of some of the following churches throughout the text and have included profiles of each church in the appendix of the book. Each church profile contains demographic information about the church, their story, as well as some of the wins and challenges they have faced.

- The Austin Stone Church — Austin, Texas
- Community Christian Church — Chicago, Illinois
- Granger Community Church — Granger, Indiana
- The Journey — St. Louis, Missouri
- Kensington Community Church — Detroit, Michigan
- Mosaic Church — Little Rock, Arkansas
- Mountain Lake — Cumming, Georgia
- RiverTree Christian Church — Massillon, Ohio
- Rock Harbor Church — Costa Mesa, California
- Seacoast Church — Charleston, South Carolina
- Soma Communities — Seattle-Tacoma, Washington
- West Ridge Church — Dallas, Georgia

growing momentum, and if we haven't already passed the tipping point, it will happen sometime soon. We are bold enough to say that adoption by the more vigorous and authentic sectors of evangelical Christianity is just a matter of time. And while, at the time of writing, we acknowledge there are few mature expressions of apostolic movements in America, the paradigm of missional church is receiving a growing acceptance by our best leaders and most progressive thinkers.

This is why we call this book *On the Verge* and the churches are described as "Verge churches." There will be times when we use the more technical and somewhat descriptive phrase "apostolic movements" to describe what we are on the verge of seeing here in the West. Whatever terminology we might employ, we do believe we're on the threshold of something that has profound significance for the future of Western, and therefore global, Christianity. What were once conflicting approaches to church (such as incarnational *or* attractional) are beginning to seriously interact. Each informs the other, and it's only now becoming clear what is emerging. Because of this intermingling of diverse and energetic idea-spaces — missional theology, new church practices, glocal cultural shifts, and breakthrough technologies — a new paradigm is emerging. Our idea or conception of church is being changed as we speak. This doesn't happen very often in the life of the church (see table on pp. 34–38), but when it does, it fundamentally alters the nature of the game.

And because it's the missional God (initiator of the *Missio Dei*) who's most invested in the church becoming missional, we have cause for great hope. And because it's the Holy Spirit who moves and shapes the church, equipping us to fulfill our purposes as God's people, this is not simply something ideological; in fact, it goes to the heartbeat and the very purposes of God's people in the world. In other words, we are on the verge of something very significant in the life of the church in the West. This book is dedicated to the articulation, the development, and hopefully the eventual triumph of what God is doing in and through his church.

Catalysts for Ecclesiological Shift

Cultural Shifts

The cultural shifting we speak of relates not so much to the overhyped rise of postmodernism alone but rather to the emergence of various large-scale cultural forces in the twenty-first century: globalization, climate change, technological breakthroughs, international terrorism, geopolitical shifts, economic crises, the digitalization of information, social networks, the rise of bottom-up people-movements, the rise of new religious movements, even the New Atheism, and others. These all conspire together to further accelerate the marginalization of the church as we know it, forcing us to rethink our previously privileged relationship to broader culture around us.

The logic of Western civilization is the increasing secularization, or at least increasing de-churching, of society as ushered in by the French Revolution. This in effect means the Europeanization of Western culture. While there are factors in American culture that work against the radical secularization of culture, the encroachment of European-style de-churching is clearly evident in the cities and population centers of the northeastern United States (for example, New York, Washington, D.C., Boston) as well as the northwest (for example, San Francisco, Portland, Seattle). However one might conceive it, there is no doubting that Christianity, as a vital religious force, is on the wane in every Western context. Many in the U.S. are just beginning to feel this, but thankfully many are also beginning to respond. *On the Verge* is one such response.

Multicultural Shifts

One of the biggest cultural shifts of our time is the increasingly multicultural nature of the West. The brute fact is that most of the evangelical church leaders who will read this book will be white, suburban, and middle-class, and the equally stark reality is that within decades, Anglo-Saxon Americans will be in the minority in the U.S.—yet our churches don't seem to be responding to this reality. In fact, the old adage that the most segregated hour in America is on Sunday mornings still holds truth. Not only is multiculturalism a missional challenge, but it's also a challenge to our ecclesiology, the doctrine of the church as Jesus designed it to be. It's going to take a lot of thinking, loving, and reaching out to correct this imbalance in the people of God.[3]

Engaging the 60:40—The Blue and Red Oceans

The Future Travelers conversation was catalyzed, in part, by the probing of questions raised by the changing role and appeal of the church in Western society. Until recent years, the church—especially in the Christendom period—retained a very significant cultural connection with the prevailing society around it. In other words, most people were within the cultural orbit of the church and open to being influenced by the ideas that energized the church. However, this has definitely begun to shift in the last fifty years.

It is our opinion, and that of the Future Travelers group, that the prevailing, contemporary church-growth approach to church will have significant cultural appeal—marketability, if you will—to about 40 percent of the American population. (This is informed opinion, anecdotal in nature because to date there is no hard research on this.)

This is *not* attendance; we know that attendance in these forms of churches is far less than that. This means that the prevailing models of evangelistic churches could likely max out at around 40 percent of the population, perhaps 50 percent at the very best.[4] However we cut it, it leaves us with two major problems.

Strategic Problem

The first one is a strategic problem. Most of our churches believe and act as if modeling on (and perfecting) the successful contemporary church approach will resolve their problems of mission. But even if they could all become successful megachurches, the vast majority of churches cannot and should not. The financial capital, managerial infrastructure, leadership ability, communication strategies, and amount of artistic talent are huge in megachurches—all making for a model that is not very reproducible.

So we have a vexing situation where probably 90 percent or more of evangelical churches in America (and other Western contexts) are aiming at becoming a model that not only is improbable for the vast majority but also (even if they could crack the codes) effectively would still just be competing with other churches for the same 40 percent.[5] This should concern us very deeply. Anyone with a sense of strategy should be immediately alert at this point.

Why? Because all our missional eggs are in one ecclesiological basket! We have no diversity of options—most of our current practices are simply variations of the same model. This is not to say it's wrong or not used by God, and so on. Please don't hear us wrong here. Clearly, God uses the contemporary church. It is simply to say it is not sufficient to the increasingly *missional* challenge now set before us.

It was psychologist Abraham Maslow who noted that when the only tool you have is a hammer, everything begins to look like a nail. The tool itself begins to define us and determine our approaches. However, if we are going to rise to the situation we face, we are going to need more tools.

More disturbing, perhaps, is that this dearth of options demonstrates a serious poverty of imagination in the way we think about the church and mission and indicates why we desperately need to innovate.

Missionary Problem

If the first problem is a strategic one highlighting the need for genuine ecclesiological innovation and a diversity of approaches, the second one is a very serious *missionary* problem taking us to the core purposes of the church Jesus built. This problem is perhaps the most important question facing us in relation to the long-term viability of Christianity in Western contexts. As Jesus' sent people, we have to ask ourselves, what about the possible 60 percent of people who for various reasons report significant alienation from precisely the contemporary church-growth model(s) we rely so heavily on? What will church be for these people? What is good news going to sound like for them? And how are they going to access the gospel of Jesus in ways that are culturally meaningful for them?

The reality is, if we expect more variations of the prevailing practices to reach into increasingly de-churched and unchurched populations, we are fooling ourselves. We're avoiding the missionary call of the church to take Christ's message to the people and nations.

In many ways, our situation is experienced in the broader world of business strategy and global markets. Leading strategists Chan Kim and Renée Mauborgne use the vivid metaphor of red and blue oceans to describe the situation.[6] The red oceans concept is used to describe all the industries in existence at any given point—the known market space. In the red oceans, industry boundaries are defined and accepted, and the competitive rules of the game are known. Here companies try to outperform their rivals to grab a greater share of product or service demand. As the market space gets crowded, prospects for profits and growth are reduced. Products become commodities or niche, and cutthroat competition turns the ocean bloody. Hence the term *red ocean*—the sharks battle it out with each other for survival.

Blue oceans, in contrast, denote all the industries not in existence today—the unknown market space, untainted by competition. In blue oceans, demand is created rather than fought over. There is ample opportunity for growth that is both profitable and rapid. In blue oceans, competition is irrelevant because the rules of the game are waiting to be set. There is no frenzied feeding, and so little competition. *Blue ocean* describes the wider, deeper potential of spiritual idea-space that is not yet explored.

Kim and Mauborgne suggest that the cornerstone of blue ocean strategy is value innovation—that is, the creation of innovative new markets to unlock new demand. According to the authors, organizations must learn how to create uncontested market space by reconstructing market boundaries, focusing on the big picture, reaching beyond existing demand, and getting the strategic sequence right.

To illustrate this point, Rob Wegner of Granger Community Church (GCC) recently told us that back in the early days of GCC (late eighties to midnineties), they were literally the only contemporary church in their community. Nobody was doing what they were doing in the region. It was unique; it was a breakthrough. They had created the buzz and set the tone. He says,

> Friends would tell friends, "You've got to check this out. This is not like any church you've *ever* seen." But nowadays there are a number of churches in this community doing contemporary church, and they serve with excellence. It is not unique anymore.... Before, we were the only church reaching the 40 percent; now we have a whole slew of churches in our community trying to reach that 40 percent. I'm excited about that. I even think our presence helped facilitate the growth of contemporary church in our community. But it's definitely a red ocean scenario.[7]

This is exactly the issue we face. We are all competing in the red waters of the 40 percent while the 60 percent remains largely untouched. It's time for some value innovation. Christian churches with a strong sense of missionary calling—while maintaining best practices in what they do—will also venture out to innovate new forms of church in the vast uncharted territories of the unchurched populations of our day. To do less is to fail in our missionary calling.

More of the Same?

It was Einstein who said that the problems of the world couldn't be resolved by the same kind of thinking that created them in the first place. And he's right, of course—we do well to take note! The popular application of this maxim comes to us in the form of what has become known as the definition of organizational insanity: trying to achieve significantly different results by doing the same thing over and over. In other words, what got us *here* won't get us *there* if "there" is missional movements in the West. Perhaps a more visual way of saying this is that we cannot dig a hole *over there* by digging *this* hole deeper—and yet that is what we seem to do most of the time.

The combination of strategic and missional problems creates more than enough anomalies to precipitate a major paradigm shift in the way we do and be church. But other reasons also have caused us to move toward more missional forms of church, namely that of apostolic movement.

The Technology of Movement

We should never doubt the power that technologies possess to seriously alter social patterns and fundamentally change the way we think and act. If futurist Rex Miller is right when he said the printing press ushered in the modern world and the Reformation/Protestant churches, and the radio ushered in the broadcast era that gave birth to the church-growth paradigm, then the digital revolution will also inevitably change the way we go about being God's people.[8] The digital era—with the internet, social media, smartphone accessibility, and so on—has the effect of democratizing knowledge and radically altering the way we think and act. The new disruptive technology is having a massive reciprocal effect on social patterns across the world. Books like *Here Comes Everybody, Linked, Wikinomics, The Wisdom of Crowds, Tribes, The Tipping Point, The Rise of the Chaordic Era, Outliers, Smart World*, and so on, are among countless others describing the profound, unalterable revolution that is literally redesigning the world we live in.[9]

And like it or not, technology—particularly information technology—*is* changing the church.[10] For one, it breaks the hold that singular, centralized institutions have had on power and knowledge. It also opens people to spiritual influence from diverse sources, rather than keeping them dependent on a priestly system to mediate information about God. The new digital democracy that technology ushers in is also realigning the way we organize ourselves. Things are getting more fluid, less centralized, more interpersonal. We celebrate this as an opportunity, because in many ways it puts us much closer to the radical, people-oriented movement of the New Testament church: the priesthood of all believers and the ordination of ordinary people.

The digital era, with the associated network thinking and acting, sets us up to experience movement again in a significant way. That doesn't happen often in the history of the church, as we shall see below. It's a huge opportunity to recalibrate back to our most primal and potent form: the apostolic movement.

Dethroning Constantine

Adopting a Verge church paradigm requires learning what it means to become a more fluid, adaptive, reproducible, viral people-movement. In other words, it means taking seriously the idea that the church Jesus built—and therefore what he intended—is meant to be more of a movement than a religious institution. The New Testament church is *movemental* to the core, and—following Jesus' prophetic critique of religious systems—it is inherently critical of highly institutionalized religion.

Christianity is designed to be a people's liberation movement, a social force, a viral idea passing from person to person through the medium of gospel and discipleship, creating gospel communities in its wake. And yet, by all accounts, most churches can be described as primarily institutional in form and nature. That is, they are conceived (by insiders and outsiders alike) as being made up of buildings, programming, creeds, rituals, denominational templates and formulas, symbols, clergy and religious professionals, and so on. Now, these things aren't necessarily wrong, but we must not confuse this with New Testament ecclesiology.

In other words, most of us mistake the forms, theology, and models of church for the church itself. We know *intellectually* that the church isn't a building but a people, but our language and actions betray what we really think. That's why we can talk about "going to church" or "getting married in the church" or "the Presbyterian church," and so on. We understand the word *church* in the context of its formal structures and institutions, rather than as dynamically located in the *people (laos)* of God. And while clearly God permits (and human societies need) structure and some level of institution, this is definitely not what the Bible means when it talks about *ecclesia*, which is the main biblical term and dynamic of *church*.

Actually, this institutionalization of our way of thinking and doing church stems mainly from the period when Christianity became the

official religion of the Roman Empire. Even though immediately prior
to the Edict of Milan, the church was developing forms, theology, ritual,
and structure, when Constantine co-opted Christianity, he fundamentally altered the way we saw and experienced ourselves as God's people.
What was largely an illegal, underground people-movement was now
given money, status, power, and legitimacy. Everything changed.

The previously subversive Jesus movement of the early church was
now given magnificent buildings at the epicenters of towns and cities,
was pressed by the emperor to standardize its theology and formulate
creeds and to develop a formalized clergy caste to guard and maintain the affairs of the church. The emperor Constantine became the
Pontifex Maximus, a title later given to the popes. The deal was that
the church became the religious and cultural center of the Roman
Empire—a pretty enticing bargain, but one that fundamentally
changed our ecclesiology. This was a radical shift, and we've never
escaped it. Constantine is still the emperor of our imaginations, of
the way we see and experience ourselves as church, seventeen centuries
later.

The Splinter in the Mind

The past 1700 years of church history following Constantine have
furthered the shift from more movemental forms to more institutional
ones. The challenge of our day is to recover the movement form again.
This has occurred in history, and when it has, it has almost always gone
viral and made a massive impact: the early church, the Celtic movement, the Waldensians, the Franciscans, Moravians, Wesleyan reviv-
als, early Pentecostalism, the Chinese underground church, the Indian
people-movements, Latin-American Christianity, to name but a few.

In order to understand these shifts and recover the more apostolic
forms of movement, we've adopted terminology that portrays the key
paradigm of each period. Here are some working definitions we will use:

- *Grassroots*: The church as a bottom-up movement; a phenomenon involving ordinary people, with very little structure or
involvement from official institutions.
- *Missional*: The church seeing itself as the primary means to
transfer God's redemptive message to the world.

- *Movemental*: The church as a more fluid structure; a social force traveling like a virus from one person to another, with leadership who lead from the front.
- *Structural*: The church as a movement at the beginning stages of cultural organization in order to give direction and focus. As the church gets a little more organized, it isn't necessarily rigid — the organization is more adaptive and functional at this stage.
- *Institutional*: The church as primarily existing in the forms, organization, liturgies, traditions, plant and resources, programs, clergy, and so on.
- *Hierarchical*: The church as a power system holding leadership and organizational structures together; where elements at lower levels are submissive to elements at higher levels.

So with these in mind, consider the following table.

Ecclesial Shifts and Paradigms

Ecclesial Shifts	Primary Paradigms	Description
New Testament church		
(AD 33–80)	Grassroots, missional, movemental	The NT church was a transformational, cross-cultural people-movement, initiated by and gathered around Jesus, engaging discipleship, worship, and mission in everyday contexts. All classes and peoples (including women and slaves) were incorporated. It was genuinely grassroots. Translocal dimensions were maintained primarily through the apostolic and prophetic ministries. Even though forms were beginning to emerge, the structure remained very fluid, contextual, organic, and adaptive.
Early church		
(AD 100–300)	Missional, movemental, grassroots, structural	As a persecuted movement, the early church retained much of the earlier ethos of the NT church and was never allowed to become an institution, but certainly (over time) thinking and practice began to define and shape the prevailing idea of *ecclesia* in an increasingly more structural manner. Persecution necessitated a more adaptive, minimalist, organic structure.

Ecclesial Shifts	Primary Paradigms	Description
Catholic Christendom church		
(AD 320– present)	Institutional, hierarchical	With the formal marriage of church and state, Christendom was born. Within decades, the movemental aspect was almost entirely ejected from the prevailing paradigm of church. From here on, it only expresses itself in protest and renewal movements within the rigid ecclesial uniformity of Catholicism. The genius of the Catholic institution would be to eventually stifle or co-opt protest and absorb the insights of renewal movement into its system without fundamentally changing the institution.
Reformational/Protestant Christendom churches		
(1600– Present)	Institutional, structural, hierarchical	Because the Reformation was basically a theological feud *within* the European church family (so to speak), the prevailing Christendom paradigm of church was never fundamentally challenged except by the so-called radical Reformers whose expressions of church were quickly marginalized, co-opted, or silenced. Even though the structures of the various Reformation churches were flattened and de-mocratized, they remained primarily hierarchical and institutional.
Historical renewal movements		
(sporadically dispersed throughout history)	Grassroots, movemental, structural	These have taken place through history, starting with early monastic movements through to charismatic renewal in late twentieth century. Basically all/most renewal movements involve a recovery of some elements of movements, such as the priesthood of all believers, the "kingdom of God" over "church," prophetic protest, church planting, mission on the fringes and among the poor, etc. (e.g., Celtic Christianity, Anabaptist variations, Moravians, early Methodism, early Pentecostalism, Third Wave). In most cases, they have also eventually absorbed into the mainstream. They have ushered in renewals in ecclesiology but failed to permanently dislodge the institutional paradigm.

continued...

Ecclesial Shifts	Primary Paradigms	Description
Contemporary church-growth churches		
(1970s– present)	Institutional, structural, hierarchical	Church growth was a movement that basically (re)organized the church around the evangelistic function. For so long the church had either forgotten this call or had outsourced evangelism to parachurches and other mission agencies. However, this paradigm basically accepted the institutional view of the church and added managerial, sociological, and marketing approaches to create the megachurch. As such, it remains highly institutional even as it reframes itself in a more contemporary manner. This is strange, because the initial founder, missiologist Donald McGavran, was a movement thinker, while later theorists (Win Arn, C. Peter Wagner) were more technical, managerial, sociological, and marketing people—which allowed the movement to lean into technocracy.
Missional-incarnational churches		
(mid-twentieth century– present)	Grassroots, missional, movemental	Arising in the middle to late twentieth century, the missional paradigm (which places mission as the organizing principle of church) begins to completely reframe ecclesiology around missiology. When missional ideas are informed by incarnational approaches, a distinctly grassroots perspective of the church is birthed. But in many cases these lack organization and structure and therefore are problematic to maintain over periods of time. Transformative movements do require a vision and translocal structure, which the grassroots movement resists. On the other hand, when missional ideas fail to embrace incarnational approach together with a movement ethos, it tends to become a rather boring technical theological discussion mainly in mainline Protestant Christianity, which is very institutional and lacks the theological funding and energy to be able to produce missional movement.

Ecclesial Shifts	Primary Paradigms	Description
Multisite megachurches		
(2000– present)	Structural, movemental	Essentially, this was the logical extension of the successful megachurch movement of the eighties and nineties that was birthed in the evangelistically driven church-growth movement. The idea of multisites was motivated largely by the desire to extend the megachurch's impact and maximize on resources through developing a regional approach to church. As such, it's a more institutional, somewhat inorganic and top-down attempt to reproduce churches. What it misses is the dynamic of bottom-up people-movements. But because multisite thinking involved the desire to reproduce churches, its key practitioners began to probe the missional math of multiplication. They are already committed to multiplication; the logic leads them to people-movements.
Reproducing churches, church-planting movements (CPMs)		
(1990–present)	Movemental, structural	Here is where the prevailing, more structural model of the multisites really begins to think and act *movementally*. Church planting becomes a major thrust, but it still tends to reproduce more institutional forms. Most church planting here is simply an attempt to reproduce the contemporary megachurch model. At this stage, it has yet to seriously engage incarnational-mission ideas. But the desire for exponential viral growth begs the question of reproducibility and what we call *movementum*. To become truly exponential, churches have to significantly de-professionalize the ministry, simplify ecclesiology, and activate the whole people of God.

continued...

Ecclesial Shifts	Primary Paradigms	Description
Apostolic movements/Verge churches		
(2000– present)	Movemental, missional, structural, grassroots	Verge churches are essentially reproducing churches that are now beginning to reframe church around the missional/apostolic function (not just evangelistic) and are beginning to restructure and organize toward exponential movement. Even grassroots dimensions are being factored into the equation as churches seek to empower all believers as agents of the King. Verge church thinks and acts like a translocal/regional movement. Micro and macro forms of church are employed in the process. The big difference between this and the missional-incarnational is that, true to its inclusive both/and approach, it's much more organized and includes hybrid forms of organization.

At the risk of oversimplifying what we have said above, we can say that the paradigm, or systems story, of the vast majority of churches in the West (contemporary and/or historical) has been primarily an institutional one. In Verge church thinking, we must recognize it's precisely this central paradigm that must be dislodged if we are going to become a viral gospel movement in our day. It is our belief that it's the overwhelming predominance of the institutional imagination—the Constantinian captivity of the church, so to speak—that is keeping us from becoming genuinely missional as well as exponential. We can picture it as in figures 1 and 2.

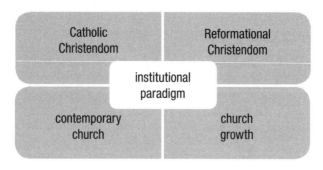

Figure 1

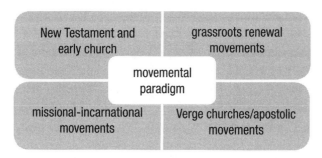

Figure 2

Verging the Church: Key Themes

The idea of pivotal design is where something that is invented or designed becomes the base design in all subsequent technologies. For instance, the airfoil designed by the Wright brothers is still the base design in all aircraft. The transistor is another example. Or even closer to the idea of movements, the Twelve-Step program; many different interpretations and applications, but the principles remain the same. All further developments build off the base one. We believe that Verge churches—or what we hope will become apostolic movements—might well provide us with one of the pivotal designs for the church in the twenty-first century and beyond.[11]

But in order to comprehend and apply the "new technology" of apostolic movements, we are going to have to do a lot of reframing our thinking and practice. Throughout the book, the reader will find we are moving from more distinctly conceptual material to that which is more concrete and practical. There is simply no way around having to do the conceptual spadework; if we wish to birth apostolic movements in our day, we cannot avoid the intellectual rigor of rethinking the paradigm, recalibrating the system, changing the metaphor, and reframing the story of church. But you will find that all the way through there are practical handles, tips, and checklists to facilitate application of what is being said.

You Gotta Move It, Move It

We insist that a genuinely apostolic paradigm of the church is by nature inclusive of all forms in service of its mission, whereas the more institutional paradigm is by nature exclusive, demanding high conformity. So we fully recognize, with the writers of *The Starfish and the Spider*, that all organizations are really hybrids of both centralized and decentralized forms of organization.[12] And while it's highly unlikely many of the prevailing forms of church in the West can become *pure* people-movements, we believe that the future viability and growth of the church requires that we have to move more and more toward embracing the forms we call apostolic movements.

We say this because (as we have seen) what has gotten us *here* will not get us *there*, but also because it's clear from church history that movements are our best and most effective expressions of *ecclesia*. Not only is it our most primal story — the New Testament church was clearly an apostolic movement — but also throughout history it appears we're at our very best when we have little or nothing of what we think constitutes the church institution. Looking at the early church, the Celtic movement, the Moravian movement, contemporary China, India, and so on, we are at our transformative best as decentralized movements, and we grow faster that way than we ever can with all the institutional accoutrements of church.

Multiplication Church Planting +

the Mission of All People Everywhere

= Apostolic Movement

The church Jesus designed is a movement and not a religious institution. If this isn't the case, then there's no way to understand why Jesus reserves his harshest criticisms *not* for the so-called sinners but rather for the religious people of his day. It also explains why he chose and empowered ordinary people and not the religious elite to take the gospel to the world. This isn't to say God doesn't like order or that there's no structure to movements; it is to say the original church structure is very unlike the kind of structures that emerged with the Christendom form of church.

We aren't saying God hasn't or doesn't use all expressions of church — clearly he does. We are not even saying that a certain level of institution is not actually necessary to maintain longevity; it is. What we are saying is that we can all do it a whole lot better, and with more theological integrity, by activating an apostolic imagination and by developing movemental forms of the church.

Discarding Either/Or, Embracing Both/And

We have shared this vision of Future Travelers and this book with our grassroots missional friends, and a common response has been, "It can't be done." We also have spent time with leaders of large established churches who shake their heads in pessimism. The truth is that both groups, being purists, are captive to the limits of their own acquired (somewhat prejudicial) thinking and are blinded to the possibilities of seeing the church become more. The problem is that for the vast majority of churches and Christians, this oppositional thinking has blocked our capacities to discern a way forward. It also implies that the only way forward for the established church is to close up shop and start again from the ground up. It is a counsel of despair for the established church and signals increasing marginalization from the mainstream for the missional movement as it now exists.

Part of the problem with this is because, to use business consultant Jim Collins' terms, they fail to embrace the genius of the *and*. Both groups are locked into the trap of either/or thinking. Seen from the perspective of either/or, these forms of church are irreconcilable, but reconceived from the perspective of the both/and, the supposed clash of imaginations begins to fade away. Collins rightly says that a truly visionary organization "embraces continuity *and* change, conservatism *and* progressiveness, stability *and* revolution, predictability *and* chaos, heritage *and* renewal, fundamentals *and* craziness. *And, and, and.*"[13]

In moving forward and engaging the issues we face, we have no doubt this must be the case.

I (Alan) admit that in my own early days as a church planter, leadership developer, and missional strategist for my denomination, I was much more inclined to this oppositional kind of thinking. The breakthrough happened for me in researching for *The Forgotten Ways*, when I came to the astonishing realization that every church, incarnational *and* attractional *and* everything in between, already has the full potential of Apostolic Genius resident in it, and all that is needed is for us to reactivate it.[14] This is a very powerful idea you should ponder for a while, because if it's true—and I am convinced it is—then it changes everything.

We'll spend time later on the process of reactivation, but we mention it here simply to suggest that every church, indeed every believer, has the full capacity for world transformation within, and when we can believe *that*, then we will begin to see the church very differently. But we have to be able to see it first. And, if we are willing, then we will find that the missional and the established forms are not mutually exclusive, because our core ecclesiology not only allows for but also champions both approaches.

But let us be clear: we believe church can be attractional and missional at the same time *only* if the organizational genetics, our core ideas, the paradigmatic brain at the center, legitimizes both impulses as important and justifiable expressions of what it means to contextualize the gospel in the Western world. It is this victory on the level of imagination — of our vision of the church as Jesus designed it to be — that makes a Verge church a real live possibility.

This isn't necessarily easy, however, because we are steeped in oppositional-type thinking and because the movement approach on which so much depends has been largely marginalized, is misunderstood, and is underdeveloped. Verge churches will be those that have somehow found the necessary intellectual freedom and imaginative space to be able to overcome the captivity to their own prevailing ideologies — and, in light of that, are willing to reframe their core paradigm from being a church to being a movement. One of the main ways to do this is to get over the impasse of either/or and imagine a church that embraces the both/and.

Mix and Match

Essentially, the new paradigm of apostolic movements is the "con-Vergence" of three distinct ways of thinking about church:

- *Church-growth theory*, which extends and maximizes traditional ecclesiology and organizes the church around the evangelistic function.
- *Exponential thinking*, as an application of the emerging science of idea-viruses and tipping points to ecclesiology. It has also stimulated church-planting efforts over the last decade or two.
- *Incarnational missiology*, which requires reorienting the entire

church around the primarily outward-oriented function of mission and recontextualizing the church into different subcultures.

We suggest a new paradigm (see fig. 3), and it will, we believe, define the thinking and practice of the church for the next few decades and present the church with its first real opportunity to reverse the long-term decline in every Western context. So when exponential/viral/networked thinking informs church-growth savvy, which in turn is being reframed around missional-incarnational theology, then history is in the making.

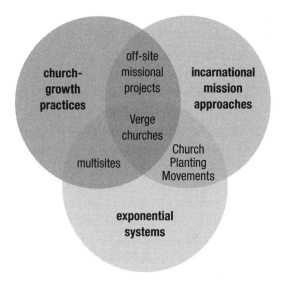

Figure 3

The reason why we feel so bullish about what is happening is because it brings together our very best thinking about mission with current best practices in church leadership and organization. The integration of the contemporary megachurch thinking with the more missional grassroots approach will result in better-resourced, better-led, savvy expressions of church, reframed by the deepest currents in the biblical story (missional-incarnational) and restructured around the world-changing organizational paradigm of exponential people-movements. What's not to celebrate?

Renovating Old Truths: Remembering the Forgotten Ways

This concept of renovating ancient truths is critical if what we are suggesting is to be understood as more than another church-growth fad. In *The Forgotten Ways*, I (Alan) suggest we can infer from the dynamics of exponential people-movements that all of God's people already have everything in them to be able to get the job done. I call this "dormant (or latent) potentials," and it fully explains why, for instance, the pre-communist Chinese church, a highly institutional form of church, can end up looking and acting just like the early church when all the institutional forms are removed because of external threat and persecution.

The only conclusion I could reach was that the full possibility of movement *was already there in the system*. All that was needed was something to activate it. Apostolic Genius, the name of the phenomenon which encodes apostolic movement in what I call mDNA, is latent in the church but is largely dormant because it's buried under the more institutional forms and blinded by the predominant mindset.

In the church Jesus built, conversion is commission or baptism is ordination, take your pick.

In the practice of contemplative prayer, we relax our well-practiced defenses and inner chatter to become alert to the God-who-is-already-there. We realize afresh that he has been there all along; it was we who were not aware. So too the solution to our situation is already embedded in the theological genetic codes of church.

The answer for the church lies in the deepest framework of our ecclesiology as Jesus designed it. We are not simply saying this as a little peppy inspirational thing; we are stating a deep truth that will help us avoid importing false and misleading ideas and methodologies into the church in order to motivate it. This is not magic but simply recognizes that God has invested his people with real potentials, due largely to the ever-present kingdom of God, the lordship of Jesus, the transforming power of the gospel, and the presence of the Holy Spirit in and among the people of God. We *are* the church of Jesus.

Furthermore, we can say, from the study of mass movements in general, that many of the same dynamics exist in all human movements. For instance, organic systems don't just serve Christian missional movements and disciple-making. Apprenticing people into a system or ideology is something all organizations can do. It's not magic; it's what living systems theorists call "distributed intelligence" and recognizes that in God's world there is inherent order and design and that systems tend to be self-organizing.

It's not as strange as it sounds at first. For instance, we can acknowledge that in every seed is the potential for a tree, and in every tree is the potential for a forest. But the potential is all contained in the initial seed. Thinking this way, we can say that in every seed there is a forest. Likewise, in every spark there is the full potential of the flame, and in every flame the potential of a massive inferno. But it's all there, in potential at least, in the tiny spark.

Apostolic Genius is a term that encompasses the six elements of mDNA, which we'll discuss later in the book. These six elements are:

1. Jesus is Lord
2. Disciple-making
3. Apostolic environment
4. Missional-incarnational impulse
5. Organic systems
6. *Communitas*

This mDNA changes everything, because it's not that we have to import some alien set of ideas into the church but rather that we must reactivate what is already there in potential. When we suggest we have to (re)activate Apostolic Genius at the very core of the church/organization, it means we're simply triggering what's already present. The approach taken in this book will therefore be to remember what we've tended to forget, and to forget some things we've tended to remember.

A Chaordic Approach to Change

The apostolic movement way of thinking should be embedded in the very heart of each church/organization; this in turn will inform innovative ethos and practices throughout the rest of the church/organization.

Dee Hock is right when he says, "Purpose and principle, clearly understood and articulated, and commonly shared, are the genetic code of any healthy organization. To the degree you hold purpose and principles in common among you, you can dispense with command and control. People will know how to behave in accordance with them, and they'll do it in thousands of unimaginable, creative ways. The organization will become a vital, living set of beliefs."[15]

He says elsewhere, "All organizations are merely conceptual embodiments of a very old, very basic idea—the idea of community. They can be no more or less than the sum of the beliefs of the people drawn to them; of their character, judgments, acts, and efforts. An organization's success has enormously more to do with clarity of a shared purpose, common principles and strength of belief in them than to assets, expertise, operating ability, or management competence, important as they may be."[16]

Hock calls this the "chaordic" principle: enough *order* at the center to give common identity and purpose, enough *chaos* to give permission to creativity and innovation. When you think of it, this is exactly how the original Jesus movement was organized, and we suggest that this is how we should strive to reframe our understanding of *ecclesia* as we move toward Verge church thinking.

It is critical to engage this process with the assumption that all lasting change needs to be systemic in nature. A system is a series of interrelated and interdependent parts. That means when one agent or part of the system is changed, the whole system is affected—for better or worse.

A Model for Apostolic Movement

Before you come to the end of this book, we want to clearly answer the very practical question, "How do I begin apostolic movement in my church?" This is what we will call "movementum."

Here is the process this book will take to get you to movementum:

Part 1: "Imagine." We will begin with the importance of missional imagination in helping us to rethink what we mean by *ecclesia*, and move on to imagining new possibilities. Imagination allows us to see the mission as Jesus sees it. The goal in this step is for each individual and the community to "see it."

Part 2: "Shift." This second section forms the paradigm-shifting heart of the book. Here we describe how churches can activate apostolic movement vision and philosophy at the heart of the church. We must reframe our basic concepts of church to understand the mission as Jesus understands it. The goal in this step is for each individual and the community to "get it."

Part 3: "Innovate." We then look into the dynamics of genuine innovation (as opposed to simple creativity), without which we are doomed to simply repeat what we already know. The church ought to do mission as Jesus does it. The goal in this step is for each individual and the community to "do it."

Part 4: "Move." In the final section, we explore what it takes to practically generate and maintain actual movement, or this movementum, throughout the church and become a Verge church. *Movementum* can be defined as the process of gaining missional momentum until we birth an apostolic movement, and movementum occurs when we are continuously taking our church through the preceding three stages: imagine, shift, and innovate.

The moves for an individual believer are the same as those of an entire community, as shown in figure 4.

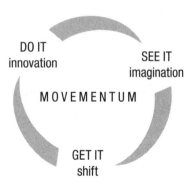

Figure 4

This isn't a change process you complete only once. This involves an ongoing cycle of renewal: to see (imagine) what Jesus wants you to see; to fully get (shift) and understand what he wants you to understand; and to obey (innovate) and do what he wants you to do. This is a constant process every church and every believer will go through over and over again with a relentless desire to see an apostolic *movement* and the mission of Jesus accomplished.

Michael Fullan, the Canadian guru on leadership and change, has observed that the two greatest failures of leaders are "indecisiveness in times of urgent need for action and dead certainty that they are right in times of complexity."[17] As we go about the task of moving to the Verge, we have to be willing to let go of prior certainties and go on a search for new, more sustainable ways of being God's people in our day. We need to feel a relentless urgency, for the time is upon us. Decisions we make now will determine the course of events. We do live on the verge of the future.

Now is that time; lean into it.

DISCUSSION QUESTIONS

Open

Would you describe yourself as driven by competition or by uncharted waters? One way to gauge this is to look at the kind of activities in which you are involved.

Explore

1. What was your gut response to this chapter? Overwhelmed, excited to continue, unsure, affirmed, convicted?

2. Looking at your current context, would you say you are attempting to reach the 40 percent or the 60 percent? How are you being relevant in the lives of those who would never set foot in a church?

3. How do the following verses support the North American church continually embarking into blue oceans? Traditionally, what arm of the local church uses these verses most?

   You will receive power when the Holy Spirit comes on you; and you will be my witnesses in Jerusalem, and in all Judea and Samaria, and to the ends of the earth.

   —Acts 1:8

   Jesus came to them and said, "All authority in heaven and on earth has been given to me."

   —Matthew 28:18

4. Take an honest look at the future of your church. Would you say your church is positioning itself to chart a course into a blue ocean or fighting to stay relevant in a red ocean? Where do you find yourself personally more drawn: red oceans or blue?

5. Within your congregation, who has the most relational potential with the 60 percent of your community who will not attend your church? How have you helped empower those men and women with the gospel?

6. We aren't suggesting that traditional or even attractional expressions of church close up shop, so how would you imagine a both missional and attractional expression be lived out in your congregation?

Move

Spend some time with your church leadership team evaluating figure 4 on page 47.

- Where does our church currently fall on this diagram?
- What are the roadblocks between where we are and being a Verge church?
- What are some steps we can take toward Verge church thinking?

Part 1

Imagine

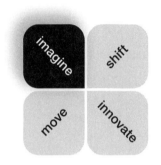

Chapter 2

The Silver Imagination

ALAN

You can't depend on your eyes when your imagination is out
of focus. — MARK TWAIN

He who rejects change is the architect of decay. The only
human institution which rejects progress is the cemetery.
— HAROLD WILSON

We are the people of the parenthesis—at the end of one era
but not quite at the beginning of the next one. Maps no longer
fit the new territories. In order to make sense of it all, we must
cultivate a vision.
— JEAN HOUSTON, PHILOSOPHER

Gordon McKenzie, in his creative book on organizations, *Orbiting the Giant Hairball: A Corporate Fool's Guide to Surviving with Grace*, describes a story from his childhood where he and his cousin learned to "mesmerize" chickens on his uncle's farm. They did so by capturing a chicken and holding its beak down to a white line of chalk until it became spellbound. The chickens would remain frozen in this position until the boy's uncle would come along and give them a kick in the backside to wake them up from their hypnotic stupor.[1]

McKenzie tells the story because he notes that organizations, like the white line of chalk in his story, can have a mesmerizing effect on people in their orbit. They create a culture of conformity that requires docility and dull obedience from their members. This stifles appropriate dissent and puts a lid on imagination and innovation. Unfortunately, churches can also tend to have the same effect on their leaders as well as on community members. Something in our traditions, theology, or inherited methodology tends to keep our collective noses down on the line. We rarely break free to do something genuinely imaginative, something adventurous, or something that challenges the status quo. Like it or not, we behave like a group of mesmerized chickens. And, like them, every now and again we need God to give us a proverbial kick in the backside to break our inertia and get us moving again.

It's Church, but Not As We Know It

Leadership guru Max De Pree noted that the first responsibility of a leader is to define reality.[2] I fully recognize that Jesus gets the privilege of decisively defining the movement that claims his name; nonetheless, leaders in his church need to take this task of defining the parameters of how people think about the church with utmost seriousness. Allowing Jesus to guide us, it is part of the leadership task to somehow manage how the rest of the organization as a whole sees itself and its function in the world. In other words, it's the leaders' job to define *ecclesia* for the people and organizations they lead.

This puts a huge theological responsibility on leadership to ensure they have a vision of the church that is consistent with the church Jesus built. We cannot shirk this, especially in moments of crisis that require accurate recalibration.

De Pree's punchy axiom highlights the leadership role very well, as it points us to that which we as leaders in the church ought to be ultimately concerned with: defining reality. In the following chapter, we will explore some mental verges that, we believe, will get us closer to the reality of seeing the church as apostolic movement; here we will simply look at the role paradigms and imagination play in hemming us in or giving us a way as to move beyond the prevailing status quo.

> Marx was right: religion is the opiate of the masses. Religious institutions dull people to their responsibilities as disciples of Jesus. Wake up.

It has been said that we don't know who discovered water but we know it wasn't the fish. For many people, church is so much part of their world that they seldom if ever stop to think about the prevailing systems-story that underlies their experience of church. Henri Matisse once noted that to look at something as though we had never seen it before requires great courage. We are framed by seventeen centuries of Christendom. Thinking about the church requires keen spiritual insight, born of prayer, to develop the theological imagination (and courage!) to be able to see things beyond the status quo of the predominant paradigm.[3] This is why any exploration of imagination must understand how paradigms operate and how they capture and/or shape our imagination. Conversely, paradigms are important because to shift from one paradigm into another, imagination is essential. The process, as we shall see, is largely intuitive and playful.

So when we talk about missional imagination, it's really describing an imagination primarily shaped by the *Missio Dei*, the kingdom of God, and the incarnation. These provide the framework for interpreting the Christian reality.

If You Can't Imagine It, You Can't Do It

Einstein, one of the greatest paradigm shifters of all time, reminds us of our sacred duty to dream God's dreams and rediscover the transforming power of the imagination. He could well have been talking of the Western church when he said, "The intuitive mind is a sacred gift and the rational mind is a faithful servant. We have created a society that honors the servant and has forgotten the gift."[4]

Einstein ascribed most of his real creativity, his capacity for creating new ways of understanding the world, to the function of the imagination. He famously quipped that if you can't imagine it, you can't do it. Elsewhere he revealingly said that when he examined himself and his own methods of thought, he concluded that the gift of imagination meant more to him than his clearly remarkable talent for absorbing positive knowledge.[5] He says imagination is in fact more important than knowledge because knowledge is limited but imagination circles the globe. With this approach, he transformed our understanding of the universe—no less than three times.[6]

What is particularly interesting here, and relevant to the role of imagination in paradigm shifts, is to note that most (if not all) of what Einstein did was not born out of real "hard science" in the lab! Rather his breakthroughs came via what he called "thought experiments"—acts of imagination—some of which came to him while sitting at a train station in Bern, Switzerland. The experiments to *prove* his thought experiments were subsequently done by other scientists. As it turns out, two of the biggest breakthroughs in physics hung on the ability to marvel at the mundane, to let imagination birth a new perspective: Isaac Newton, with a falling apple; and Einstein, with the trains in Bern!

Geoff Maddock, a dear friend of mine, recently reminded me that Jesus is a big believer in the human imagination. Over and over again Jesus uses stories and parables to capture the imaginations of those around him. And yet he isn't just a storyteller trying to entertain; he is a great teacher who knows that whatever gets our imagination (and attention) will ultimately capture our entire lives (Matt. 6:19–21).

We give ourselves over to what we conceive to be good and worthy of our efforts and resources. We also, regretfully, give ourselves over to sinful impulses. Jesus teaches that how and what we imagine is truly serious and profoundly spiritual. If we allow our imaginations to be caught up in the kinds of things Jesus taught and the kinds of miracles Jesus performed, we will be ready to live like him—according to the will of the Father and in the power of the Spirit. How might we see greater transformation in believers if people invited Jesus into their imaginations?[7]

Telling an Alternative Story

Although all of us have heard about successful attempts to revitalize existing churches, we have to acknowledge that the overall track record is very poor. Few congregations ever achieve positive growth curves again once they've begun to decline. What's more, church leaders report that their attempts to revitalize their churches don't yield the desired results. A lot of energy (and money) is put into change programs, with all the usual communication exercises, consultations, workshops, and so on. Like fad dieting, it achieves short-term results but not long-term solutions.

In the beginning, things seem to change, but gradually the novelty and impetus tends to wear off, and the organization ends up settling back into something of its previous configuration. So instead of managing new organizations, leaders end up managing the unwanted side effects of their efforts. The reason for this is simple, though often overlooked: unless the paradigm at the heart of the culture is changed, there can be no lasting change. Change must come from deep inside the paradigm; anything less will simply be external and cosmetic.

Ivan Illich, the educator and philosopher, was once asked what he thought was the most radical way to change society. Was it through violent revolution or gradual reform? He gave a careful answer: *neither.* Rather he suggested that if one wanted to change society, one must tell an alternative story.[8] Illich is right; we need to reframe our understandings through a different lens, an alternative story, if we wish to move beyond the limitations of the prevailing paradigm that clearly dominates our current approach to leadership and church.

Telling the different story means reframing the central story that defines our understanding of church. It also means allowing that reframed story to seep into our ethos and practices. This reframing

> Discipleship is key to Verge church effectiveness: it is critical to credibility, embodiment, and transmission of our message.

of the all-determining paradigm, effectively the brain of the organization, is essential to change, growth, and impact. For those wishing to activate the Verge church approach, it will require exercising the latent apostolic capacities lying at the heart of the church Jesus built. To mix up some metaphors, we have to reframe our thinking, rescript the story, rewrite the internal program—take your pick!

A great example of offering an alternative interpretation, an alternative meaning to our story, comes once again from Rob Wegner of Granger Community Church. He reports that over the last year, every time he taught, he would deliberately reframe the story of GCC as *movement*, both locally and globally. He says, "A few months back I spent half a message 'retelling' GCC's entire story through the filter of movement, tying it back to the early church. The people that are reading this from a megachurch background will probably have stories of 'micro-movements' from their history too. For example, in the early days of GCC, when there was no permanent building and the pioneering spirit was everywhere, it had the vibe of a movement. When a new ministry becomes a 'breakout,' it has the vibe of a movement.... We have to find those reference points in our own story and then tie them back to the Acts [early church] identity as movement, proclaiming, 'This is who we are meant to be!' "

This is exactly what is needed: a reframing of our narratives in light of our most primal stories—the apostolic movement of the early Christian church and other amazing apostolic movements in history.

Paradigm-eh-tic?

So what, then, is a paradigm? Thomas Kuhn, who did so much to help us understand the complex nature of paradigms, suggests that they are a way of trying to both understand our world and solve the *problems* of understanding by relying on a set of assumptions—which in turn help us interpret our situation and therefore give rise to possible solutions.[9] These solutions are breakthrough advances in learning and understanding that trigger new paradigms, thus outdating previous ones. For instance, paradigm shifts explain how Copernicus changed our view of the universe and of our place within it, and how Einstein changed the game from physics to quantum theory.[10]

Similarly, David Bosch, one of the key missiologists in the twentieth century, suggests there have been six paradigm shifts in missiology.[11] For instance, the shift from the pre-Constantinian church to the post-Constantinian one involved a massive paradigm shift. The Reformation was another. Although the Reformation did not fundamentally affect our ecclesiology, it certainly changed the way we thought about God, the gospel, salvation, and so on. In our day, the missional conversation is now fundamentally changing the paradigm; we are smack-bang in the middle of this shift right now.

Imagination Is the Key

If paradigms determine our interpretation and frame our understanding, then the way to comprehend and develop them must take place at the level of imagination. Imagination is soaked in possibility; it can see around corners and make the intuitive leaps that trigger paradigm shifts. But in order to unlock the power of imagination, we first need to understand the nature of paradigms. So get your thinking gear on and seriously grapple with this, because it is key to advancing the cause of the church in our time. (See fig. 5.)

For our purposes, we can say that the paradigm (systems story, ecclesial genetic code, organizational brain, or whatever you wish to call it) is made up of the following:

1. Unspoken assumptions and beliefs that over time take on the power of controlling *myths* or *codes*.
2. Primary *metaphors* we use to describe ourselves (body of Christ, church as organism, family of God, local fellowship, and so on).
3. A *working model*: the protocols, policies, and templates that guide behavior and choices (clearly the most visible/explicit part of the paradigm).
4. Manifestations of organizational culture (the "petals" in the diagram), composed of rituals, symbols, language, power arrangements, and so on. While these are important and overt, the core paradigm is maintained in the myth-metaphor-model structure.

theology

myths/codes
background assumptions, scripting,
and underlying belief system
generated in organization

rituals and
routines

symbols

metaphors
shorthand descriptions of underlying belief system

**The paradigm or
systems story**

control
systems

models
strategies or ideas in action

exemplars

organi-
zational
structures

Figure 5

Every organization is built upon this underlying paradigm or genetic coding. This is not the same thing as the church's beliefs or theological systems. Rather the paradigm determines how an organization feels, thinks, and thus acts. This paradigm therefore determines the way an organization behaves, no matter how the organizational chart is drawn. The paradigm explains and then guides behavior, and because of this it's the primary template that shapes all other things. Restructure the organization but leave the original paradigm in place, and nothing will change within the organization.

The truth is that most change programs concentrate on the petals; that is, they try to effect change by looking at structures, systems, and processes. Experience shows us that these initiatives usually have a limited success. Veteran church consultant Bill Easum says it this way: "Following Jesus into the mission field is either impossible or extremely difficult for the vast majority of congregations in the Western world because of one thing: They have a systems story that will not allow them to take the first step out of the institution into the mission field, even though the mission field is just outside the door of the congregation."[12]

It's important for the Verge process to note that it's futile trying to change the church, or a denomination, without first changing the paradigm or genetic codes that guide it.

It's because of this that reframing the central paradigm of church is one of the keys to change and much-needed innovation. A paradigm shift is a change to a new game, a new set of rules. And this in turn means we must reactivate our underutilized imaginations.

Verge church thinking therefore is first and foremost an exercise in a distinctively *apostolic* imagination—we have to (re)imagine the church in light of its apostolic design and imperative. If we fail to reframe the issues on this most fundamental level, we won't activate apostolic movements. We are back to needing to dethrone Constantine in order to advance Verge church thinking; to do this, we need the original (and originating) apostolic imagination that inspired and shaped the world's most transformative Jesus movements.

> Verge church thinking therefore is first and foremost an exercise in a distinctively apostolic imagination—we have to (re)imagine the church in light of its apostolic design and imperative.

I Was Blind but Now I See: The Problem of Paradigm Blindness

The Zenith Drilling Company prided itself on being the best drill-bit-producing company in the world. In many ways, they had revolutionized the industry, using tungsten-tipped drill bits. The problem is, the competition caught up with them and began to erode Zenith's market share to the point where profitability was in question. The board of directors decided to get a new CEO who could perhaps help the company recover its previously held market-leader status.

The new CEO called all the leaders and managers to a three-day crisis conference, where he asked everyone to clarify what they thought the mission of the company was. After much conversation and deliberation, they decided that their mission was not only to make drill bits but also to make the best drill bits in the world. They all agreed this was an excellent purpose for the company.

At this point, the new chief executive said, "No! Your job is *not* to make the best drill bits in the world; rather it is to make the best holes in the world!" They went on to innovate laser drilling and become the best hole-making company in the world.

This is a good example of seeing the same thing but from a different vantage point. And in many ways, this same change of perspective helps us understand how preconceived notions and paradigms have blinded people to how God was really working. Much of the theology of John is built on this concept, and it's seen in scriptural encounters such as Luke 24, where the disciples were at first prevented from "seeing" Jesus (v. 16) and then had their eyes opened as he broke bread with them. Like an Escher painting, a change of perspective changes *everything*.[13]

We need to exercise what we call the paradigmatic imagination, because any prevailing paradigm, ecclesiological or otherwise, acts as a kind of mental lens that helps us understand the world. As such, they are necessary and unavoidable in framing our sense of reality and functionally negotiating our way through our world. But paradigms also impose limitations of how far thinking can go, because they selectively screen out important facts to fit the internal mindset, wishful thinking, and emotional overinvestment in maintaining the status quo. In other words, they blindside us, creating the situation where those who dance are thought to be quite insane by those who cannot hear the music, as Angela Monet so famously said.[14]

That paradigms conceal as much as they reveal also explains why the formation of a new paradigm opens up new ways of perceiving and acting that overcome the limitations of the old one. This is why, as Thomas Kuhn showed in his definitive book on the subject, paradigm shifting is how every major new discovery is made in all spheres of knowledge and endeavor.[15] But paradigm blindness also shows how development and growth can be blocked and why it's important to be passionately committed to finding new and imaginative ways forward.

The creative role of the paradigmatic imagination, as well as its capacity to blind us, is very much echoed in the biblical use of the word *heart* in both Old and New Testaments. While the Bible never uses the term *paradigm*, the heart and imagination are portrayed as being the seat of intellectual and emotional functions (Ps. 14:1; Lam. 2:11) as well as the origin of will and intellect. It's the heart that provides us with the ability to "see": to give direction, make choices, and discern between lies and truth (Jer. 17:9; Eccl. 10:2). The link between a passionate and unrelenting love of truth and the capacity to see is clearly referenced by Jesus when he says in Matthew 5:8, "Blessed are the pure in heart, for they will see God" (that is, they will be able to imagine/perceive him rightly). It also implies that the paradigmatic imagination can block our seeing when we are bound too closely to a certain paradigm or framed way of seeing.[16] This has both frightening as well as thrilling aspects, as is seen in Jesus' application of Isaiah 6:10: "This people's heart has become calloused; they hardly hear with their ears, and they have closed their eyes. Otherwise they might see with their eyes, hear with their ears, understand with their hearts and turn, and I would heal them" (Matt. 13:15).

In some cases, the dominance of a paradigm can approximate what the Bible means by *stronghold*, because there is no doubt our thinking can sometimes profoundly lock us into patterns. Religiosity is a classic example. The Pharisees were highly dedicated scholars and passionate people, and yet they missed the Messiah they so ardently searched for (John 5:39–40). They studied the Scriptures to learn about God, and yet they entirely missed what God was doing! How? The only way to understand this is to recognize that they were blinded by their own paradigm. Similarly, we are instructed by Paul to demolish such mental strongholds and take every thought and imagination captive to Jesus (2 Cor. 10:1–6). This means, among other things, that we must allow Jesus to frame our most fundamental paradigm: Christology.

To illustrate paradigmatic imagination and paradigm blindness, consider the well-known image that, depending on how you perceive it, looks like either a young woman or an old crone. The issue is that generally we see one to the exclusion of the other, but both are there. We choose one or the other, and we can't see both at the same time. On the one hand we see, and on the other we are blinded.

It's the paradigm itself, the hidden and determinative assumptions we hold about life, that help us to see. But our paradigm also deters us from seeing a better way when it presents itself to us. If we are to break out of the established ways of doing things and find a new and better way, we are going to have to allow our imaginations to be (re) infused with ancient truths. Bill Easum says, "Churches wanting to break free from the quagmire of their dysfunctional systems and climb out of their downward death spiral must learn to feel, think, and act differently than they do now. The times in which we live require us to change our Life Metaphors, something akin to rewiring the human brain."[17]

The Bible calls this repentance (*metanoia*, or turning in the mind), and it is critical if we are going to lead the church into the apostolic movement forms of the Verge church.

Changing the Game

Before we look at practical ways to engender fresh and imaginative thinking, we believe it is vital to comment on the dynamics of paradigms and of paradigm shifting. Thomas Kuhn gave us the foundational text on this subject in his seminal book *The Structure of Scientific Revolutions*, in which he describes the transitions between various scientific worldviews and how they were affected.[18]

Seeing that the church is also meant to be a community embracing the search for truth, Kuhn's book is a tremendous resource in our attempts to reframe the mission of the church in the new millennial context. It also serves as a warning to us as to how easily vital new perspectives can be stifled by a predominant paradigm, something that has sadly been so much a part of historical Christendom. It's important for the church to know something about the shift from one paradigm to another.

A paradigmatic shift involves the following stages (see fig. 6):

1. *Structure/normalcy.* We begin with a well-established paradigm, a captured (or closed) imagination, if you will, that dominates the thinking/consciousness, of the scientific philosophy of a period.

2. *Anomalies.* An increasing sense of anomaly develops from within the paradigm, that is, a feeling that something is wrong. Or, at least, the prevailing mode of thought cannot resolve all the problems the paradigm itself faces or achieve its own vision of truth. Paradoxically, it is those who have mastered the prevailing paradigm who are most often the first ones to break from the consensus — for example, Einstein and Heisenberg in science, or Calvin and Barth in theology. The

real experts are the ones most able and likely to perceive when things are wrong! Thus begins what Kuhn calls "a roaming of the mind," a new sense of freedom to engage anomalies without recourse to the preconceived assumptions and set of solutions. Again, imagination and intuitive leaps are vital in shifting the paradigm.

3. *Crisis.* Slowly a growing (but inexorable) recognition is made by more and more people that something is basically wrong in the prevailing conception of things; eventually a tipping point (crisis) is reached, and the trickle becomes a flood. A group of dissenters emerges, followed by a flurry of new theories in search of an alternative understanding of things.

4. *Transition/restructuring.* A new paradigm (answer) begins to emerge, most often with opposition by those who still hold strongly to the established paradigm — for example, Copernicus saved his neck only by recanting from the "heresy" implied in his theory but was still imprisoned for life. This is probably because some have invested their sense of selfhood in the paradigm and so receive their legitimacy from it. This is also why denominations seldom permit a questioning of their core organizational beliefs (commonly called sacred cows).

We mention this here because paradigm shifting, which is precisely what is required for us to become an authentic apostolic movement, will go through something of the process above. Another reason is because paradigm shifts involve exercises in imagination and creativity. They point us toward the need for the kind of innovation we will explore later in the book. Also, this particular illustration of paradigm shifting highlights how imagination (and not simply acquired linear reasoning) plays a crucial role in helping people shift from one paradigm to another.

Playing Our Way into a New Future

As followers of the Way, we must remember that imagination is not only the realm of fantasy and children's games but also the proper place to locate our prayer, worship, and action — and, in our case, our desire to creatively lead the church into its missional calling. The sci-

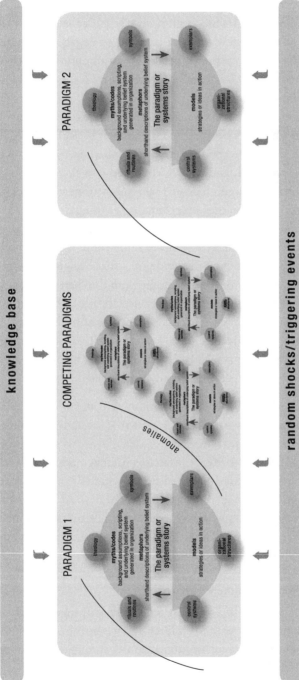

Figure 6

Paradigm Shifts in Organizations. Adapted from Hasan Sisek and Karen Louis, "Organization Change as Paradigm Shift," *Journal of Higher Education* 65, no. 6 (November–December 1994).

ence of ideas also fully recognizes the critical role of the imagination, intuition, and insight in the development of breakthrough creativity.[19] And there is a science to it! Imagination is the ability to visualize possibilities, to form images and ideas in the mind (especially of things never seen or never experienced directly), and to resolve problems while being guided largely by the nonlinear logic of intuition and insight.

Imagination derives from the creative part of the mind where new ideas, thoughts, and images are first conceived and formed. Analytic reasoning is important (and in the church, we rely on it through our well-developed theological rationality), but it takes imagination to get us beyond the impasse of any prevailing paradigm to genuinely innovate and find our way into breakthrough creativity. This is what is called "looking around corners."

Imagination requires that we be playful with the various elements in the organizational mix. Imagination is therefore, by nature, metaphorical thinking; it compares ideas that normally would not be related. By using a metaphor, a comparison of one thing to another, you intellectually connect disparate ideas. Once this connection is made, the metaphor is extended and the two things are allowed to grow, merging the two ideas together. The extension of the metaphor creates the framework for your new idea. The combining of ideas gives birth to a new thing. George Lucas combined mythology and science fiction to produce *Star Wars*. Mark Zuckerberg used the metaphor of a college yearbook and social networking to produce Facebook.[20]

To unleash the power of imagination, we need to allow ourselves to explore possibilities we have never thought of before. William James once said genius means little more than the faculty of perceiving things that have become habitual in an unhabitual way.[21] Because it's a dimension of the human heart, real imagination requires a radical openness of mind and a willingness to *repent* of previous understandings when they seem to no longer fit. Similarly, as we've seen in our critique of the institutional paradigm, we've become profoundly habitual in our ecclesiology, our way of thinking about church. In

> The fundamental job of apostolic imagination is to produce out of the church we now experience a vision of the church Jesus wants us to experience.

order to advance, we will need to be willing to let go of the inadequate understandings blocking us from becoming a movement again.[22] And here's where the apostolic imagination will help us think differently about things assumed to be right.

World-famous U2 front man Bono challenges his audiences to dream up the world they want to live in, to dream out loud, at high volume. He is appealing to the inherently human capacity to create new possibilities and futures. If this is true for all humans—and clearly it is—then the godly imagination, because it is grounded in the gospel and inspired by the Holy Spirit, is hopeful, creative, and transformative. Applying this, we would then say that *the fundamental job of apostolic imagination is to produce out of the church we now experience a vision of the church Jesus wants us to experience.*

The Verge-ination: Reimagining Church in Apostolic Perspective

It's no coincidence this book is being released in the same year as my book *The Permanent Revolution*, which thoroughly explores the nature of apostolic imagination and practice for the contemporary church in the West. In "Shift," the next section of this book, I will suggest the model of Apostolic Genius, composed as a system of six interrelating elements of what I call mDNA, the most coherent model of apostolic imagination and thinking I can offer. For now, I want to simply suggest that the following areas will need to be the focal points, or theological/organizational verges, around which we are to reimagine the church for our time. All of these are directly addressed, and I believe answered, in the Apostolic Genius concept we will explore later.

Christology

In essence, the church needs to constantly return to its Founder in order to chart its way forward. He has full defining rights on the way the church defines itself in the world. We are Jesus' people, and we are designed to reflect his purposes, his teachings, and his lifestyle and to fulfill his intended design for the church. Perhaps a way of saying this is that Jesus retains full rights regarding the church's core intellectual property. And so any attempt to imagine a new future needs to ensure it is fully representing what the Founder wants and intends in the first place. If this was to be said theologically, it means Christology lies at the heart of church renewal in any time and place we find ourselves. This is perhaps the most radical thing we can do, because it takes us back to the root *(radix)* of the church. This process, what I have called "reJesusing the church" (in a book titled *ReJesus*), allows us to imagine futures consistent with God's dream for the world; in the Scriptures, that dream is called the kingdom of God.[23]

Missiology

Missiology explores the reasons why mission is integral to the life of faith as well as develops methods of how we might fulfill our calling as God's missional people. The methods it develops ought to be consistent with the nature and purposes of the sent God who in turn sends us. In other words, it's a thoroughly theological process (and not just a pragmatic one) that requires that our imaginations be inspired by who God is and how he engages the world. We also are inspired by the way the New Testament church so creatively extended this mission. We look to Jesus, we study the life of Paul, and we discover that mission does not simply involve attracting people to "church," but rather it is about being sent into our worlds, into every domain, and going deep into culture.

Mission inspires innovation, deeper cultural engagement, and calls for more integrity in our witness. And because mission is tied to the very being of God and to the work of Jesus, it offers the imagination a profoundly rich resource in engaging culture, incarnating the gospel, sharing faith, and forming faith communities. Reengaging missional ways of doing church is a direct route to renewal of our theology and ecclesial imaginations.

Organization

Organization is a social arrangement allowing people to pursue collective goals, control the performance of the members of a group, and distinguish the group from other groups. Because of this, it shapes so much of what we do and how we think. We all know this and experience it every day of our lives, and certainly we need organization of some form or another to get anything done collectively. But organizations can, over time, develop into impersonal institutions that tend to impose conformity (that is, crush creativity), are change-resistant, and become controlling entities that resist the promptings of the Spirit and undermine the "people dynamic" of the gospel.[24] We simply have to apply our imaginations to the issue of organization, because if we fail to do so, it will inevitably undermine all of our attempts to become a more fluid and adaptive apostolic movement.

Discipleship

Another area of focal concern for imagination should be around the issue of how we form and empower the people of God. This is no small issue, because if we fail to activate every believer in their God-given calling to be an agent of the King, it's doubtful we will ever become a dynamic movement at all. If we don't disciple people to be like Jesus, not only is our witness distorted, but also we can never hope to develop Christlike leaders.

We have to admit that our imaginations are stuck here. So much of our current energies are put into pastoral programming and worship, but these understandable emphases have by and large failed to develop mature disciples. If we put similar effort into apprenticing people in the way of Jesus, we can expect significantly different results.

Once again, all four of these Verge focal points (Christology, missiology, organization, and discipleship) are addressed, and I believe resolved, by applying the Apostolic Genius (mDNA) model we'll explore later in the book.

An Imaginative Solution

In the first chapter, we suggested that the church in the West faces two major problems arising from the endemic shift to post-Christian culture in the West (the 60:40 problem). We saw that the first problem is a strategic one, because most churches focus on a diminishing segment of the population and effectively compete for the same slice of the market. The other issue is the distinctly missionary one and raises the problem of how we get our message to an increasingly unchurched, alienated, and culturally diverse audience. So how does missional (apostolic) imagination help us resolve these two major problems?

Addressing the Strategic Problem

As I've stated before, Einstein noted that the problems of the world couldn't be resolved by the same thinking that created those problems in the first place. In other words, the kind of thinking (the paradigm) that got us to this point in history cannot generate the solution to the very problems it has created for itself. We need to break the monopoly of the institutional paradigm in order to morph into an apostolic movement again. As we've noted, this is exactly where apostolic/missional imagination helps us.

By following the radical, living, upside-down Messiah/Prophet, we are actively drawn into a kingdom that can't be contained in human institutions. When we allow our imaginations to be profoundly shaped by the doctrine of the *Missio Dei* and the incarnation of God in Jesus, we are inspired to find new ways to meaningfully live out the good news to people around us. When we reimagine organization in terms of networks and living systems, we will generate new forms of *ecclesia* and allow them to develop; these in turn become the seeds of the future church. The church imagineered around these invigorating themes ought to be a highly creative, multicultural, multidimensional, diverse, highly innovative enterprise. This is especially true because as a missionary agency incarnating the gospel into multiple contexts, it ought to mirror the wonderful cultural diversity making up the world. Seen in this light, institutional conformity is damaging to the commitment to incarnational ministry. We are meant to be culture creators, not cultural resisters.

To overcome the fact that most contemporary churches focus on the same diminishing 40 percent of the population (and therefore compete against each other for the same slice), we must have *more* than just one arrow in our ecclesial quiver. The way to have a really good idea is to have many ideas, and the answer to the diversity of Western culture is diversity of church expression. One size will not fit all anymore. If our only answer to the strategic challenge we face is another tweak of the same institutional paradigm that got us here, then we must expect

> We need a blue ocean strategy: ecclesial innovation inspired by King Jesus, incarnational mission, living systems — all dedicated to creatively activating disciples. This is the answer to the infertile sameness of the prevailing forms.

to be (and will be) sorely disappointed, and church attendance will continue its long-term trend of decline. We need a blue ocean strategy: ecclesial innovation inspired by King Jesus, incarnational mission, living systems—all dedicated to creatively activating disciples. This is the answer to the infertile sameness of the prevailing forms. Inspired by the Holy Spirit, we have to dream up the church we want to worship in—there is no silver bullet, but there is a silver imagination.

Much of this book is dedicated to helping churches develop more diverse and innovative expressions of church. This is the kind of church we must become if we are to get over the current impasse; we must become a movement again. It's worth noting again that the movemental paradigm we are suggesting in this book is *inclusive* of all forms of *ecclesia*, including ones that are more institutional in expression. Whereas, the institutional paradigm is by nature *exclusive*—it cannot make space in the paradigm for more-fluid and adaptive forms of *ecclesia*. In other words, the movemental paradigm is by nature a both/and form, while the institutional form maintains a stance of either/or.

I'm in no way suggesting we abandon the current forms, but simply that we allow for the significant experimentation, development, and innovation of new forms. The seeds of the future *ecclesia* will be found in the new forms that come out of the Verge process and others like it.

Addressing the Missionary Problem

The related problem comes from the likelihood that around 60 percent of America's population (much higher in Europe and Australia) is increasingly alienated from the prevailing forms of church. In missionary terms, it means they are culturally distant from us. As a *sent* and *sending* people (that is, missional people), it is *our* task to take the message to them and deliver it in ways meaningful to them. This means we need to reassess the situation in the light of best-practice missionary approaches.

We need to ask the question, what is the gospel for this people group? What would sound like good news to them? This means we must attend first to the existential and religious issues people are facing, before we can communicate how the gospel addresses them. Think of it this way: don't plant churches; plant the gospel, and the church will grow out of it. This will mean we go back to our primal message and allow it to reframe the way we see church—not the other way around. It's imagination fired up by the gospel and its missional implications that drives the church to become more authentically *evangel*ical.

If we persist with the current status quo, we are in effect asking the nonbeliever to do all the cross-cultural work in coming to church! Remember, we are the sent ones—not them. So we not only bring people to church (that will work for the 40 percent); we also take church to the people (to reach the other 60 percent and growing). We can't front-load church into the equation of mission. We must go to the people group and—once we have understood their culture a whole lot more—then ask ourselves the question, what is church for these people? We can't presume we have the answer up front. We can only know it from the context of mission.

It's easy to see how these questions force us to innovate. Because culture and cultural context differs, it will mean we have to reimagine how we express *ecclesia* and how we communicate good news.

One of the major keys in reimagining church is unleashing all of God's people as missional agents of the King, commissioned to represent him in every sphere and domain of society. The institutional paradigm, because it so identifies the church with its formal institutions (buildings, clergy, programs, and so on), effectively blinds its members to the profoundly missional capacities of the people of God as a kingdom of priests.

The church doesn't consist of its institutions; it consists of the people of God. We know this in our theology, but our practice is almost entirely at odds with this belief. We have so identified the church with its rituals, theology, denominational templates, symbols, and professional clergy that we can't see this remarkable truth.

Everyone in a movement, and not just the so-called religious professionals, must be activated and thus play a vital role in extending Jesus' mission on earth. Everyone is in full-time ministry, and most of us express this outside the more formal church community, but it is still *full-time* ministry. In fact, this false distinction in what constitutes ministry is one of the major hurdles we have to overcome if we are going to activate as Jesus' people.

When you add to the ministry of every believer the idea that each carries the full potential of the whole movement in them, you're seeing church very differently. You are thinking *movement*. Reflecting on people-movements, missiologist Donald McGavran once said that "in every apple there is an orchard." If we could just realize this amazing piece of truth—that every believer carries the full possibility of an *ecclesia*, and every *ecclesia* in turn has the full possibility of a movement—we will be well on our way to becoming the world-changing movement God designed us to be.

It is only when the people of God as a whole are activated in a movement that real-world transformation takes place. In *Right Here, Right Now*,[25] I described a movement as comprising both the more formal, organized aspects of mission (what I call apostolic mission) and the "mission of the people of God." Diagrammatically, it looks like figure 7.

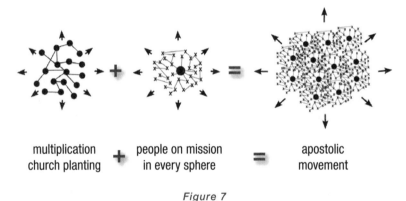

| multiplication church planting | **+** | people on mission in every sphere | **=** | apostolic movement |

Figure 7

What we have here is reproducing churches (the round nodes) and disciples dispersed into the spheres of society (the *X* nodes). When both these aspects come together, we have centers and hubs that provide the platform for launching the mission of every believer into every sphere. So both multiplication church planting and the mission of the people of God create apostolic movement. This way of looking at the church is *paradigmatically* different from the predominant way we see it now, and yet it is much closer to the image of the church in the New Testament and in all apostolic movements everywhere. Once again, we can imagineer our way to a more authentically missional, and therefore more biblically consistent, Christianity. I know that all this talk about paradigm shifting seems somewhat overwhelming, but before we rush to the how-to, we need to make sure we really understand the why. (Don't worry, the how-to is coming.) I can't overemphasize how important it is to take this all in now, because the answers that so readily suggest themselves to us at this point come directly from the toolbox inherited from the prevailing paradigm, and they are insufficient to change the game. (Remember, doing more of the same will not produce different results.) We must do the hard work of recoding (telling a different story), and to do this, we must learn to work with conceptual tools of intuition and imagination. The next chapter will look at this, which is what I call the mission to the mind.

Winston Churchill remarked that in light of the fading of the British Empire, the empires of the future would be the empires of the imagination. This is profoundly true for the church in our day, particularly as we find ourselves on the back foot in every Western cultural context. If imagination is so important in change and development of human civilization in general, then for the church, apostolic imagination is a resource of almost inestimable worth as we once again negotiate becoming the kind of movement Jesus designed us to be in the first place.

Dave's Response to "The Silver Imagination"

God is not only creator but also creative and constantly creating and reimagining. We see this in Isaiah 43. First God challenges us to give up our old paradigm: "Forget the former things, do not dwell on the past." Then he pleads with us to open up our imagination: "See, I am doing a new thing! Now it springs up; do you not perceive it?" (Isa. 43:18–19). From the beginning, throughout the Old Testament, and into the future, God is reimagining his mission and almost begging us to see it! It's as if you can hear God's voice saying, "C'mon, people, don't you see what I'm doing?"

This is the premise of Neil Cole's *Church 3.0*, in which he explains, "There have been two major upgrades in church formation since Acts that have changed the entire system. The first occurred dramatically

during the rule of the Emperor Constantine. The church shifted from
an underground, grassroots, organic movement [Church 1.0] to a more
institutionalized organization [Church 2.0].... I believe the second
major shift is occurring now in our lifetime [Church 3.0—Apostolic
Movement]. Many people want to go back to the beginning again. As
much as I am enamored of what I learned about the church of the first
century, we simply cannot go back; we can only go forward."

God is advancing into the future, and God's people must go with
him. And for us to move forward with him, we must open the eyes
of our missional imagination and see what new thing God is doing.
In far too many corners of the church, the puritan (or primitivist)
impulse is alive and well. The creative tension we're called to occupy
sees the rich wisdom of the past while being open to the Holy Spirit
in order to become truly adaptive and anticipatory when it comes to
future embodiment of God's kingdom on earth.

The power of missional imagination is something I have experienced firsthand. It was on the back of a napkin while sitting alone
in a little Mexican restaurant that I first drew a map of Chicago and
then dozens of little circles representing future sites of the church we
had just planted. I had never heard the term *multisite*, but in that
moment I allowed the Spirit of God to infuse my imagination with
his mission for my life and our church. God was doing a new thing,
and I could see it. Fast-forward to several years later, and we are now
one of the fastest-growing churches in the country, with eleven sites
in the Chicago area and a network of more than one hundred church-
plants around the world through NewThing. I know the power of
missional imagination. Despite all that, I find myself looking at blank
napkins again these days and wondering what God has next for us.
The reimagining process Alan just described isn't a one-time event
for a follower of Jesus, a leader in his movement, or his church. It is
a continual process of imaginational reuptake and creative destruction—it's putting yourself "out of business" before institutional calcification does it for you.

The systems story for Community Christian Church is that we
are a missional church which is all about reproducing. We were good
at reproducing large; we knew how to train up leaders from within
and deploy the very best of them as staff, campus pastors, and church

planters. While we were successful at reproducing new sites and churches with hundreds of people, we still had thousands of people sitting on the sidelines who were not fully engaged in the mission. We knew if we were going to see a movement, it would require reimagining our future.

Being absolutely convinced the future would be won or lost in the minds of our people, we brought Kim Hammond from Melbourne, Australia, to join our staff as the director of missional imagination. Kim had been Alan's right-hand man for the Forge Training Network in Australia, and he brought the experience and knowledge we needed. One of my first conversations with Kim was about movies, and that talk revealed a lot about the paradigm shift we needed to make. I told him I'd just seen a movie I really liked, *Invictus*—the story of Nelson Mandela and how he changed the entire direction of his country, South Africa. Kim said he too enjoyed *Invictus*, but his recent favorite was *Blindside*; he loved the story of how a stay-at-home mom changed the life of one disadvantaged teenage boy forever. Then Kim said to me, "You like the story about the leader who comes in and brings massive changes to millions of people, but I prefer the story of one-on-one life change by an everyday person. Do you see the difference?" He added, "We need both. Community has been great at reproducing macro; now we need to help people see how we can be great at reproducing micro."

It is a continual process of imaginational reuptake and creative destruction—it's putting yourself "out of business" before institutional calcification does it for you.

Kim was right. We had created a culture where people would sacrifice money, move their families, and change careers to be a part of a new site or new church—and that's good. But we didn't have a culture or practices that expected the mobilization of all people for mission into every sphere of life. Over the next several months, Kim met with paid and volunteer leadership from every campus to begin taking us through a reimagining process, with Christology, missiology, organization, and discipleship as the focal points.

In an effort to make this painstakingly practical, let me make a few suggestions regarding how to move through the process of missional imagination.

Solitude and Prayer

Most of us leave solitude for the pull of the crowd. And when we think of creativity and imagination, our first reaction is to pull together the most creative people we know to brainstorm an idea. This thinking took off with the 1953 bestselling book *Applied Imagination*; however, more recently, Yale researchers have found that brainstorming can actually reduce a team's creative output, and the same number of people can generate more and better ideas separately than together.[26]

So encourage people to spend time in solitude and prayer. Solitude has long been considered critical to the creative process. And if that is true, think how much more creative we can be when we are alone with the Creator. I'm convinced God passionately wants every one of us to understand our part in his mission and is willing to speak to us. That is why Jesus told us, "The harvest truly is great, but the laborers are few; therefore pray the Lord of the harvest to send out laborers into His harvest" (Luke 10:2 NKJV). Solitude, retreats, and silence are a great means for hearing from God and engaging our missional imagination.

Life-on-Life Apprenticeship

People get mission when they see mission lived out; that is why apprenticeship (what Alan calls discipleship) is critical for reimagination. Our best estimate is that 10 percent of the people in most churches seem to understand that they are sent by Jesus and that they are Spirit-empowered to incarnate the gospel in their context, as Jesus was. They may not use this language, but they are living it out. We need this to rub off on others. This is exactly what Jesus did with his apprentices. Notice what he does right after he called his first followers together: "After this, Jesus and his disciples went out into the Judean countryside, where he spent some time with them" (John 3:22).

Doesn't sound like a big deal — Jesus *spent some time* with his disciples. The word for "spend time" is *diatribo* (pronounced *dia-TREE-bo*), which is a composite of two words: *dia*, which means "against," and *tribo*, which means "to rub." So *diatribo* means "they spent time rubbing off on each other." *Diatribo* occurs in an apprenticeship. What the leader does rubs off on the apprentice. In a life-on-life apprenticeship, people will begin to see Jesus, they will see mission, they will see discipleship, and they will see how organic systems reproduce to create movement.

Experiential Teaching

Alone, teaching on mission can be helpful, but it becomes a powerful tool for engaging the imagination when it is coupled with experiences. A special series at a weekend service or a series of workshops which include stories of people on mission and the commissioning of new people into mission are powerful examples of experiential teaching. I've seen it done where a series of workshops will include a testimony from someone who is active in mission and then concludes by commissioning someone new into ministry in their context. It was very compelling. There are studies that show that actual or simulated experiences in other cultures have proven to increase creativity. For instance, just watching a forty-five-minute slide show on the history of China will increase creativity in participants for one week.

And of course the best kind of experiential teaching is a field trip. Whether the setting is local or global, if you are in a place where real mission is being lived out and you can teach from there, it promises to spark the imagination of every participant.

Leaders Spark Imagination

Many churches are like gun powder; at first glance, it appears to be latent, dry, and easily blown away. But leaders can spark the missional imagination to create a great explosion in any church. If you want to see an explosion of missional engagement, start with the leadership. The best and simplest definition of leadership is *influence*, and when leaders live out life on mission, it will influence the whole!

When Michael Stewart of Austin Stone Church moved into an under-resourced neighborhood in Austin, Texas, it sparked the imagination of an entire church toward transforming that community. When Jon Ferguson moved his family from the suburbs into the city of Chicago, it sparked in

If you are a leader, the best way to turn missional imagination from a blurry phrase found in a book to something your people see with 20/20 vision is for you to live it out.

Community Christian Church the imaginative possibility of impacting both the suburbs and the city. If you are a leader, the best way to turn missional imagination from a blurry phrase found in a book to something your people see with 20/20 vision is for you to live it out. When leaders are *being* the change they want to see, they spark the missional imagination of all who follow, and fan into flame the gift God has given them. If the fires of an apostolic movement are going to burn bright, they will be sparked by leaders who lead from the front and live it out.

The 2.5 Percent Spark Imagination

In every group there are innovators: those who ignite the change before all others. The 2.5 percent of us who are innovators spark change in the 13.5 percent of those who are early adopters, and when you reach 16 percent of the group, the mission burns so red-hot, everyone can feel it.

Our first efforts to spark the missional imagination of the people at Community came when we identified the innovators — the people who were already doing it and/or trying to do it. This small group of people came together several times to share what efforts they were already piloting on their own and to learn from one another. From this group came some successes and also a lot of failures. We learned some things about what didn't work and what does work, and we put together a library of stories that would ignite the imagination of any Christ follower toward mission. It is by experimentation and pilot projects that you first enroll the 2.5 percent, who in turn influence the 13.5 percent and, over time, the whole church.

Alternative Stories Spark Imagination

A predictable story is like a bedtime tale you've heard a hundred times — it's designed to lull you to sleep. But telling an alternative story is like pulling the fire alarm in the middle of the night: it awakens everyone out of their slumber to a new reality. Alone, teaching on mission can be helpful, but it becomes a powerful tool for engaging the imagination when it's coupled with stories and experiences. The commissioning of new people into mission can be a remarkable awakening for others. I've seen the commissioning of young artists to do ministry in each gig they play, the commissioning of a stay-at-home mom to do outreach in her neighborhood, and even the commissioning of a student who plans to lead a Bible study at school. Seeing others commissioned, especially in such alternative stories, is compelling.

These alternative stories don't have to be our own. We did a workshop called Discover the Dream, where we not only taught on mission but also took people on an imaginary journey with Fridtjof Nansen, the great Norwegian explorer and Christ follower who saved millions of lives. We allowed participants to live through Nansen's story. One participant said afterward, "At Discover the Dream, God pushed my clenched fists open and placed back in my hands the idealistic dreams of my late teens of working with and loving street people. Since that experience I have moved into a neighborhood where I am living out that dream and mission."

And of course the best kind of story is your own story. When you bring people into new experiences, it allows them to write a brand-new chapter in their stories. Whether the setting is local or global, if you put people into a setting where real mission is being lived out and they can experience it, it promises to spark the imagination of every participant.

Like the character of Neo in the film *The Matrix*, we are all asking the rhetorical question, "I can't go back, can I?" The answer is obviously no. But the good news is, we have a God who is advancing into the future, and for us to be with him, we must open the eyes of our missional imagination and see the new things he is doing.

DISCUSSION QUESTIONS

Open

When you were a child, what did you imagine you'd be doing by the age you are now? How did you imagine your life looking?

Explore

1. What do you think is the current "story" of your church, as most of your attenders would tell it? What are some things you wish they'd include? Exclude?

2. "This people's heart has become calloused; they hardly hear with their ears, and they have closed their eyes. Otherwise they might see with their eyes, hear with their ears, understand with their hearts and turn, and I would heal them" (Matt. 13:15).

   How have we become calloused and paralyzed to a particular way of doing church? While we must be careful to gently convict, how could a refocusing on the person of Christ help us reframe our way of doing church?

3. Where is your church within the four steps of paradigm shifting (pp. 64–66): structure/normalcy, anomalies, crisis, transition/restructuring? How will you move to the next step?

4. Why is imagination so important in helping people make the missional paradigm shift? Is it possible to expand people's capacity to imagine?

5. "Forget the former things; do not dwell on the past. See, I am doing a new thing! Now it springs up; do you not perceive it?" (Isa. 43:18 – 19). What does your church need to stop dwelling on from its past? What new thing do you sense God is doing in your church/community?

Move

1. Have everyone on your team imagine/dream what your church could look like in five years. Have each person share one God-sized (but doable!) dream and one crazy, "out there" dream (for entertainment).

2. Alan encourages us to determine what the gospel looks and sounds like in the context of those your church is attempting to reach. What is the gospel for this people group? What is good news to them? Come up with your answers as a team.

Chapter 3

Mission to the Mind and Heart

ALAN

Sometimes I try to think of six impossible things before breakfast. — *ALICE IN WONDERLAND*

It's easy to come up with new ideas; the hard part is letting go of what worked for you two years ago, but will soon be out of date. — ROGER VON OECH

New opinions are always suspected, and usually opposed, without any other reason but because they are not already common. — JOHN LOCKE, PHILOSOPHER

Gordon McKenzie, who did much to foster the art of creative disruption at Hallmark, tells stories of going into classrooms full of kids at different levels. He would ask, "How many artists are there in the room? Would you please raise your hands?" He reports that the response was always the same: all first-grade kids considered themselves artists, in second grade about half of the kids put their hands up, in third grade about 30 percent of the kids identified themselves as artists, and so on. By the time he reached sixth-grade classes, no more than one or two put their hands up — and even then rather guardedly, fearing rejection by the other kids for identifying themselves as artists.

The point he makes with this is that schools participate in the suppression of creative genius, and that something akin to this is at work in all organizations that suppress creativity in the cause of protecting the status quo.[1] The loss of creative imagination is a direct result of trying to preserve the status quo in any organization, including the church.

The result of this suppression of the artful imagination is that churches and Christian organizations find themselves "stuck in a moment" (as Bono sings in the U2 song), and they struggle to break free from the limitations inherent in their current way of thinking. As we've seen, paradigms can effectively become psychic prisons we need to break out of. I really believe that our long-term captivity to the Christendom (or institutional) paradigm is directly related to our loss of the original, and *originative*, imagination that fueled the early church and all other exponential movements since. And I equally believe that the original apostolic (or missional) imagination of the church is the key to breaking out. As we shall see later, this is coded into Apostolic Genius, and it is latent in the church.

What Got You Here Won't Get You There

In the previous chapter, we saw that the institutional paradigm (or systems story) of the church resolves some dilemmas in preserving the faith, by encoding it (in rituals, theological traditions, ecclesial templates, and so on). However, in doing so, it creates a whole new set of problems it cannot resolve from within its own frame of reference. In other words, while on the one hand the prevailing paradigm has provided the church in the West with a viable framework for understanding our nature and function for many centuries, it can no longer function as a suitable map for the new, post-Christian, increasingly unchurched, missionary context we are now having to negotiate. Furthermore, in trapping our imagination, screening our thinking, and prohibiting certain approaches, it has also blinded us to other, more productive and missionally dynamic possibilities inherent in the apostolic movement paradigm of church.

It's time to suggest ways we can change the paradigm by reconceiving the primary frameworks, conversations, and metaphors of how we see ourselves as God's people. We are now ready to explore how these help us transition from a more institutional paradigm closer to that of an apostolic movement. Figure 8 is an elaboration of figure 5 on page 60 of the preceding chapter.

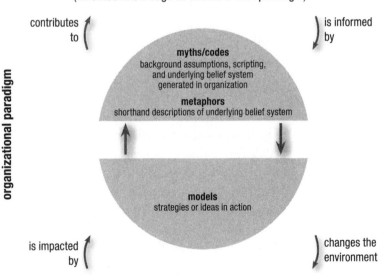

prevailing body of knowledge about church
(inherited knowledge as source of root paradigm)

contributes to

is informed by

organizational paradigm

myths/codes
background assumptions, scripting, and underlying belief system generated in organization

metaphors
shorthand descriptions of underlying belief system

models
strategies or ideas in action

is impacted by

changes the environment

internal and external organizational reality
(particular settings, conditions, and context)

Figure 8
Church as Paradigm. Adapted from Hasan Sisek and Karen Louis, "Organizational Change as Paradigm Shift," *Journal of Higher Education* 65, no. 6 (November–December 1994).

Myths/Codes

Remember, organizational myths (what can also be called codes or scripts) are the background assumptions which are generally the abstract and subconscious dimension of organizational paradigm. Often they come with the territory: the inherited beliefs that are simply taken for granted because they are seldom subjected to serious questioning. These beliefs and codes take on the character of myth because they are so deep-seated and resistant to change. It's only when serious anomalies call into question the viability of the paradigm that we begin to become consciously aware of them. Actually, this is part of the function of prophetic ministry and why it's so important. Through prophetic dissent—or through the increasing awareness of anomalies—a crisis occurs, where the organization's viability is called into question. We have to recode the organizational paradigm in order to survive.

Recoding is a tricky but essential matter to negotiate, because survivability and effectiveness is often at stake.[2] But it can also be a very creative time as people go on an adventurous search for workable new alternatives. In our time, the major shift to a genuinely post-Christian, unchurched culture has forced the church in the West to seriously rethink our paradigm (remember the 60:40 issue). What an opportunity!

Remember, the answers to the crisis won't come from within the current thinking. We have to both transcend and include our surroundings in order to go on a search for new answers. Key leadership must initiate and guide this journey, first by getting other leaders in touch with this sense of disorientation, anomaly, and crisis. Second, leaders should try to resolve the problems without recourse to the prevailing thinking, with its overused repertoire of solutions.

Following are some examples of deeply entrenched myths I believe are part of the institutional paradigm. Try these out on your team.

- *Build it and they will come.* This has been a predominant myth over the last fifty years but has deep roots in Christendom thinking. This one lies at the root of what I have called the attractional-extractional church. It has worked for many years, but changing conditions in our context are seriously challenging its viability.

- *The church is the bastion of family values.* This might express itself positively, as in "ours is a family church." Well, of course it is, but surely the church Jesus built should also be *more* than that. Furthermore, when interpreted from within the predominantly Western experience of (and assumptions about) the middle-class nuclear family, it can seriously limit—perhaps even damage—our understanding of the mission of the church.[3]

- *The church is the guardian of society's morals.* Again this seems hard to disagree with, but it really does come from the Christendom assumption that we're the central religious institution of society, that we have the inherent right to speak with authority into the moral situation. In a post-Christendom, post-church, secular culture, the church no longer has that kind of status, legitimacy, and permission. (Shouting louder ain't going to help!) Besides, this kind of myth can tend to make Pharisees of us all. Rather than trying to resolve this, we must return to the image of *witness* and not presume we have the cultural right to correct other people's morals.[4] We point to Jesus through faithful witness, not prescribed behaviors.

> Every believer a church planter. Every church a church-planting church.

- *We need clergy, buildings, and Sunday services in order to be a real church.* Again we can see the predominantly institutional paradigm impressing itself on our imaginations here. But this myth cannot explain the very best, and most impactful, Christian movements in history—which are often persecuted (therefore underground and without buildings) and are patently *not* run by seminary-trained professionals. Yet the myth persists even in contemporary churches; for example, we say that it is "pastor so-and-so's church" and that we "go to church" (meaning the building). Ask most people in the church what ministry is, and they will say it's something that the clergy do. If the people have anything at all to do with it, it's seen as volunteering for something and it's temporary. This myth is very deeply embedded into our codes, and we have to deliberately recode it before we can advance to becoming an apostolic movement.

- *We are a Bible-teaching church.* The subtext here is that if we simply teach more Bible (and teach it better), things will automatically change. The reality is that this is far from the truth. The Western church has more theology, commentaries, training, and intellectual tradition than at any other time in history, and it certainly hasn't produced the desired revival—perhaps it has even influenced the opposite! This is not to say we ought to be biblically illiterate, but we must remember we are perfectly designed to produce what we are currently producing. I'm sorry to say this, but more beautifully delivered three-point sermons are not going to solve your missional problems—or any serious strategic problems, for that matter! If they could do that, we would be there now. Remember, the Pharisees knew their Scriptures better than anyone and missed the whole point of God in Jesus (Matt. 23:24; John 5:39–40).

Because conventional thinking serves very often to protect us from the painful job of thinking for ourselves, ruthless honesty is needed when exploring our myths and assumptions about the church. Furthermore, many of us have bought deeply into the paradigm and have even gotten our sense of legitimacy from it, so we are personally involved; we might well find ourselves getting defensive here.

For instance, it's very hard to critique the seminary from which one earned one's degree without devaluing one's hard-earned sense of self-worth derived from the degree. This is what makes myths so hard to change.

We all know the story of the emperor who had no clothes. It takes a child to expose the collective spell myths have over us. So we too will need to approach this as a little child (Matt. 18:1–4). We need to be willing to give up every preconceived notion, follow humbly wherever the Spirit will lead us, and laugh at our own nakedness. If you are too protective of your own assumptions and myths, you will learn nothing. Some questions to ask: What myths have guided us thus far? What anomalies have led us to question their viability? How do these myths aid or hinder our effectiveness in becoming an apostolic movement?

I have focused on exposing examples of more *negative* myths here because these are the ones obstructing the latent potential Jesus has placed in every church. Many assumptions held about church are good and consistent with Verge church thinking, but again this highlights the need to take a myth audit. Take the bad assumptions out, and the good ones will do what they are meant to do: make us a whole lot better.

Metaphors

Metaphors, on the other hand, are powerful, highly compact language bites that give us insight into the implicit (and hidden) assumptions of any organizational paradigm. They are therefore wonderfully convenient shorthand descriptions of your belief system or myth, but they can't provide the whole picture, only a window into aspects of it. Rob Wegner reminded me at this point that Jesus always used images and metaphors, and the reason why is that stories, metaphors, and images don't have less truth than abstract propositions; *they have more truth*. A great story or metaphor invites you to come in. You almost intuitively find yourself in it, and it has a subversive life of its own. Metaphors and stories not only speak to the mind; they capture the heart, mind, and will all at once.

> Metaphors and stories not only speak to the mind; they capture the heart, mind, and will all at once.

The reason why metaphors are powerful descriptors is that they filter and define reality in a simple fashion (for example, "Richard is a lion," "the brain is a computer," or "organizations are machines"). Even simple words like *amoeba, beehive, fort,* and *cookie cutter* provide clues as to how people see and experience paradigms in relationship to organizations. For instance, if I said that such-and-such church was an elephant, what images come to mind? What if I had used the term *starfish*? Each metaphor will convey different information about reproductive capacities, mobility, strength, wisdom, personality, courage, and so on. Identifying the metaphors thus offers significant clues about where to focus the efforts at shifting the paradigm. And what is more, change the metaphor, and you change the imagination. Advertising (and education, for that matter) tries to do this all the time.

Get people to list the words and phrases that for them most accurately describe their church or organization. The problem in church circles is the vast array of metaphors people have picked up from the Bible but don't necessarily believe. So maybe you want to ask people to use the biblical metaphors they think most accurately fit, and then ask them to use nonbiblical language. Try identifying the ones people are most emotively bonded to.

Do this individually (and then also corporately) with samplings from all over the organization. Collate the information and identify the dominant metaphors. You might also want to ask people to add adjectives to describe the metaphor (for example, *efficient, sloppy, controlling, decentralized*). By the way, Clotaire Rapaille's book *The Culture Code* is a brilliant resource in helping understand the codes of behavior in organizations and culture.[5]

In the "Shift" section following this, I will suggest many alternative metaphors more consistent with Verge church thinking.

Models

Models (the recognizable collection of typical organizational protocols, strategies, and policies) are directly drawn from the dominant myths/codes and guide the action in any organization, including churches. Models therefore provide the scaffolding any organization needs to fulfill its function. And make no mistake, how a model is framed and played out directly shapes behaviors and actions in the organization.

The model activates, embeds, and maintains the paradigm and therefore needs reimagining if we are to transition to becoming a Verge church. Because we will deal thoroughly with this later, we will simply note this here since it's part of the paradigm that needs to be assessed.

A Whole New Mind

Imagination and intuition are clearly functions of the right brain. So in many ways we are suggesting that in order to develop Verge church thinking, we need to at least counterbalance our overreliance on methodology, ideology, and techniques, with a recovery of intelligent imagination and intuitive responsiveness. I find Daniel Pink's *A Whole New Mind* very useful at this point.[8] He suggests we need to cultivate a much more right-brained approach in ourselves as well as in the organizations we lead.

Cultivating this right-brained approach involves the following:

A Quick Checklist of Reimagining Skills

Much of this material will resonate with the sections that follow: "Shift" (processing change from inside out and outside in), "Innovate" (implementation of imaginative solutions to old problems), and "Move" (generating momentum and creating movement — that is, *movementum*). But I couldn't resist putting in some great ways to provoke imagination.[6]

- *Create holy dissatisfaction.* Reach into your deepest commitments to the King and his kingdom and ask people if we have yet reached perfection. Most likely, the answer is no, with the understanding that we as God's people are called to do something about that. We are created for good works, after all (Eph. 2:10), and I guess we can always improve on the delivery.
- $L = P + Q$. This is the formula for learning organizations. Learning (L) takes place when programming (P) is subjected to questioning (Q). Learn how to ask the right questions and to initiate a genuine quest for the answers. For instance, you might simply ask what it is you're measuring. And then ask if what and how you are measuring are clues to what you value. Finally, ask how effectiveness could be measured differently.
- *Take more risks.* This is a major issue in churches that have largely become socially conservative and profoundly risk-averse. Conformity is the result of obsession with safety; diversity and adventure will come from a willingness to take risks. Simply putting yourself out of your comfort zone is likely to create new learning opportunities.[7]
- *Think like a beginner, not an expert.* This is a classic way to think differently about things. As the expert of your sphere, you have ready answers that suggest themselves to you. Approach the problem as a beginner, and you have to learn again from scratch. Ask, if I had to do this all again, and differently, how would I do this?
- *Sell the problem before you sell the solution.* Help people get in touch with the problem. Once they see (and especially *feel*) the issue, they can get very creative indeed. All people can be highly imaginative and innovative when their life depends on it!

This mention of *feeling* things differently opens up a whole new issue for us to consider.

1. *Using beauty: aesthetics.* We must develop ways of thinking
   that factor artistic and emotional beauty into the equation.
   Pink calls this "design," and it means we must move beyond
   looking at the church in a merely functional way to looking
   at it as something beautiful and emotionally engaging. We've
   tended to see the church in far too mechanistic ways in the
   twentieth century, and therefore most expressions of evangelical church are pretty artless. (If you don't agree with us, then
   just ask any artist.)

2. *Living out of a big story: narrative.* The ability to use story to
   engender movement and open-endedness is key. This is what
   Pink simply calls "story," and it is vital in weaving people and
   organizations together. We recognize that at the heart of any
   healthy understanding of the church lies a compelling narrative
   that goes beyond a simple line of reasoning. It invites others
   to join and take a role in the unfolding narrative. Again this
   is precisely what the gospel does to us. For too long, Western
   Christianity has emphasized thoroughly rationalized doctrinal
   formulas over narrative and diminished the power of story to
   form Christian identity and create movement. An apostle is
   a theological storyteller, and apostolic movements understand
   and skillfully navigate the power of stories. We suggest that the
   recovery of story which has taken place over the last twenty or
   so years is at least one of the factors opening us up to see the
   paradigm church as an apostolic movement now.

3. *Seeing pretty patterns: discernment.* We have to improve our
   ability to detect patterns and take advantage of new opportunities presenting themselves. According to Pink, the greatest demand today isn't detailed *analysis* but rather big-picture
   thinking, systemic approaches, nonlinear dynamics, and syn-
   thesis. He poetically calls this "symphony," and it involves
   (among other things) the ability to put together seemingly
   disparate pieces of information, to see relationships between
   seemingly unrelated fields, to detect broad patterns rather
   than deliver specific answers, and to invent something new
   by combining elements no one else thinks to pair.[9] In fact,
   we think this is exactly what is required for us to "see" as well

as experience the power of Verge church ecclesiology. (In this book, this symphonic understanding of the church is what we call Apostolic Genius.)

4. *Feeling all right: empathy.* This word *empathy* is what Pink uses to describe a capacity to understand others and forge significant relationships; others have called this emotional intelligence quotient (or EQ). Empathy involves the ability to motivate and inspire from deep within a rich relational bond, and it shouldn't be strange for us as we seek to develop real community, or *communitas*, in churches. Empathy also creates a deep human bond between those related in such a way. Again, this gets us much closer to what the Bible means by inspirational leadership: "Both leaders and followers raise each other to higher levels of motivation and morality by engaging each other on the basis of shared values, calling and identity. They are in a relationship in which each influences the other to pursue common objectives, with the aim of inspiring followers to becoming leaders in their own right."[10] Movements thrive on — and are held together by — such relationships!

5. *Learning to play: chillax.* The ability to simply chill out and enjoy life must sometimes be learned. Pink's advice here is very useful to evangelicals, who can tend to be somewhat task-focused, life-denying, and sometimes just plain uptight. Learn to play! Seriousness has its place, but everyone needs some lightheartedness and time to have fun. This not only creates good connections but also allows space for creativity and freedom of expression within the broad guidelines of apostolic theology and ministry. God is good, and pleasure (when rightly ordered in relation to God) is a great motivator.[11] Take time to enjoy his goodness together. Einstein said, "Games [playfulness] are the most elevated forms of investigation." Play is one of the major sources of innovation.

6. *Managing meaning: heart connection.* Meaning, the final element of Pink's *Whole New Mind*, is clearly something we as God's people should well understand. People act from their deepest (and highest) motivations only when something is *meaningful* to them. Connecting people and a grander

meaning lies at the heart of all ministry and mission. In Verge churches, we must motivate people through what has sometimes been called the "management of meaning." Meaning might well require ideology but reaches beyond the mind to the heart and makes the connection between God and people. This is the reason why movements hold together and how leadership can operate in and through distributed networks. And it also highlights why good theology is a vital part of the equation—it makes the connection between Word and world, between God's mind (and actions) and the human heart.

All this requires us to seriously reconsider the role of the Holy Spirit in organization, mission, and ministry. Clearly, the Spirit brings life, creativity, and inspirational courage to his people while at the same time requiring intuition, risk, responsiveness, and flexibility from us. If we want to move to the Verge and become an apostolic movement again, we must allow God's Spirit to play a leading role. We simply have to ask ourselves hard questions about the extent to which we have replaced the leading of the Spirit with technique, ideology, and top-heavy, left-brained thinking in the life of the church. Movements are movements of the Spirit of God before they are anything else.

So what's not to like about right-brained thinking? Particularly when we see this as a corrective (and not as an overbalance) to the other side—we could do with a whole lot more intuition/imagination and a little less rationality and technique. This does, however, raise significant and very practical issues for us. Like all paradigm shifts, it will likely also require repentance from us if we are to progress healthily into the Verge church paradigm.

First, it's obvious that left-brained approaches will tend to yield left-brained results, and vice versa. Clearly, we need both. However, at present, most leadership is overwhelmingly male, even though most ministry on the ground is performed by women. Remember, we are perfectly designed to achieve what we are currently achieving, in that our organizations tend to reflect a predominance of male thinking (which tends to be more left-brained and can tend to exclude right-brained thinking). The results are the loss of creativity, diminished relationships, and a whole lot less by way of symphony. Let's be honest:

women tend to be better at this than men, and in order to be genuinely movemental, we need a whole lot more women in leadership. It's time to balance up this equation.

At the risk of overgeneralizing, what Pink is describing with this right-brained approach can be characterized as being much more "feminine" in style and approach to organization and leadership. Movements need "masculine" technique and structure, certainly, but they also require us to be more fluid, responsive, and intuitive in order to develop—especially when we need creative solutions in order to thrive/survive. In other words, we need a balance of masculine and feminine energy in the church, radiating from leadership out. It's no coincidence that about 65 percent of the leaders in the Chinese underground church are women, and even more in the many rapidly expanding movements in India and elsewhere. The same is true for the post–New Testament church; women played a very significant and active role in the expansion of early Christianity.[12] And consider that of the fifty thousand cell churches within Yoido Full Gospel Church, the world-influencing church led by the apostolic leader Dr. Yonggi Cho, over forty thousand are pastored (yes, *pastored*) by women—which indicates a massive change of thinking from Dr. Cho's early days.

> It's not so much that the church has a mission but that the mission has a church. Church follows mission, not the other way around.

No matter how we choose to interpret the Pauline texts (and for what it is worth, both Dave and I are fuzzy complementarians), it's clear in the New Testament and from history that women bear together with men the image of God, are integrally part of the body of Christ, are fully empowered agents of the King, and are commissioned in their conversion to Jesus' ministry and kingdom. It's high time to balance out the male dominance in church ministry and leadership. If we do not, we can expect more of the same (somewhat one-brained) results we're currently achieving.[13]

Second, few churches and Christian organizations make space for serious experimentation, research, and development—space now known in the business world as "skunkworks" projects. Not only does this lack of space diminish our capacity to dream up new futures and solve significant problems; it will inevitably mean that we'll lack creative options precisely when we need them, because we haven't valued and invested in creativity. In times of uncertainty and adaptive challenges, this can prove completely disastrous. The best way to have *one* great idea is to have *many* ideas; the best way to negotiate the conditions of rapid, discontinuous change isn't to have *one* ten-year plan but to have *many* one- to three-year plans.[14]

The movement itself is its own R&D department. Best thinking and practices in the business world reflect this — they have to. Failure to innovate means inevitable demise in a global economy. The missional situation we face demands that we have more creative irons in the fire and that we invest in research and development (R&D); this means embracing the right-brained approach more often.

Truth is that most of the R&D and skunkworks projects for churches would cost nothing (or very little indeed). For instance, Rob Wegner notes, "Every church has loads of people who are just itching to do this, as well as people who would personally fund it. All these folks just need encouragement, permission, training, and coaching along the way. Ask five people who are interested to read *The Forgotten Ways Handbook* together or *The Tangible Kingdom Primer* by Hugh Halter and Matt Smay, and over six months encourage them to go and *do it* where God has already planted them. Then make sure you harvest the ideas and learnings that flow out of their experiences ... it's that simple."

Alex McManus, a colleague in Future Travelers and a missional architect for Kensington Community Church, adds that tapping into the initiatives of adventurous missional leaders will coax churches and their leaders out from within the four walls and into the world, where God is waiting for them.

The movement itself is its own R&D department.

Changing the Conversation

As a Word community, the church fully understands the power of words; they shape reality. Theology itself is built on this very idea. In general, words mediate by signifying or triggering appropriate thoughts in our minds. Like the imagination to which they appeal, they make or imply associations and therefore shape the way we perceive reality. In many ways, we can say that words even *define* reality;

change people's language, and you will in the end change their way of thinking. The whole study of linguistics and semiotics has made a science of this, and the power of it (for good and evil) is undeniable. As we've seen, imagination uses metaphor, words, and images to probe possibility, solve problems, project into the future, look around corners, and (in the end) evoke action. So too Verge churches must recover this capacity to develop powerful words and phrases that help people think and act differently. In fact, it's our hope that this book is a virtual cache of missional slogans to help fire up apostolic movement.

The Power of a Slogan

"The slogan is ... probably the best people mover this side of earthquakes, court orders and guns."[15] This is because a slogan is as easy to remember as it is hard to forget and plants itself in the consciousness by rhythm, rhyme, pith, or brevity. Once there, it works not only by whatever imagery it carries but also by the latent emotions it mobilizes, either calming or inflaming an audience—depending on purpose. As such, "the slogan lurks as a sort of floating hook in the psyche. Properly tugged, it can impel people to coalesce, to divide, to fight, to sacrifice, to vote, to buy."[16]

Consider the following slogans, all of which still carry great ideas that are sticky, motivational, and viral: "Yes, we can!" recently helped propel the first African-American president into the White House. Pope Urban II's rallying cry "God wills it!" fired up the First Crusade. Luther's "Here I stand, I can do no other, so help me God" ignited the Reformation. "Speak softly and carry a big stick" evokes the now-vanished world of Theodore Roosevelt's America. Horace Greeley's popularization of "Go west, young man" not only helped inspire California-bound migration but even today conjures up appealing images. "No taxation without representation." "Make love, not war." "Give me liberty or give me death." "We shall overcome." "Hell no, we won't go." Each of these captured social imagination, focused emotion, and fueled various people-movements.

Never underestimate the power of a theologically loaded slogan to ignite apostolic movement. Consider, for instance, the theological force gathered up and communicated in the apostolic church's timeless rallying call "Jesus is Lord!"—not only is this a whole worldview

(Christocentric monotheism) in three words, but it is a thoroughly sneezable slogan that has galvanized countless viral movements in history. The sheer movemental power of "Every believer a church planter, every church a church-planting church" is quite remarkable. Viewed in the light of the power of words to shape and transform behavior, thinking, and culture, the gospel itself is the most powerful idea-virus in the history of the world.

Here are some slogans from Future Travelers churches:

Granger Community Church: Blowing it up to blow it out.

Community Christian Church: Helping people find their way back to God.

The Journey: We are a community on mission, not a mission of community.

Soma Communities: We don't *go* to church, we are the church.

RiverTree Christian Church: Your mission is your life.

Making It Schtick

But generating great slogans isn't always easy. We need to make them as sticky as Velcro and as contagious as viruses. Sadly, we should expect the automatic rejection of the obvious, without thought, inspection, or experiment, in all forms of human endeavor, perhaps especially in church circles.[17]

In their stimulating book *Made to Stick*, the Heath brothers suggest some principles in order to "sell ideas" and to be able to develop what they call "stickiness."[18] It is therefore important for innovative missional leaders to remember that developing the best evidence and practices is often even less than half the battle. Ideas that spread and stick need to be sold well too.

Incidentally, the reader can easily discern the direct use of, and appeal to, the imagination and right-brained thinking throughout these six principles. They are:

1. *Simplicity.* "To strip an idea down to its core, we must be masters of exclusion. We must relentlessly prioritize. Saying something short isn't the mission — sound bites aren't the ideal. Proverbs are the ideal. We must create ideas that are both simple and profound."[19]

2. *Surprise.* "We can use surprise—an emotion whose function is to increase alertness and cause focus—to grab people's attention.... For our idea to endure, we must generate interest and curiosity."[20]

3. *Concreteness.* "We must explain our ideas in terms of human actions, in terms of sensory information.... In proverbs, abstract truths are often encoded in concrete language: 'A bird in hand is worth two in the bush.'"[21]

4. *Credibility.* "Sticky ideas have to carry their own credentials. We need ways to help people test our ideas for themselves...." Ronald Reagan asked, "Before you vote, ask yourself if you are better off today than you were four years ago."[22]

5. *Emotions.* "How do we get people to care about our ideas? We make them feel something.... We are wired to feel things for people, not for abstractions. Sometimes the hard part is finding the right emotion to harness."[23]

6. *Stories.* "How do we get people to act on our ideas? We tell stories.... Hearing stories acts as a kind of mental flight simulator, preparing us to respond more quickly and effectively."[24]

A Tithe to the Lord

Having made all these statements about intuition and insight, I'd like to offer an intuition of my own here (and Dave thoroughly agrees with this as well): Taking a cue from one of the slogans, that *every church has in it all that it needs to get the job done*, I suggest that there are many people present in your church who already intuitively understand Verge church thinking. For some it might be a vague sense of holy discomfort with the status quo, for others it is already a well-informed grasp of the dynamics of people-movements, but these intuitive thoughts are still seeking expression. I dare suggest there may be *as many as 10 percent* in any progressive contemporary church who will already have a positive heart-response to the various issues we raise in this book, even if they might not be able to fully articulate their thoughts yet. *You can work with this*; massive movements were started with far less—our New

> Movements, like human bodies, start small. We start as single-cell organisms—and if all the conditions are right, we can grow very, very big indeed!

Testament church ancestors being a case in point! Movements, like human bodies, start small. We start as single-cell organisms—and if all the conditions are right, we can grow very, very big indeed!

This suggestion of 10 percent buy-in—a missional "people tithe," so to speak—is an intuitive guess, but it does square well with Everett Rogers' theory called Diffusion of Innovation, which states that in any given population there are a range of people with different responses to new ideas, including the progressive wing composed of innovators and early adopters (fig. 9). It's a leader's job to understand that these people are present and are vital in changing the organization, and indeed for innovation itself. The same theory of knowledge would suggest that all you need is 16 percent of the most progressive sectors of a population for the idea to be inevitable in that system![25] Gladwell's *Tipping Point* simply confirms Rogers' basic thesis and develops it.

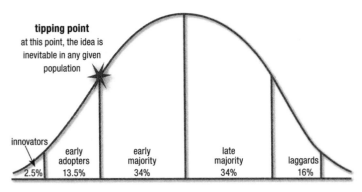

Figure 9

This is a well-tested theory, and it ought to be used to further apostolic movement. It's surely a strategic task of leadership to identify these people (the "berry-eaters," who are first to try the new fruits at risk of their own lives), legitimize their concerns, fertilize their thinking, give them oodles of permission to dream, and then harvest the results. In other words, create a homegrown think tank and use this as a generative source of imagination, leadership, and ideas.

From Here to There, Funny Things Are Everywhere

A final word about transitioning to the new paradigm: it's not going to feel comfortable at first. It's just not. (Deal with it.) We are so used to operating in the existing paradigm that it feels natural to us, and it will be the new that feels rather strange and unnatural. It might just feel ... *eccentric*, but I suggest that all new ideas feel that way at first. What is now accepted as normal once felt abnormal and eccentric.

Verge churches are just that: on the *verge*. And because their primary paradigm is deeply grounded in inherited institutional ideas of church, a more movemental approach isn't necessarily going to feel easy, at least at first. Abraham Maslow's scale of learning might be as useful here as it is later, in the final section, "Move," where we talk about movementum and change management. You see, Maslow maintained that in relation to awareness and embracing of any idea, action, or paradigm, people will move through four distinct stages:

1. *Unconscious incompetence.* Here people are simply not aware of the new paradigm at all. Clearly, the task is to raise awareness so learning can begin. Apart from selling the problem before suggesting the solution, leadership should appeal mainly to the latent imagination and sense of obligation to God's mission that all true believers feel.[26] It's good to remind ourselves at this point that in order to change our perception, we have to first experience some level of frustration in our actions, or a significant change of purpose.[27] Holy discontent accompanied by an imaginative search for answers will move people toward ...

2. *Conscious incompetence.* Here there is a dawning awareness about the Verge paradigm, and — as a result — people become increasingly aware of their individual and corporate deficiencies in this area. The trick is not to get cynical or give up. What is needed at this point is a real commitment to learn and grow, to try things out, and so move to the next stage. To increase the levels of competence and confirm the truth of the paradigm, leaders should directly model the change they wish to see and should encourage lots of experimentation, with plenty of permission to fail. Help the church get over its risk averseness and get to ...

3. *Conscious competence.* This phase happens when people understand the basic dynamics of the new paradigm but still need to concentrate in order to operate well; it is not yet second nature or automatic. Like a new driver, navigating the road takes concentration and practice, but the natural reflexes will come. The slogan "Practice makes perfect" might well apply here, until the final phase comes ...

4. *Unconscious competence.* Here the paradigm becomes instinctual — it's hard to see it any other way. Those at this stage are true insiders of the paradigm. They are now competent to teach others about apostolic movement thinking.

Leaders will need to help others adopt innovation, by providing broad-based access to knowledge, by actively persuading people about the viability of the new paradigm, and by encouraging others to give it a go (not just once but a few times, because it's going to feel clunky at first). Eventually the innovation will be fully embraced.

Dream On ...

Peter Drucker once stated, "People in any organization are always attached to the obsolete — the things that should have worked but didn't, the things that once were productive and no longer are."[28] The task of visionary leaders, therefore, is not only to make sure things advance into some preferred future but also to ensure that outmoded ideas and processes are discarded along the way. This is partly what a mission to the mind is all about. It's relatively easy to come up with new ideas; the really hard part is letting go of what worked two (or four or eight) years ago but will soon be out-of-date! We need to unlearn as much as we need to learn. We need to be remissionalized at a very deep level. And to do this, we need imagination, but even more so we need *apostolic* imagination.

We need to unlearn as much as we need to learn.

I end this chapter where I started, with a reminder that the first task of leadership is to *define reality.* As Christian leaders, this reality isn't something we arbitrarily determine; rather it's based on a biblical view of things. It's critical that leadership, at every level, come to grips with the profoundly biblical nature of Verge church thinking. The previous chapter suggested four Verge focal points, or paradigms, that are needed to reimagine the nature of church and mission as apostolic movement (Christology, missiology, organization, and discipleship). With this as a guide, we can begin to move away from the prevailing imagination/paradigm of church, one that has served the gospel for centuries but now blinds us to more dynamic forms of church.

Your primary responsibility as a leader will be to awaken what is already there, by calling people to see beyond their current constraints, to wake up to the ever-present reality of Jesus, and to fulfill their deeper destinies as disciples of the King. You will need courage and conviction to do this. But know this: when awakening the deeply embedded missionary calling and instincts of the church, you have the Holy Spirit on your side. This is what apostolic ministry is about, and (dare I say) what it means to be a true *apostolic* visionary in our day.

Dave's Response to "Mission to the Mind and Heart"

The challenge to recapture the missional imagination of God's people in the West may be more daunting than we first thought, because there is not only a crisis of creativity in the church; there is also a crisis of creativity in the United States. Gordon McKenzie's hunch about the loss of imaginative creativity, which he tested by asking first- through sixth-graders, "Who is an artist?" is now substantiated. After analyzing almost three hundred thousand creativity scores from adults and children over the last fifty years, Kyung Hee Kim at the College of William & Mary found that creativity scores have consistently declined for the last twenty years.

Kim commented, "It's very clear, and the decrease is very significant." So creativity is not only a great challenge for the church; it's also a challenge for the context of the church. The battle for the future of the Western church will be won or lost in the minds of people. We must recapture the imagination of God's people with his compelling vision of transformed lives and communities, or we'll die a slow death, trapped in the same paradigm as our brothers and sisters in Australia and Europe.

The response to this challenge by churches that are part of the Future Travelers has been swift and definitive in at least three ways:

challenging existing assumptions, creating new metaphors, and exploring new models. Let me give you some examples of each.

Challenging Existing Assumptions

The Austin Stone Church in Austin, Texas, was born out of a Southern Baptist tradition and, because of this, inherited denominational assumptions about baptism. The assumption was that if you wanted to be baptized, you had to come to a church-sponsored service and have an elder or pastor baptize you. This is a perfect example of the kind of unwritten code that supports an institutional paradigm of church that creates a chasm between the clergy and laity. It's my view that baptism was given to us not just for the benefit of the person being baptized but also for the baptizer. It's like payday after doing the work of an evangelist. Think of all the people who have prayed for a friend or neighbor and spent hours talking to them and finally introducing them to Jesus, only to have some "professional" step in and do the baptizing. How de-motivating! I know it isn't about gaining personal reward, but neither should the reward be going to some pastor who never met the person.

At the Austin Stone Church, they began to reimagine the experience of baptism as they reread the Great Commission: "Go and make disciples of all nations, baptizing them in the name of the Father and of the Son and of the Holy Spirit, and teaching them to obey everything I have commanded you" (Matt. 28:19–20). One staff member confessed, "We realized we were letting them go and teach, but when it came to baptism, we were saying, 'Bring them to us to be baptized.' We were only asking them to follow two-thirds of the Great Commission."

So the unwritten code saying that only elders and pastors could baptize (and it had to be done in church) had to go away. Today Austin Stone is baptizing more people than ever, and they have people in their communities baptizing in their pools, hot tubs, lakes—wherever there is water! This particular unwritten code is just one of the many assumptions that must be challenged if we are to see a paradigm shift in the churches we lead. Making that shift will require courageous use of our imaginations.

Creating New Metaphors

Granger Community Church is a sprawling megachurch in northwest Indiana. They had heard Alan say, "Change the metaphor, and you change the imagination" and knew it was true. They also knew that if you asked anyone in the Granger area about their church, they would point to the fifty-four-acre physical campus and say, "Granger is over there." The leadership knew that the primary metaphor for their church was their building and that—if they ever wanted to see an apostolic movement—they needed to create new metaphors, starting with their facility. The new metaphor had to inspire people to *go* and not just *bring*. So the leadership of Granger began to imagine new metaphors for their campus and came up with the following possibilities they are still working through:

- *Incubator:* a facility nurturing new missional expressions
- *Boot camp:* a facility training people for full missional engagement
- *Airport:* a facility sending you to another place, not keeping you inside it
- *Notre Dame University* (which is near Granger): a facility training alumni who spread worldwide after graduation
- *Community center:* a facility reprogrammed to provide for the community and not just for the church

The consistent use of any of these metaphors (and the practices that must go with them) will be a huge help in transitioning Granger from an exclusively attractional paradigm to a gathered *and* scattered church.

The hard work of identifying current metaphors and reimagining new ones is critical for creating a new systems story for any church.

Exploring New Models

With more than fifteen hundred people from around St. Louis, Missouri, in community groups, the Journey church had seen tremendous success connecting people into smaller groups. While this impressive number of people had been successfully assimilated into the life of the larger church, the leaders of the church knew that most were not personally engaged in mission. The church's existing model was perfectly designed to achieve what they were currently achieving, but they wanted more! They wanted to see a missional movement throughout the St. Louis region. They began to explore other models and designed a website called *Community Loop*, where community group leaders could go to connect their groups with a variety of missional causes throughout the city. The reimagining process created a new model that provided ways for their small groups to stay intact and move forward on mission.

In a culture whose imagination is slowly slipping away, we have within us the source of all creativity, the *imago Dei*. We are all made in the image of our God, and that includes, among other things, the ability to be imaginatively creative. And when the church is in the act of imagining, we access the *imago Dei* within us and within our communities of faith. That imagination has the capacity to make visible what was only implied, to connect matter with spirit. Holy imagination is able to help us rediscover our primal story, an alternative story that has the power to move us forward into God's future.

DISCUSSION QUESTIONS

Open

What is the best business slogan you've heard recently? How about the best church or ministry slogan? What makes them stick with you?

Explore

1. What myths and/or metaphors are present in your current church structure? "Our church is like _____." (See p. 86 for some examples.) From where do these myths originate? Which ones hinder and which ones aid in becoming an apostolic movement?
2. On page 97, Dave writes, "Change people's language, and you will in the end change their way of thinking." In what ways does your current language inhibit your church from Verge church thinking?
3. What do you think your greatest challenges will be in addressing the creativity crisis in your context? How can you prepare ahead of time to combat those challenges?

4. What are two or three steps you can take to encourage the 10 percent in your church who intuitively understand Verge church thinking?

5. "Live in me. Make your home in me just as I do in you. In the same way that a branch can't bear grapes by itself but only by being joined to the vine, you can't bear fruit unless you are joined with me. I am the Vine, you are the branches. When you're joined with me and I with you, the relation intimate and organic, the harvest is sure to be abundant. Separated, you can't produce a thing" (John 15:4–5 MSG).

   How does a person make his or her home in Jesus? How do you personally make your home in Jesus? What does an intimate and organic relationship look like? How is this vital to unleashing our missional imaginations?

Move

1. Spend some time with your leadership team "de-mythifying" your church. Brainstorm these metaphors and myths, weeding out the ones that are confining and holding on to the ones you agree are central to mission.

2. This is not simply an attempt to be hip or cool in a changing culture but a Spirit-led process, reshaping the people of God to be more effective in the Jesus mission. With this in mind, commit to spending time allowing Jesus to keep you focused on him. Sit quietly for fifteen minutes and meditate on John 15, particularly verse 5: "I am the Vine, you are the branches. When you're joined with me and I with you, the relation intimate and organic, the harvest is sure to be abundant. Separated, you can't produce a thing" (MSG).

Part 2
Shift

ALAN

It is impossible to travel south without turning one's back on north.   — A. W. TOZER

He who rejects change is the architect of decay. The only human institution which rejects progress is the cemetery.
  — HAROLD WILSON

Our nature lies in movement, complete calm is death.
  — BLAISE PASCAL, *PENSÉES*

Introduction to the "Shift" Section

Having described the silver imagination and the mission to the mind required to become an apostolic movement, we now come to the very heart of this book. Here I will put forward a unique, distinctly *movemental*, model for change. Nowhere, as far as we are aware, has there been offered a change process to develop churches into apostolic movements. And while the process might itself be innovative, it is developed on best practices as it relates to systemic change.

But a few things need explanation and definition before we can engage the shift process.

From Verge Paradigm to Verge Practice

To this point, we have explored the nature of the paradigm, or cluster of paradigms, needed to shift toward being apostolic movements in the West. We have also looked at some ways in which we can unleash imagination and creative thinking in the life of the church or Christian organization. Here I will suggest a process that will allow churches to engage the Verge paradigm and begin to genuinely embrace apostolic movement.

This process assumes that all organizations, and indeed humans, work from a paradigmatic center which operates as a kind of ideological DNA. Furthermore, it assumes that this genetic basis provides the basis of values, or ethos, and that ethos in turn is what generates meaningful actions. If this is true, that the paradigm determines outcomes, then all true and lasting change must first take place at the deepest level, at the level of the genetic codes of the organization—the paradigm.

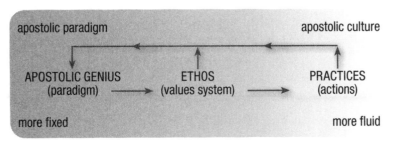

Figure 10

As mentioned before, if we don't change the paradigm, then all attempts to change at the other, less causal, more expressive, elements of organization will likely fail, because the default will just reassert itself when the pressure of change is relieved. The genetic coding of the church determines everything else; ethos and praxis are expressions of how we see and interpret our world. As a result, they are, to greater or lesser degrees, more fluid and adaptive than paradigms.

Because of the intangible nature of the paradigm, and because of the power of the scripting of our codes, it is much harder to work at this level, because it requires significant theological awareness and understanding of organizations and paradigms. The work here is conceptual; we have to reframe assumptions and change imaginations (hearts and minds). Nonetheless! If this is done, and done well, we can expect cascading missional change to result, because when we do this, we are working as Christian organizations should work—from the inside out. That's why God needs our hearts in order to get everything else. Our hearts, remember, are our paradigmatic centers.

Discipling the Whole Shebang

In many ways, what I am talking about here is *discipleship*—however, not discipleship that merely includes every believer but discipleship that also goes on to transform the whole system we call church and organization. We need another kind of administration that goes beyond organizational transformation, one that can address not just the transformation of an organization but also the transformation of the human heart. For that, there is one possibility—only one. There is a carpenter, a young rabbi, and his name is Jesus. He announced the coming of such a new organization that is a living organism made of people: the kingdom of God. You might want to call it the society of the transformed heart. And since that day two thousand years ago, governments and civilizations and political movements and economic systems come and go, they rise and they fall. But Jesus remains the single bright light of the human race for heart transformation.

If this is so—and it's hard to dispute it—then we have to ask ourselves, what's our plan to pursue both organizational and personal transformation? How does Apostolic Genius awaken in the heart of each follower of Jesus in our church?

Philippians 2:13 says that "it is God who works in you to will and to act according to his good purpose." The reality is that I can't really change myself; only Jesus can; only God does heart transformation. But I'm not passive either. I'm not just treading water, because verse 12 says, "My dear friends, as you have always obeyed—not only in my presence, but now much more in my absence—continue to work out your salvation with fear and trembling."

Paul says, *"work out."* There are activities and practices to which we commit in order to be able to join God in the process. This is something we do. We must arrange our lives around certain practices that deliberately serve to awaken (and "work out") Apostolic Genius and make it the central paradigm and ethos of our lives and church.

Consider Dallas Willard's work on VIM; in many ways, it offers an *exact* parallel to the shift process we suggest in this book (paradigm → ethos → practice).[1] While referring to the transformation of the heart, Willard says we need a VIM:

- *V* stands for vision (the Jesus dream)
- *I* stands for intention (the Jesus decision)
- *M* stands for method (the Jesus way)

If we want to pursue the transformation of the heart, we have to have a *vision* (paradigm)—a picture, a dream of what this new life would be like. And then, flowing out of that somewhere along the line, we've got to make a decision that we will pursue this; that's *intention* (ethos). Then it involves a *method* (practice) — a rearranged life, a way.

If we embed the Verge paradigm properly, we can *expect* an authentic Verge culture to emerge. As you are about to see, the shift process involves the embedding of Apostolic Genius (with its symphony of six elements of mDNA) at the heart of the organization. Next, through a profound engagement with our deepest identity as an apostolic movement, we will go on to develop a movemental ethos. And finally, out of a theologically well-funded ethos, we develop apostolic movement practices.[2]

Initiating and developing (discipling) movements — and even more so, reframing existing organizations as movements — is likely to require some serious change management. Dave will delve into this in the final section, called "Move." In this section, however, we will explore the central process for moving from the apostolic movement *concepts* to sustainable and consistent *practice*.

Putting the Apostolic Genius into Apostolic Movements

In this section, we will articulate what we believe is the epicenter of Verge churches. The first chapter in this section deals with the core codes of a Verge church. I use the term *Apostolic Genius*, a phrase I coined in *The Forgotten Ways*, to describe the paradigm at the heart of apostolic movements. Apostolic Genius is the total phenomenon, but it is in turn composed of six elements, what I call mDNA. The use of genetic language here is very deliberate; as in all living organisms, genetics plays a determining role in shaping the organism as well as in reproducing it. The same is true for the living system that is the human organization. There are deeply embedded codes at the heart of the organization that determine identity and shape resultant behavior and actions.

I use the word *mDNA* here because it distinguishes the ecclesial genetic coding from its biological counterpart and because I believe that Apostolic Genius actually describes nothing less than the *internal, transmitted genetic code of all apostolic movements in history*.[3] Please hear this carefully, because it's a big claim: I am saying that *wherever* we see an apostolic movement — the type of Christian movement that experiences an exponential growth curve, high impact, and "spontaneous expansion"—these six elements will be present and dynamically interrelating in the movement's system! It is vital for the reader to understand what is being said here, so let me say this another way: assuming God's presence and activity, *where the six elements come together and begin to create and inform a Christian organization, apostolic movement appears to be inevitable.*[4] If you can track with this, then in Apostolic Genius we are onto nothing less than the key to bringing movements into play!

So having identified and briefly described the phenomenon of Apostolic Genius, now we are ready to concisely identify the six elements of mDNA that together make it flare up. They are:

- *Jesus is Lord.* This is the spiritual heart and theological soul of apostolic movements and will require that we take Jesus with all seriousness in every possible way.
- *Disciple-making.* This is the way Jesus lives his life through us, and the way in which a missional ethos is embedded throughout the organization. Essentially, it is a process of being apprenticed to Jesus.
- *Missional-incarnational impulse.* This describes the ways in which the church follows the missional God in its engagement with the world. It will mean we take seriously the issue of how we engage culture and extend the mission of God through his people.
- *Apostolic environment.* This is how the church's ministry is expressed in at least five forms, allowing for growth and maturity. Here we will tackle the idea of developing a missional ministry and leadership for a missional church movement.
- *Organic systems.* This looks into the way decentralized movements are set in motion and then subsequently organized. We are going to have to look at ways in which we can reconfigure ministry to incorporate more reproductive, fluid, and adaptive forms of church and church organization.
- *Communitas.* This strange word describes the kind of comradely community that forms in the context of spiritual challenge, adventure, and risk. Here we deal with issues relating to *esprit de corps* and overcoming the risk averseness of prevailing forms of church.

The Remembered Ways

Another vital thing to note is that this Apostolic Genius is present but forgotten, latent but unused, in every church, and in fact, in the same way that DNA is in every cell in a body, mDNA is also present in every cell of the body of Christ. In other words, every believer carries the church's potential for world transformation, and every church has the selfsame potential infused into its system. And before you think this is some spooky New Age idea about human potential, we suggest it has more to do with the power of the gospel and the presence of God the Holy Spirit working in and through human agency than with some idealized view of human power and ability. Yes, it is Jesus who will build his church, but make no mistake, we are real players in the kingdom equation, and God has created human beings with incredible potentials, mDNA included.

As far as I can tell, this is the only possible conclusion from the study of apostolic movements, particularly demonstrated in the persecuted forms of movement.[5] Like DNA, the full genetic coding laced throughout every cell of your body, every component in the church's living system has the full capacity for the whole. To employ another useful metaphor, the church that Jesus designed is more like a starfish than an animal with a central nervous system.[6] Each piece of a starfish has the full potential of a new starfish; twenty pieces lead to twenty starfish! Viewed in this perspective, there are literally thousands of (potential) starfish contained within just one of these creatures. A church of a thousand disciples has a thousand *potential* churches contained in itself!

People might argue that not everyone can do a church. But this seems to work against what we see in people-movements everywhere. Very ordinary people get to be very significant agents of missional church. Actually, this is exactly what happened in the New Testament church! It is certainly on current display in China, India, and Latin America, in budding pockets of churches throughout the West, and so on.[7] Our inability to see it means that our current institutional paradigm blinds us to the reality of dormant potentials in all of God's people. This is one of the things that must be overcome if we are to operate as a Verge church.[8]

This is exactly what the Verge church process seeks to do: activate the latent potentials that are already present but largely inactive within most churches. It is important to recognize this, because we are not suggesting that you import some alien system of ideas into your church; rather we suggest that we must *remember what we have forgotten.* In effect, we are not imposing the six elements of mDNA but rather re*activating* them and establishing them at the epicenter of our thinking—at the root of where all ecclesial identity, ministry concepts, and missional actions are formed.[9] Beginning with the end in mind means starting with a vision and paradigm of apostolic movement if we are to truly become an apostolic movement. We suggest that Apostolic Genius (with its six elements of mDNA) provides us with the apostolic imagination needed to become apostolic movements. And when it is recognized, understood, activated, and applied at the very base of our thinking, it will change *everything*; here is the paradigm shift, the genetic codes, for Verge church movement.

And so applying this to the Verge church process will mean embedding these six elements of mDNA at the center of identity and consciousness. It will look something like figure 11.

Verge church process mDNA level

core practices

core ethics

core mDNA
systems story
paradigmatic center
comprising:
1. Jesus is Lord
2. disciple-making
3. missional-incarnational impulse
4. apostolic environment
5. organic systems
6. *communitas*

Figure 11

The mDNA core requires a constant return to the center to legitimize any ethos and praxis that come out of it. We will be continuously engaging all six elements at any given time. They will need to be constantly referred to if they are to operate as the effective guiding center of the church/organization. This means constant study of, and attentiveness to, Apostolic Genius with its six elements of mDNA.

Other Aspects to Consider

Think Systems: It's the Whole That Counts

The six elements of mDNA provide us with a system, a way of seeing movements in their wholeness. It is not a one-dimensional look at the simple characteristics of movements; rather it describes the phenomenon of movements in their wholeness—as a system of interrelating and interconnected elements. To think systems, all you need to do is consider your own body and try to remember, from your biology class at school, how intricate and wonderfully interactive it all is. Mess with one part, and you mess with the whole.

The claim made in *The Forgotten Ways* is that *all six elements are evident in all Jesus movements that achieve spontaneous expansion.* In other words, Verge church thinking is inherently systemic in nature, and therefore it is critical that you keep your eye on the whole while focusing on any of the singular elements. We cannot emphasize this too strongly. Remember, there are no single silver bullets; however, there definitely is a silver imagination that emerges when all six elements, powerful in their own right, come together in Apostolic Genius. Never lose sight of the fact that a true apostolic movement needs all six elements to make it cook. It's the whole, not just the parts, that counts.

With this in mind, we would *highly* recommend that those who wish to pursue a Verge process use the mPULSE approach to both diagnose the organization and develop strategy using the Apostolic Genius systems approach. This tool is more thoroughly described in Alan's response to chapter 9 (p. 271), but readers can familiarize themselves with this by going to *www.theforgottenways.org/mpulse.*

Ending with the Beginning in Mind

If beginning with the end in mind is wise, then we should also endeavor to end with the beginning in mind. If only a good tree can bear good fruit, it is also true that only good seeds can produce a good tree. Work hard at getting it right at the beginning, because what you do then determines what you end up with later. Mutations at the genetic level of the movement (mDNA) will lead to some serious problems later on.

If You Love Something Long Enough

If you love something long enough, it will reveal itself to you. In many ways, this is the way Alan discovered the six elements in the first place. It was a refusal to stop probing the issue of what factors come together to initiate and sustain apostolic movements. It took three years of probing the problem every day: reading, researching, interviewing, observing, theorizing, testing, discarding aspects that didn't fit, starting over again, and so on. This is not always easy, but as we indicated in the chapter on imagination, leadership has to define what reality is for any organization, and that requires conceptual work. For many, this will feel difficult because it is so intangible and because we all suffer paradigm blindness caused by the institutional paradigm of the church. But no matter how you configure it, in the end it's going to mean prayerful study and passionate pursuit of a greater manifestation of the kingdom than we currently experience. We need to cultivate a certain type of spiritual hunger for more. So prayerfully and passionately keep at it; you will eventually "see" it in a flash of revelation, and then you will wonder why you hadn't seen it all along. Do this with your teams and friends.

Win Hearts and Minds

A Verge church will need to come forth at the level of both heart (volition and imagination) and mind (rationality and theology). This is vital in initiating and maintaining *any* movement; minds *and* hearts must be constantly engaged. This will be developed robustly in the "Move" section, which is all about momentum and movement.

Chapter 4

Apostolic Genius
The Genetic Code of Movement

ALAN

The only way to propagate a message is to live it.

— JIM WALLIS

The most probable assumption is no currently working business theory will be valid ten years hence.... And yet few
executives accept that turning around a business requires
fundamental changes in the assumptions on which the business is run ... [that] it requires a different business.

— PETER DRUCKER

121

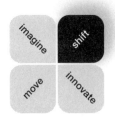

During the Chinese Communist revolution of the twentieth century, leaders of the underground Chinese church learned to adapt pretty fast — not only their lives but also the very survival of the Christian church in their country was at stake. What they experienced as a terrible adapt-or-die experience gifted us one of the most remarkable revelations about the most fundamental nature of the church as Jesus designed it to be: Apostolic Genius. The Chinese underground church phenomenon of the last sixty years, where against all odds the persecuted church grew from about 2 million to over 120 million, is quite possibly the most remarkable manifestation of Apostolic Genius in the history of the church. And it is a gift to us because it teaches us about ourselves as a different cultural expression of the very same *ecclesia*, with all the same latent potentials as of those Chinese peasants.

The most amazing thing that is learned through the Chinese experience, along with every other apostolic movement in history, is that the church Jesus started already has *everything* in it to get its job done. Read that sentence again: *ecclesia* is *perfectly* designed to fulfill its mission and purpose. This is as true for them as it is for us, because Jesus is the Founder and Designer of the church wherever it might manifest. What is more, we can say that every believer — and by extension, every believing community of Christ — has the same full potential for world transformation present in even the smallest part. Apostolic Genius is latent within the *ecclesia*, and given the right conditions, it can be reactivated and can transform the church into a potent movement of the gospel.

What these great movements learned through sheer force of circumstance, we are going to learn and apply in a much more deliberative and determined way. In this book, we are trying to do precisely that: this chapter will focus on describing the essentials of the paradigm. Our aim in the Verge church approach is clear: we hope to revive the same dormant potentials in your church/organization that existed within the early church, the Chinese church, and every other exponential missional movement in history — nothing less. But in order to do this, we have to effectively dislodge the predominant institutional paradigm by replacing it with the more movemental one. How do we do that? By reactivating Apostolic Genius that already resides in your church. Remember, Apostolic Genius is by nature an inclusive paradigm of church; therefore it is able to incorporate and include the more institutional expression while making real shift toward diverse new forms.

Apostolic Genius is a paradigm, a way or model of thinking, but it is also more than that. It actually describes the intelligence, the "genius" that is distributed throughout the system that in the New Testament is called *ecclesia*. It has everything to do with God's Spirit, the transformative power of the gospel, and the way that God has created human systems and people-movements to generate and organize. In fact, apart from the "Jesus is Lord" factor, every other element of mDNA can be found in other movements, Christian or not! For example, "discipleship" is simply the church's language for identity formation and developing its adherents, and "organic systems" is just a way we can frame what happens in all distributed networks everywhere.[1] *Communitas* is experienced by something as common as a sports team every time they play!

> Monday is as spiritually important as Sunday.

I say this very carefully, but phenomenologically speaking, Al Qaeda exhibits all the elements except for the central defining one—Jesus is Lord! Yes, they use different terms, and there will be some disparities, but the phenomenon itself, as a manifestation of a people-movement, is remarkably analogous. We are a Jesus movement, and they are a (in this case, particularly violent) Mohammed movement, but this most essential difference highlights the similarities. What this shocking comparison illustrates is that in a generic sense, something akin to Apostolic Genius is already coded into the created order, not just into the church. Much as C. S. Lewis observed that the Christ story is the "true myth" that provides the scaffolding from which all other great myths flow (see, for instance, the prodigious work of Joseph Campbell), so mDNA is the deep architecture of all movements, however distant they become from our living and vital Source. In the church, Apostolic Genius simply takes its very specific, Jesus-shaped form!

This is hopeful for us because it allows us to see that we are not foisting something onto the church as if it were some alien imposition, but rather we are activating something that is dormant, something that is already there! In some ways, we simply have to remember what we have forgotten.

Apostolic Genius

What follows here is really a working summary of what I explained more fully in *The Forgotten Ways* and have tried to elaborate in all my subsequent writings. It should provide an adequate, and I hope convincing, description of the core ideas necessary for movement. However, if a church or organization is really serious about applying the Verge process described here, then I strongly suggest that the entire leadership team undertake a serious study of the basic text as well as the associated handbook.[2] Hopefully, it is clear by now that there is no way around the need for leadership to have a real grasp of movemental paradigm if they are going to lead the church into the new possibilities of movement. If this seems too difficult, or if there is no collective will to transition, then we suggest that it is probably best to leave things as they are. As we have seen, paradigms are not birthed easily, and it requires prayerful processing of change, some deep thinking, the political will to get the job done, along with some serious strategic planning if we have any chance of successful transition to becoming an apostolic movement. I don't want to make this sound unnecessarily complicated; gaining missional movementum is simple but challenging. It is simple (and it has to be, if anyone can do this) because it is based on these six elements, but it is challenging because of the nature of change and reversing momentum.

The process of becoming an apostolic movement ought to be holistic and should be applied systemwide. This is not to say that there are not real benefits in applying each element of mDNA on its own; for instance, there clearly would be an improvement if a church made disciple-making a core task or activated fivefold forms of ministry and leadership. Each of the elements, if successfully applied, will bring the church closer to the kind of church Jesus designed in the first place. But if we wish to see our church become an authentic missional *movement*, one capable of rapid, sustainable expansion, regional impact, and high influence, then all six elements have to be activated and correlated in ways that usher the entire system into a new form of *ecclesia*, a new and yet ancient way of being the church — that of apostolic movements.

So what are the elements, and how do they change the way we are and do church? Diagrammatically, it can be represented as in figure 12.

The Structure of Apostolic Genius

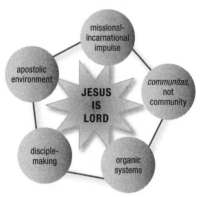

Figure 12

Jesus Is Lord

When Christians dream about the growth of the church, we can become highly excited by the success of exponential movements. But a critical, often neglected consideration with such movements is the question, what exactly are we multiplying? What is the church's core message, and are we delivering it properly? This takes us directly to the gospel and to Jesus and his role and function in the life of his people, anytime and anyplace. In theological circles, this is called Christology, and it's the most basic but poignant theological touchstone of the church. It is our North Star, our compass, and our central criterion as Jesus' people.

At the center and circumference of every significant Jesus movement, there exists a confession that is both simple and complex: what we can call a *simplex* confession. Simple, in that it can be easily understood and passed on from person to person; complex, because it carries the full weight of biblical monotheism. The way this was expressed in the New Testament church and in later movements was simply, "Jesus is Lord!" With this simplex confession, they changed the world.

Massive theological weight loads into these three words; in fact, there is a whole worldview in these three words! There are at least two aspects to this.

First is the aspect of lordship, or sovereignty, that Jesus is *Lord* (or Master or King or Messiah). When we use this phrase, in the context of the biblical understanding of YHWH's lordship, it goes to the very heart of the biblical revelation of the one true God. The teaching that God is Lord over his creation, what theologians have called ethical monotheism, or what Jesus himself calls the kingdom of God, is the subterranean message undergirding all of Scripture. It doesn't get any deeper than that!

Whatever meanings the Old Testament applied to the idea that YHWH is Lord are transferred fully to the New Testament claim that Jesus is Lord. What's more, this is an exclusive claim; it means we always turn to God from false lords and idols (Rom. 1:18; 1 Thess. 1:9), and God thereby claims exclusive loyalty over his people. Monotheism is therefore a direct challenge to all polytheisms ancient and modern. There can be no idolatry admitted into the life of true worship — this refers not just to animistic fetishes but also to the myriad of idols prevalent in all cultures: money, sex, power, ideology, and all things that claim to bring meaning and demand the loyalty that should belong to God alone.

The kingdom of God is a healing, redeeming force in human history, to be sure, but it also demands a certain lifestyle characterized by holiness and love. That is why we call it *ethical* monotheism: it forms the basis for the lifestyle we call discipleship or apprenticeship.

The other aspect captured in the phrase "Jesus is Lord" lies in that it's *Jesus* who is Lord, and not some other person. It matters very much *who* it is that is sovereign Lord and King. It is *Jesus*, the radical, irreligious, merciful, always-surprising redeemer of our souls, who qualifies the nature of that lordship. Change the name, and the whole character of lordship changes accordingly. To get a feel for this, replace the name Jesus with Mohammed, Moloch, Mammon, or Ba'al and try to discern the different impact of each. Everything changes when the king changes.

A true understanding of Jesus is therefore vital to authentic Christianity. It is the particular historical revelation of Jesus that sets the tone and character of Christian discipleship and community gathered in his presence. What is more, he is the location of our saving covenant with God—he is Savior as well as Lord. So whatever we as the church might know of God, it must be mediated through the lens of the revelation given to us in Jesus the Jewish Messiah, empowered by the Spirit and exalted by the Father to become Savior of the world (1 John 4:14). This means that Jesus must always play the central role in the life of the disciple and the church.[3]

Whatever else he is for us, Jesus is the Founder. Because of this, he gets the defining rights to what it means to be a Christian and, by extension, what it means to be the church. This means we must always return to Jesus in order to authenticate ourselves as followers and as the church who claims his name. When the church loses this kind of defining contact with Jesus, when we lose the central focus of Christianity, some other ideology tends to take Jesus' place, and we end up with something less than what was intended in the first place. At times, people have managed to concoct an all-out toxic religion—a Christless form of Christianity—that has seriously damaged many people and the gospel. The church needs a constant checkup, and the most appropriate—no, make that the *only*—place to go is to Jesus, our Founder and Lord.[4]

How does this play out in the Verge church process described here? Well, when we place this absolute commitment to Jesus at the very epicenter of church life and consciousness, it functions as an inbuilt theological touchstone, an internalized criterion for ongoing authenticity, and thus the true principle of ongoing renewal of our spirituality, discipleship, mission, and worship. As this works its way out in the life of the community, it will mean we'll present an expression of Christianity that looks a lot like Jesus. The church should reverberate with a distinct Jesus vibe.

This lordship of Jesus is both the center and circumference of apostolic movements. As an element of mDNA, it functions as the touchstone that organizes and informs the others. That Jesus is Lord changes, directs, organizes, and qualifies the other aspects of mDNA: disciple-making, missional-incarnational impulse, apostolic environment, organic systems, and *communitas*.

Disciple-Making

This element of mDNA is the one most associated with the centrality of Jesus, and it is that of discipleship and disciple-making. Essentially, this involves the irreplaceable and lifelong task of becoming like Jesus by embodying his message as well as his interior habits. Disciple-making (or apprenticeship) is a core task of the church and needs to be structured into every church's basic raison d'être—it must become a pervasive ethos felt at every level of the organization. When we embed discipleship and disciple-making at the mDNA level of the church, we ensure that the life of Christ flows throughout, because it will practically express itself as a commitment to be like Christ, to live like him and to rightly represent him in everything we say and do. It isn't hard to see how and why this will profoundly affect the character and expression of the church's life and worship. When an apprentice blacksmith studies under his master, what happens after time and experience are gained? He becomes a blacksmith! Similarly, being apprenticed to Jesus, we become little versions of Jesus ourselves.

Although the language of discipleship does float in the ether of some church vision statements, the *reality* of being apprenticed in the way of Jesus is largely missing. The net result is that we are being apprenticed, but not by Jesus. There is, sadly, no neutral ground, spiritually speaking. In Western culture, our identities, actions, and sense of community and meaning are deeply shaped by the prevailing forces of mindless consumerism (the alternative religion of our day) and mediated through a very sophisticated system of formation driven by mass media and billion-dollar budgets. Mammon is alive and well; his temples are everywhere. And the church, as the focal point of this spiritual warfare, has lost significant ground in the battle because of passivity and inaction. If we don't apprentice people, the culture surely will.

The reason why discipleship is such a critical key to Verge church thinking is because movements grow only in proportion to their capacity to make disciples—followers of the living Messiah. We can say this with some authority: no disciples, no movement. *Some* disciples, *some* movement. But having many disciples creates a real basis on which movements generate and develop. And so discipleship and disciple-making are in fact the strategic missional activities in our time.

So much is bound up here: not only the heart of Christian spirituality—that Jesus actually *lives within* his people—but that our lives lived in and through him are also lives lived *like* his. We are imitators of Christ and not merely his fan club! Our very authenticity as Christians is bound to our capacity to rightly represent our Lord; surely a life that fails to mirror Jesus' own earthy resplendence is but a dim reflection of who we're created to be.

Our willingness and ability to live lives like Jesus' life, what I called "embodiment of the message,"[5] is the basis of the spiritual authority we have as disciples, individually and corporately. In the New Testament, authority (*exousia*, or literally "out of one's life/being") is directly associated with the capacity to live consistently with the message we seek to convey. Jesus has authority because in him, message and deed are utterly congruent—he is the active Word of God. Likewise, apprenticeship, involving as it does the embodiment of the gospel message in and through our lives, brings personal authority but also brings us credibility in the eyes of those around us. Again discipleship shows itself as crucial to our witness and our mission.

Another aspect of apostolic movements is directly related to this element of mDNA: leadership. Leadership is directly proportional to discipleship. If we aren't making disciples, we shouldn't wonder about the un-Christlikeness of the leadership evident in many churches. Discipleship is a prior condition of leadership in the church that Jesus built. That's why the Bible says little directly about leadership. In fact, its wisdom on the subject is deeply subversive (the last will be first, leaders should serve, not many should presume to be teachers, and so on); rather than being about leadership, everything is about apprenticeship to Jesus.

Such discipleship is the key to cultivating a missional ethos. If we fail to generate a movement composed of authentic followers of Jesus and instead focus on making converts who turn into consumptive church attenders needing constant entertaining and "feeding," we'll never see apostolic movement take place. Remember, the Great Commission is about making disciples, not "decisions." Our friends at 3 Dimension Ministries (3DM) have understood this well,[6] and we'll refer to their story throughout this book. If you locate missionality where it belongs—smack in the center of God's gratuitous love—

then mission comes out of the core of who we are and isn't just an external task and obligation.

Discipleship is the key to implementation of movement, and that's one of the reasons why it's an irreplaceable part of the six elements of mDNA. The Verge church process requires that this become part of the ideological epicenter of the church, along with the other elements. Like Jesus' lordship, it will qualify and condition all the other elements.

Missional-Incarnational Impulse

With the rise of the Christendom church (the institutional paradigm) — resulting from Emperor Constantine's marriage of the church to the state — the prevailing idea or conception of church became fundamentally nonmissional. Historically, the reason for this, of course, is that all who were born within the geographical realm of the Christendom civilization were considered Christian. In the American expression, Christianity was not married to the state (as in Europe) but is nonetheless seen to be an inextricable part of American culture and identity; until the last thirty years or so, if you were an American, you were a Christian, with few exceptions (Native Americans, Jews, and so on). But the net result of either hard (state-mandated) or soft (cultural) Christendom is to effectively create a domesticated civil religion which no longer challenges and transforms society but rather is co-opted by it.

The disastrous result of Christendom (for the mission of the church) was that the way we thought about ourselves as church became ruinously detached from the catalytic impulse of the mission of God, or *Missio Dei*. We forgot that it's not so much that the church has a mission as that the mission has a church. Missiology became a subset of ecclesiology, rather than the other way around. No longer was the church seen as a result of God's prior initiative in sending his Son, his saving mission in the world; mission was downgraded to being an inferior function of the church, a subcommittee composed of about 2 percent of the church and largely concerned with overseas missions to "pagan" lands. Mission was marginalized and then ejected from the church's sense of identity and practice. Mission no longer set the agenda for the church's life and ministry.

As a result of the overwhelming power of the Christendom paradigm, even many who claim to be missional Christians still think of mission as a subset of ecclesiology. For instance, many still think that because a church *does* mission, therefore it *is* a missional church. Not so! All churches have always done some form of mission — even the most institutional. Simply reaching across cultures, even in our own neighborhoods, doesn't mean we are *missional*. Rather, a truly missional understanding of the church arises from the fundamental recognition that mission is the catalyzing principle, that it actually forms and informs the church. The church takes its cue from the mission of God in the world, not the other way around. Mission shapes the church; church takes it cultural cues from mission. We ought not load ecclesiology up front in the equation. This is a very important paradigm shift in itself; it requires a conversion of sorts, and unless it can be made, there is no way to truly become missional in nature.[7]

One of the Future Travelers churches reframed the issue this way, moving mission from being a "department" to being the determining factor that informs *all* the departments (fig. 13). It's a powerful visual clue to what is being said here.

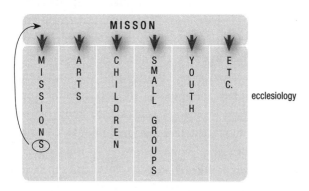

Figure 13

God is the Redeemer, and we, God's redeemed people, are the result of God's love. This also means that the church emerges out of our joining God's mission in the world. This is a liberating alternative to deadlocked church bureaucracy, because we recognize that God is already doing mission and that we can join with him. Jesus will build his church as we listen to his voice and engage in the *Missio Dei.*

What about the incarnational piece; how does that fit? If the missional approach requires that we take this *sent*ness (for the Latin *missio* means "sent") of the church seriously, then the *way* we are sent must be influenced directly by how God engages the world in Jesus. This takes us straight to the incarnation as our primary model of how we should engage the world. God enters into the world, fully into a given context, concretely loving a people as an insider; he meets people where they are. And so the Verge church takes incarnational mission very seriously. As commissioned missionaries, we go to unchurched people where they are, and we work hard at speaking meaningfully from within the culture and so demonstrate and live out the love of God for them in Christ.

Missional is not just an adjective we attach to church; it is an adjective that must be attached to our faith.

Deriving as it does from our deepest theology, this element of mDNA goes on to shape (even prescribe) how apostolic movements extend themselves into new situations and contexts. The two terms in the phrase (missional-incarnational), though clumsy, are important because they each qualify and inform the other.

Getting practical, and building an appropriate model of engagement out of these essential theological truths, we can say this: on the one hand, the missional impulse describes the outward-bound impulse that urges the church to reach beyond itself to its immediate neighbors, often across cultures and class, and eventually to the whole world. It is how the gospel is "sneezed" into the world and grows exponentially (in a viral way) as it extends itself over time and space. On the other hand, the incarnational impulse describes how the gospel is embedded deeply into a culture. As the seed of the gospel falls on cultural soil, it takes root, and Christianity thus develops within that culture, in ways that make sense within that culture. It is how Christianity is contextualized into cultures and subcultures anywhere and everywhere. The missional impulse takes its cue from the *Missio Dei*, and the incarnational impulse takes its cue from the incarnation of the Son of God into human context. Missional God leads to missional church. Incarnational God leads to incarnational church.

When the missional-incarnational impulse (or imperative) is placed alongside the other elements of mDNA, at the epicenter of the church's self-understanding, it maintains the movemental impulse to partner with God in his redemption of the world. It creates the internal pressure outward into mission and downward into culture in incarnational engagement. Theology informs methodology, and methodology is held in check by deep theology so as to avoid thoughtless and harmful syncretism.

Apostolic Environment

This element of mDNA relates to the type of leadership and ministry required to sustain metabolic growth and impact. For one, it means taking seriously the role of apostolic ministry in our day. This means we must open ourselves to the fertile and distinctly missional vision and energy it creates, and how it is vital in initiating and maintaining exponential missional movements. Not surprisingly, the Latin word *missio* has the same meaning as the Greek word *apostello*: "sent"! Missional church *is* apostolic church. Any talk about missional church that doesn't also legitimize apostolic ministry is doomed to frustration. I can't encourage you enough to look seriously into this, so much is at stake here.

Many churches, and whole denominations, deny any possible legitimacy to this. But this denial itself comes directly from the inherited paradigm and is one of the major reasons why most of these selfsame churches and denominations are struggling to reverse their decline. The great irony of course is that most of these denominations, when they were still in movemental forms, were started by apostolic people! Even if the term itself was not always used, there is no doubting the impact of its ministry. Apostolic is what apostolic does.

But beyond just the recovery of apostolic ministry in our day, this mDNA really requires we significantly broaden our understanding of ministry. We need to break away from the inherited understanding of ministry as maintenance. In other words, a pastor/shepherd framework or teacher/theologian framework can (and often does) exclude other, perhaps more *generative*, forms of ministry. Said in another way: *if we want missional church and movements, then we will simply have to have a missional ministry to go with it.* There can be no way around the central importance of Paul's description of ministry in Ephesians 4 in this regard. Ministry in Verge churches will therefore be at least fivefold in form. I, for one, simply can't get away from the feeling that Ephesians 4 is critical genetic information about the ministry of the church. We avoid this to our great detriment.

I deliberately use the term *ministry*, not *leadership*, here because Ephesians 4:7 – 11 indicates that this fivefold gifting relates to *all* the people in the church and not just to those who lead. How can we say this? Because this is a general letter, packed with concentrated Pauline ecclesiology, to be read aloud in the churches. (And the churches were made up of men and women, slaves and nobles, and so on.)

Ephesians 4:7 – 11 explicitly says that grace is given "to each one of us" and that it is Christ who gives it. In other words, it's not primarily a leadership text! Rather it describes the ministry of Christ expressing itself through the body of Christ. Leadership is implied in ministry, not the other way around. Remember, everyone gets to play. This is a very radical text indeed!

It also means that every church is packed with all kinds of ministry potential; churches aren't just playgrounds for pastors and teachers. We've found a useful acronym in this passage of Scripture: APEST.[8] It's an outline for Jesus' playground.

Think of it this way:

Apostles are architecturally and missionally oriented.
Prophets are questioners of the status quo, demanding faithfulness.
Evangelists are recruiters to the cause — the infectious people.
Shepherds (pastors) care and create community.
Teachers bring wisdom and understanding.

Wouldn't the church (or any organization, for that matter) be better off by having all five of these players present and operative? Of course! How could we fulfill our mission and purpose without them? Answer: we can't.

Ephesians 4:11–16 unambiguously declares that we can't mature without APEST! Read verses 1–16 again: verses 1–6 represent the unity factors, verses 7–11 describe APEST, and verses 11–16 describe the resultant maturity in the body of Christ. How did we ever think we could possibly mature with just the anemic twofold form of shepherd/pastor and teacher?

When this is placed in the paradigmatic heart of the church (along with the other elements of mDNA), it will legitimize and activate a far more potent, comprehensive, multidimensional ministry that can both initiate *and* maintain Verge churches. It will also call into question the sorely limited view of ministry and leadership we have inherited from the more institutional and missionally neutered forms of church handed down from Christendom. Churches that have active and authentic APEST forms of ministry are almost always movemental in nature.[9]

Organic Systems

The truth is, over centuries the church has been (largely) taken captive to an institutional and structural way of organizing. When we think of church, we think of the institution of church (for example, its buildings, clergy, creeds, rituals, denominational templates, symbols). It's very hard for anyone, even non-Christians now, to think of the church in any other way. But this isn't the way the original church manifested itself, and it certainly isn't our most potent expression, which is namely that of apostolic movement. The problem with an overly institutional conception of church is that it basically overconcretizes and freezes in time the way we see ourselves as the people of God—and this is problematic.

This is not to say that institutional structures are all bad; certainly, their intent is almost always good. Even so, concretized institutionalization does tend to block some of the most powerful aspects of *ecclesia* as Jesus intended it: a potent social force and gospel phenomenon that sweeps through populations. Any reading of history, Christian or otherwise, shows us that institutional religion can become repressive, stifling creative expression.

One of the most fundamental reboots we need to do in our day is to rediscover ourselves as the same potent, transforming people-movement that started with Jesus and went on to change the world. The institutional forms have gotten us where we are now and can't take us much farther. We need to become a people-movement again.

We need to take the New Testament's meaning of *ecclesia*/church again with utmost seriousness. I'm more and more convinced this word contains the full meaning of what we are trying to articulate about apostolic movement. *Ecclesia* in the Bible doesn't refer to some building or religious institution (no scholar would argue otherwise); rather it was borrowed from the process of Roman city assemblies — it means "gathering." But even more significant, as far as I can determine, *ecclesia* has four distinct levels:

1. *Ecclesia* as the people of God expressing the ministry of Christ in every sphere and domain
2. *Ecclesia* as the local church
3. *Ecclesia* as the citywide church
4. *Ecclesia* as the universal church

The term applies at every level of expression and organization! In other words, *ecclesia* is movement! We've allowed this big word to come to mean something profoundly different than what it originally meant — we have had a nasty case of long-term paradigm blindness, and it's time to move.

What we now have are somewhat inflexible, backward-looking, often fearful and defensive forms of church. What we need are missionally responsive, culturally adaptive, organizationally agile multiplication movements. Verge churches — because they are apostolic movements — mobilize the whole people of God, are reproducing and reproducible, are structurally networked (avoiding centralization of power and function), and employ missional leadership and ministry modes.

Both Dave and I have no doubt that if there is to be any advancing of the Western church in the twenty-first century, it will be marked by the recovery of the apostolic movement form of church. In fact, we suggest that if we fail to somehow rediscover this mode of church, we may eventually lose all significant cultural impact and become a footnote to Western history. In the final section of this book, we will present a detailed approach to what it means to activate movements, but at the very least:

- *Movements mobilize the whole people of God.* The real revolution comes when all the people of God get to embrace their God-given destiny as active agents of the King. Surely, one of the most potent ecclesial doctrines in the New Testament is the priesthood of all believers, yet it's one we've seldom lived out. Clergy and professionals can be control freaks. We need to recognize that Jesus is well able to lead his people and doesn't require professionals to keep us on track!

- *Movements are reproducing and reproducible.* In truth, much of what we do as church is unwieldy and very hard to reproduce—largely because of our captivity to institutional forms. In contrast, exponential missional movements thrive on rapid and spontaneous expansion and can be achieved by all agents in the system. That's why they're able to achieve what Roland Allen calls "spontaneous expansion." To say it another way, reproduction necessitates "reproduce-*ability*," and reproducibility requires an ecclesiology simple enough for any disciple to reproduce.

The church Jesus designed, the one in the pages of the New Testament, is precisely that: a grassroots people-movement with a vision for the transformation of society, operating as a decentralized network, spreading like a virus, and profoundly reproducible by every active agent in the system. Verge churches must be willing to reconceive themselves as people-movements. They can no longer simply see themselves, through an institutional lens, as "churches"; rather they must see themselves as embryonic movements in the making. (In other words, they must become *ecclesia*!)

When we are willing to see that every believer can be a church planter and every church can be a church-planting church, then we will reorganize to make that happen, and things will change.[10] Verge churches recognize the power of this form of *ecclesia* and are willing to increasingly move in this direction. For instance, Soma is one of the Future Travelers churches that has already morphed into the early stages of movement envisioned here.[11] Others are heading in the right direction,[12] but it's important to note that in order to be a decentralized movement, we need to activate all six elements of mDNA and not just one.

This is not to say that pure movemental forms are the only true manifestations of missional structure. By God's common grace, there are many ways in which humans organize, some more theologically consistent and missionally potent than others. But it is to say that intentional movemental forms are most consistent with the reality of being an apostolic movement. Most likely, Verge churches will have elements of centralized organization in them — they will be hybrids of sorts — but they will definitely need to learn what it means to operate as a decentralized network if they are determined to move beyond the limitations (and costs) imposed by hierarchical organization. Much will depend on whether these churches can activate the whole people of God, but when and if they do, they will almost certainly need to learn the power of the more fluid, networked, movemental structures. If we can't become a fully-fledged organic underground movement like the one in China (and that is unlikely, given our context, culture, and history), we can certainly begin to approximate it by moving in that direction.

Communitas

The word *communitas* captures the idea of the enhanced forms of community that emerges from the context of a shared ordeal, a common task, an organizational challenge, even danger. The context of the challenge forces a restructuring of the basic relational fabric of the group. In such situations, people move from being associates to becoming comrades, from being acquaintances who happen to bump into each other at church-related activities to being partners bound together in common cause.

Communitas is easy to spot once you've seen it: sports teams, leadership teams at work facing deadlines, short-term missions teams, friends painting a house together. It forms a fundamental code that informs almost every story of coming together against the odds, whether in film, comics, or novels. People are moved outside what is perceived as safe, predictable, and normal, only to find themselves and others in a new and profound way. It forms the most basic aspect of the human adventure.

Relating this to the most current expressions of church will mean we become far less risk-averse, more missional, and more willing to experiment by engaging in open-ended learning together. It will also mean we need to lean into the future and engage with our cultural contexts, as these will force us to more adaptive expressions of *ecclesia*.

As we have seen in the section on paradigms and innovation, too much concern with safety and security, combined with comfort and convenience, has lulled us out of our true calling and purpose and has effectively blocked our God-given creativity.[13]

A Mindset, Not a Technique

We suggest that any church wishing to move toward being a Verge church will need to really study the paradigm shifts necessary to become an apostolic movement (see the resources section in the back of this book). But if God is in the details, so is the Devil! Don't let annotated bibliographies keep you and your community from (as John Wimber used to put it) *doing the stuff!* Trust what God has put into you; be willing to follow your deepest instinct in living it out.

What you should be inspired by here is the sheer vigor of a church that can combine all six elements of the mDNA in Apostolic Genius: when a church takes Jesus with utmost seriousness and refers all matters of its life to him, when it embeds discipleship as a defining activity at every level, when it activates a broader missional ministry based on Ephesians 4, when it learns to organize and operate as a decentralized people-movement, engaging in incarnational mission and being willing to takes risks and learn, you can be sure it's spiritually healthy and transformative. When this happens, it not only describes the possibility of movement; it *is* movement.

Please note: I do not mean to suggest some sort of ecclesiological "technique" or church methodology here. Apostolic Genius is a *mindset*, an approach, a phenomenon, a way of thinking and doing church. It is the much-needed silver imagination for our times. There are internal checks and balances within it to keep it from degenerating into a mere technique. For instance, commitment to Jesus' kingdom at the heart of the church—together with the willingness to become more and more like him (apprenticeship)—ensures the spiritual health of the movement, at the heart of the movement. A movement of radical disciples worshiping Jesus as Lord cannot but be a worshiping, praying, Spirit-led, Spirit-empowered church.

Now pause.

Take a deep breath: *God is good. Selah.*

If you feel like you've absorbed too much in this chapter, *let it go.* But circle back to it again later and read the material more slowly, leisurely. Anything worth knowing is worth knowing thoroughly, and we needn't make ourselves frenetic wrecks while doing so. This is a vital discipline in our media-saturated world. You'll be shocked at how much clearer everything will become on a subsequent read.

This is the *Missio Dei*, and to participate in it is the highest calling you can possibly imagine, so relax and enjoy it. Let your longing lead you. The vision we're seeing for the church can be summed up in this quote by Antoine de Saint-Exupéry: "If you want to build a ship, don't summon people to buy wood, prepare tools, distribute jobs, and organize the work — rather, teach people the yearning for the wide, boundless ocean."

Dave's Response to "Apostolic Genius: The Genetic Code of Movement"

While Alan took the lead on this chapter, I fully endorse and believe the inherent truth in what he calls Apostolic Genius, and I wholeheartedly agree that it gives us the genetic code of all apostolic movements. I believe this in part because it's supported by my own research, observation, and personal experience as a church planter (Community Christian Church) and leader of an emerging movement (NewThing). The other reason is because I have heard Alan very humbly and privately talk about the six elements of mDNA as a grace that God gave him for the church. He would tell you that his understanding of Apostolic Genius is not merely a product of his own intellect but came to him almost supernaturally as a gift from God for the church, and I believe him.

While I don't want to elevate this apostolic paradigm to the level of Scripture, I am saying that both the source of this revelation and my own practice of it tell me that what we have here is a missional archetype from the primal heartbeat of God.

Beware of Being Too Familiar

As a practitioner in the midst of interacting with this apostolic paradigm, let me offer some words of caution. The elements you think you know the most may be the ones you know the least. As I have interviewed church leaders transitioning their churches to movemental thinking and behaving, a common reaction to looking at the first two of the six elements is, " 'Jesus is Lord' and disciple-making? We got 'em! Let's move on." And they move on to the more exotic-sounding elements of missional-incarnational impulse, apostolic environment, organic systems, and *communitas*—all the while leaving their culturally conditioned assumptions about Jesus' all-pervasive lordship and thoroughgoing apprenticeship unexamined. The last four, because they sound less familiar than the first two, capture our attention and our energy.

Here is my caution: beware of being too familiar with "Jesus is Lord" and disciple-making. There's a lot to be unpacked in these potent-but-overused phrases.[14]

The Familiarity of "Jesus Is Lord"

More than one church leader has confessed to me that while making this paradigm shift early on, they got the missional virus and started infecting everyone around them. They communicated vision and strategy for people to be on mission, and they genuinely and fervently prayed that their people would get it. But along the way, *mission* became the *a priori*, not Jesus. Missional became a new form of legalism. As is often the case in sick systems, if we aren't careful, we can replace one addiction for another rather than discovering the cure. In this case, they replaced self-righteousness with mission. Mission became more important than Jesus, because the mission was where people looked to find their identity. Their value was not in Jesus but in "being on mission" and in what they accomplished for "the mission."

What they discovered is that mission is a terrible lord. The mission will always ask and expect more from you than you can deliver and will ultimately abandon you and leave you disappointed. One church leader confided, "I recently moved my family to an underresourced part of the city in the name of mission. What I discovered is that I am prone to using living in the inner city as a trump card to give me more influence and power, because I have a tendency to love influence and power more than I love Jesus."

Warning: don't let your infatuation with mission allow your love for Jesus to wander. Don't let Jesus become too familiar. Jesus is a great Master. Jesus enjoys you and takes pleasure in you and delights in you, and he will be a great Lord. He won't kick you to the curb when you let him down. We're not selling Amway here, friends! Multilevel empire-building isn't the name of the game. Entire Christian movements have been built on these premises devoid of a living encounter with Jesus, and wrecked lives are always the result. Missional living is really about allowing Jesus to be Lord of your life and then telling the good news of what Jesus is doing in your life. Mission only works when we make Jesus Lord and his mission flows out of that.

The Familiarity of Disciple-Making

Just as churches think they already know what it means to make Jesus Lord, even more churches will say to themselves, "Oh, we understand disciple-making." But the Reveal study conducted by Willow Creek was a wake-up call that churches don't get it. What they understand is their old paradigm of disciple-making. And the old paradigm is more about consuming cognitive content and not engaging in missional action. The old paradigm of disciple-making is about an individual's ability to get a passing grade on a subject matter, rather than being led by the Spirit 24/7 to follow after Jesus and to trade their life for the mission. It's indoctrination without transformation.

The introduction of new language is crucial for reshaping paradigms and getting people to think differently about the movement of Jesus. For that reason, I intentionally use the word *apprentice* as opposed to *disciple*. While *disciple* is a brilliant word, it doesn't mean today what it meant in the Bible. When Jesus called people into discipleship, it was a calling into the Father's mission and into preparation in every way to accomplish that mission.

You may choose to continue to use disciple terminology, but that choice may get you the same kind of static thinking and behavior you're trying to change. I much prefer the term *apprentice*. The power of *apprentice* is that it clearly says you not only are a learner but also are in a relationship to take on more responsibility to further the missional movement of Jesus. First and foremost, we must apprentice with Jesus, and second, we must bring someone alongside us whom we will apprentice, just as Paul did when he encouraged churches to "imitate me, just as I also imitate Christ" (1 Cor. 11:1 NKJV). The apprenticeship process not only inherently has a missional intention but also has a movemental outcome because built into it is the ongoing reproduction of other Christ followers.[15]

Thinking You Know, When You Don't

Within the macro paradigm shift to apostolic movement are the six micro-shifts in regard to each element of mDNA. As I've already explained, the shifts in regard to "Jesus is Lord" and disciple-making are often the most challenging, because churches and leaders think they know what they don't know. The last four shifts of missional-incarnational impulse, apostolic environment, organic systems, and *communitas* are often not as challenging, because in most cases churches and leaders *know* they don't know. The steps we take along the journey of Apostolic Genius remind me of then – Secretary of Defense Donald Rumsfeld's quixotic words of reflection during the buildup to the Iraq conflict nearly a decade ago, taken verbatim but arranged as poetry by the online magazine *Salon*:

> As we know,
> There are known knowns.
> There are things we know we know.
> We also know
> There are known unknowns.
> That is to say
> We know there are some things
> We do not know.
> But there are also unknown unknowns,
> The ones we don't know
> We don't know.[16]

When we interact with the stuff of God and destiny and eternity, we will often be the ones who "see through a mirror dimly." But as long as we are oriented Godward, being led toward Christ by the compass of the

Holy Spirit, we are safe. As we progress in learning and action, we will begin to enjoy the unknown unknowns, becoming ever more responsive to the wisdom and leading of the Incarnate God in our midst.

DISCUSSION QUESTIONS

Open

Do you remember finally mastering something that previously seemed impossible to grasp? Maybe it was a math technique, a critical play in the playbook, or when you finally understood how the opposite sex thinks! Who did you tell; how did you celebrate?

Explore

1. Of the six elements of mDNA — Jesus is Lord, missional-incarnational impulse, *communitas*, apostolic environment, disciplemaking, and organic systems — which was the most difficult to grasp? Explain.
2. After reading this chapter, how has your understanding of the following passage of Scripture been altered? Do you agree that this is not exclusively a leadership text? If so, how does that change your perspective of those within your church?

> It was he who gave some to be apostles, some to be prophets, some to be evangelists, and some to be pastors and teachers, to prepare God's people for works of service, so that the body of Christ may be built up until we all reach unity in the faith and in the knowledge of the Son of God and become mature, attaining to the whole measure of the fullness of Christ.
>
> Then we will no longer be infants, tossed back and forth by the waves, and blown here and there by every wind of teaching and by the cunning and craftiness of men in their deceitful scheming. Instead, speaking the truth in love, we will in all things grow up into him who is the Head, that is, Christ. From him the whole body, joined and held together by every supporting ligament, grows and builds itself up in love, as each part does its work.
>
> —Ephesians 4:11–16

3. Before taking the online APEST assessment, how do you predict that the roles of apostle, prophet, evangelist, shepherd, and teacher will be evident in your life, in order of emphasis? PEATS? ETASP? Are you A PEST? What evidence do you have to support your guess?

4. What is your reaction to Dave's strong warning on page 140, concerning the assumed mastery most of us think we have over the lordship of Jesus and disciple-making?

Move

The best way to fully grasp the concepts within this chapter is to study them. Spend some time using the following tools to help solidify your understanding of what this chapter covered.

- Take the online APEST assessment: *www.theforgottenways.org/apest.*
- Read and discuss *The Forgotten Ways* or *The Forgotten Ways Handbook* with a small group.
- Read and discuss *Exponential: How You and Your Friends Can Start a Missional Church Movement* with a small group.

Chapter 5

Verge Vibe

The Operating System of Apostolic Movement

ALAN

Ethos (n.) the character, sentiment, or disposition of a community or people, considered as a natural endowment; the spirit which actuates manners and customs; also, the characteristic tone or genius of an institution or social organization.

— *WWW.LEXIC.US*

There are essential differences between institutions and movements: the one is conservative the other progressive; the one is more or less passive, yielding to influences from the outside, the other is active influencing rather than being influenced; the one looks to the past, the other to the future.... the one is anxious, the other is prepared to take risks; the one guards boundaries, the other crosses them.

— H. R. NIEBUHR

A nation's culture resides in the hearts and in the soul of its people.   — MOHANDAS GANDHI

Whatever happened to Starbucks?

Starbucks emerged seemingly out of nowhere in the 1990s and made drinking coffee cooler (and more expensive) than ever by the early 2000s. Though existing as a seller of coffee equipment and beans since 1971, Starbucks was grown in the late eighties by entrepreneurial buyer Howard Schultz, who knew there was money to be made in crafting a space in which to both sell and enjoy brewed coffee and espresso. Through a number of wise business and cultural moves (including striking a lucrative deal with the also-rising Barnes & Noble bookstore chain in the nineties), Starbucks crafted a genuine "third place" vibe of quality, community, and cool-factor.[1] You could say that its branding was pitch-perfect.

Flash-forward to the second decade of the twenty-first century: many twenty- and thirty-somethings—the once-loyal customer base that made Starbucks what it was in the previous decade—have begun to *dislike* Starbucks, complaining of rising prices, the homogenized feel, and the sense that the pro-employee, pro-environment, and pro–fair trade stance might be more hype than reality. What was once lauded as cool is now often panned as corporate. This loss of cultural cachet, coupled with the difficult economy, has slowed the once-impossible growth of the beverage behemoth, causing many hipsters to defect to independent coffee shops (which are experiencing a bit of a renaissance) while blue-collar people are returning to Dunkin' Donuts or even McDonald's, which has been aggressively marketing their new coffee lineup against Starbucks (and winning). While Starbucks still sells a lot of coffee in a lot of locations, the uniqueness and shine of their brand is dulling, and they are now closing more stores than they are opening.

Starbucks has taken a hit because of a dwindling cultural identity. They once had good ethos, but it wasn't cherished, stewarded, and renewed properly. So now they face a *crisis of ethos* in their corporate culture and in the hearts and minds of their baristas, customers, and most notably ex-customers. The church is at a similar crossroads in this second decade of the twenty-first century. The attention to developing a consistent brand and ethos is similarly vital to becoming an apostolic movement.

Ethos As Pivot

Developing an ethos is pivotal, because it is here where the Verge paradigm begins to inform and create an explicit Verge *culture*. A metaphor from the world of computing might help us understand the function of an ethos: There are basically three levels of relationship between hardware and software in personal computers. First, there is the machine language—the code hardwired into the hardware itself. Then, second, there is the operating system, which mediates between the hardware/machine language and the programs, which are in fact the third level. However necessary each of the three levels are, most of us will only ever interact at the programs level, and so it is with practices of the Verge church.

What we have called an apostolic movement paradigm corresponds to the machine language; the ethos, to the operating system; and the practices, to the programming (fig. 14). A computer is a system and the hardware is vital, as are the programs we use. But the interpretive core is the operating system. There is no way you can use your programs on your computer without the operating system. In the same way, ethos interprets Apostolic Genius (the hardware) into the system and makes it useable.

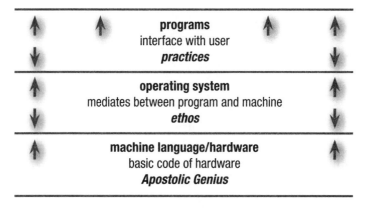

programs
interface with user
practices

operating system
mediates between program and machine
ethos

machine language/hardware
basic code of hardware
Apostolic Genius

Figure 14

As the operating system, the Verge ethos—drawing deeply from the Apostolic Genius paradigm/hardware and code—creates the necessary platform for consistent activity, influencing the core practices of the organization.

The pivital nature of ethos can also be seen in figure 15; like an operating system, it is the layer between paradigm and practice. If the first part of the Verge church process required the (re)activation of the ever-present, always latent Apostolic Genius at the paradigmatic center of the church, then this chapter looks at the next step—how paradigm becomes that which we value and how this in turn will guide our choices and behaviors.

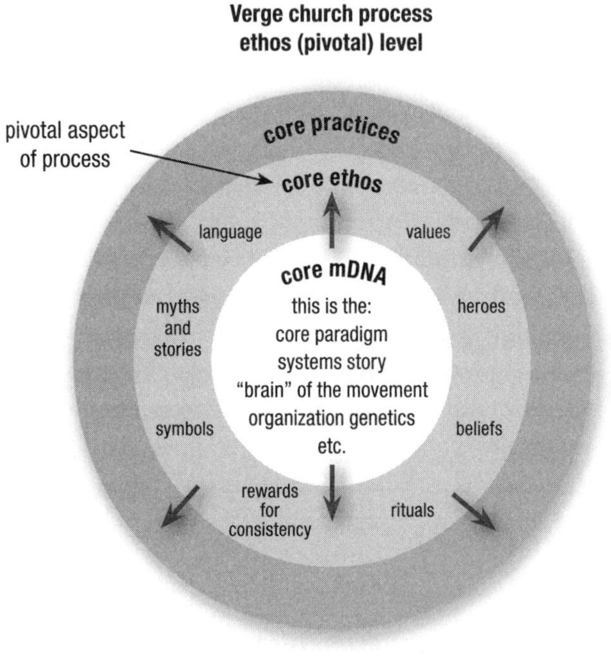

**Verge church process
ethos (pivotal) level**

Figure 15

As is true of all attempts to develop a living ethos in organizations, we are dealing to some degree with beliefs and ideas that lie beneath the level of corporate consciousness. Sure, people tend to be more aware of values and beliefs than they are of their paradigm(s). Though they all have a paradigm, it doesn't always mean they can articulate it, or that they haven't uncritically adopted ideas from general culture, ones that are inconsistent with the way of Jesus. In fact, we would argue that all people, and therefore many churches, have indeed uncritically assumed the values of prevailing culture to some degree or another.

Part of the discipleship process (an element of mDNA, of course) is to instill a basis of theologically grounded and biblically consistent values, which in turn will set the culture and guide behavior and action. As an extension of the apprentice-making ethos, it's therefore within the tasks of the leadership of Verge churches to create the right complex of values (an apostolic ethos), which is true to the genetic code of the church as Jesus designed it. When it comes to developing an authentic Verge church culture, this will mean we have to weed out missionally incompatible values and be very deliberate in articulating, as well as demonstrating, an ethos that *directly* draws its inspiration and direction from the core of mDNA at the paradigmatic heart of the church. We have to bring what is previously unarticulated (and therefore implicit) out into the explicit consciousness of the community.

An ethos should begin to explicitly (and implicitly) bring to light what we truly value. In other words, we have to name the values, make them *explicit*, and so develop a living ethos that will in turn set the cultural tone of the church/organization (fig. 16).[2]

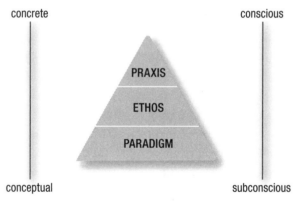

Figure 16

It's All in the Ethos ...

Just so that we are clear, to develop ethos, you will need to consciously do the following:

1. Identify and Develop Beliefs

As Christians, our beliefs are of fundamental importance—we have an innate need to *know* that what we are doing has authoritative roots in the revelation of God in Christ and in the Scriptures. But the process of learning to believe rightly isn't automatic; it needs to be a deliberate, in-depth engagement with God through the Bible and in relation to context. This highlights the need for church leadership to be working theologians. While it's crucial to let the felt-needs and questions of our native culture inform our spirituality, if we aren't deliberate about thinking theologically and systemically about beliefs, then we hand the systems story of the church over to pop culture, mere pragmatism, or the many other prevailing forces that simply co-opt our thinking and doing.

Still, we need to be careful. All of us tend to select what is convenient to our dominant paradigm. That is exactly how the institutional paradigm has been able to legitimize itself (and thereby dismiss other forms) for over seventeen centuries! It also accounts for how we can screen out so much of the Bible's teaching on idolatry (for example, money, sex, power) and justice (for example, care for the poor, economic disparity, gender relations) and focus on what suits us. Watch the selectivity with which we engage the Bible!

2. Formulate Values

Values are often implicit, but through a process of bringing them into the conversation, these should be made explicit and then sorted as to their relative weight and significance. In other words, we should become clear as to the difference between general values and *core* values. Core values get us all passionate and worked up. In fact, Dave suggests they're what bring about spontaneous applause. Once we are clear about what we truly value, we can then begin to reorder our thinking and choices around them. In such a way, values become guides to thinking — shaping attitudes and behaviors.

In the next chapter, we will explain how core values form key practices, so it's important to clarify them. If you have never gone through a process of clarifying core values, we suggest that you should. We will give you stacks of possible Verge church examples in the second half of this chapter.

3. Develop a Verge Vocabulary

If you can shape the various conversations that go on in the community, you can shape the culture. As we've said before, language shapes our consciousness. Words are the main bearers of meaning for people. If you can change the language, you actually restructure the way people process information and communicate at a very deep level. In many ways, this is why the Bible is so strong on verbal integrity and against the sins of the tongue. Developing our vocabulary must not be done manipulatively, but we must recognize that it's extremely important to shape the organizational discourse—to shape how members talk about church, mission, heroes, and so on.

So we suggest you actually define or redefine common terms and create a commonly understood vocabulary consistent with the central paradigm of the church. For example, use the word *movement* and not *church* to describe who you are. Why? Because most people have a very concrete idea of church; it has fixed meanings and a definite shape that isn't always useful to developing apostolic movement. When you start calling yourself a movement, you'll eventually begin to act like one. Also, use the phrase *incarnational mission* and give it real meaning (resist throwing around the term like a verbiage fad), and it will inevitably change the way you do mission in the church. If the word *movement* is too much for you, try using the word *ecclesia* and then try to live into what the Bible means by it.

But be wary of simply using trendy catchphrases. You've got to be intentional and use them in consistence with their meaning. Without care and intention, the words will have a negative effect on the community and weaken the ideas they represent.

4. Identify Movemental Heroes/Exemplars

This sounds rather strange, but our heroes are those people in our world (current or historical) who demonstrate through their lives what we think is truly valuable. They live out what we all hope to be. Heroes and their stories inspire us because they reach into, and embody, the vision of what we want to be and become. Show me your heroes, and I will show you who you are! Quite literally, I can tell a lot about an organization by asking who it is the people within it deeply admire.

For instance, if your church's hero is a brilliant scholar and preacher, well then, everyone gets the message that it is teaching, rhetoric, and scholarship that are most prized. If, on the other hand, the hero is the church planter/pioneer, people get the message that missional entrepreneurship is highly esteemed. The same is true for prayer warriors, miracle workers, and so on. These are your living examples of what you are seeking to achieve. Don't underestimate the importance of everyday heroes—they are embodiments/carriers of change, especially when empowered by the esteem of leadership.[3]

5. Reward Verge-Consistent Behavior

Similar to the idea of creating a hero system, this means giving social reward to those who are living in a way that is consistent with the vision and ethos of the church/organization. Again, this shouldn't be seen as some sort of elitism, and certainly not as a manipulation of the people, but by rewarding individuals, publically or otherwise, your people will get a profound message about what your church/organization values—your ethos.

Use rituals in your gatherings—laying on of hands, telling of stories, giving of gifts, even have some sort of "People We Are Proud Of" section on the website, whatever works in your context. Distinguish those who really deserve to be singled out; otherwise this will be of little value—if everyone gets a certificate of accomplishment for their wall, then it's of no real value. Future Traveler Jeff Vanderstelt calls this "gossiping the good stuff." *Tell* the stories of success.

6. Brand Your Movement

We have to be very careful when using this term, because branding is used in a profoundly manipulative way by advertisers and spin doctors. Nonetheless, it would be naive to think that managing the "brand" (how people perceive the movement) isn't involved in creating a healthy missional ethos in the church. The reality is that all organizations, simply because they *have* a distinct identity and interact through it (even if it's just their name), have to manage how people perceive them.[4]

Think of a brand as a promise kept. A good brand keeps its promises, and a bad one doesn't—it disappoints. This is a good way to think about branding: what promises are you making, and are you keeping them? Your brand is your church's identity, and it's the projection of that identity into the world. A humorous example: I use an iPhone (which I love). The problem is that in the U.S., the iPhone is bonded to AT&T, a brand which I have come to out-and-out loathe because of so many embarrassing dropped calls. I am conflicted enough to get rid of the iPhone because of the bad branding of the carrier. (By the way, this is a useful metaphor for how people feel about Jesus and the church: *Jesus? Yes. Church? No.*)

In other words, branding has to do with how you want to be known by those coming into contact with your church/movement. In many ways, the ethos can automatically be incubated from within. But it would certainly not harm your cause to make sure the symbols/words/ideas you project to the outside world are consistent with who you are and what you are all about.

7. Set Measurement Criteria

Decide what constitutes success or failure for your movement. For instance, Bob Roberts Jr. says that every church that values multiplication will measure success or failure outside its walls. *Touché*, Bob! This is a great clue to the missionality of the church. What we measure indicates what we value, so how we measure is very important.

A missional measurement, for instance, might not be how many people are attending the church or the size of the annual budget, and so on, but rather it could be the extent and reach of people's relationships into the non-Christian community. Or another example is the lowering of divorce rates in the local community. This might be a great indicator of healthy impact. And so, moving beyond the standard measurements is a useful way of changing culture.

When you mix these beliefs, values, language, identity, heroes, symbols, rituals, and measurements together, you create a very distinct culture — and *culture* is what people interact with. The culture in turn creates an atmosphere, the vibe that people coming into contact with the organization can feel in the ether of the community. Or to use another metaphor, the ethos is like the "spirit" of the organization. This organizational spirit has an effect on people. In the same way that a magnetic field has an influence on various metals, the aura of your movement will impact people coming into it.

We all have experienced this: you can go into any church or corporation and somehow sense the atmosphere of the place. No one has to tell you how to behave; you simply know it intuitively. For instance, we can safely guess that Saddleback Church in Southern California has a very different vibe (and invites different responses) than St. Paul's Basilica in Rome. Likewise, McDonald's emits a different vibe *(eat quickly, get out)* than Outback Steakhouse *(stick around and work your way through the menu)*. In the same way, different leaders create different emotive/cultural fields. Some are stern, some creative, and so on. For instance, Nelson Mandela strikes us as a really joyous, embracing man—maybe fun to spend a weekend with. But if Adolf Hitler were alive, you'd be unlikely to want to vacation with him. (It's all in the ethos!)

An ethos thus identifies and develops the core beliefs, values, hero system, and so on and weaves them all together to create the organization's culture and vibe. It communicates (verbally and nonverbally) through symbols, actions, and experiences what we really think and what we truly value. An explicit, well-developed ethos is crucial in determining behavior, making the right choices, developing programming, allocating resources, and setting the overall direction of the organization. (I'm pretty sure Starbucks would raise a cup to that now!)

Verging the Vibe and Vibing the Verge

When we talk about having a Verge church ethos, we mean an ethos that is consistent with what it means to be an authentic apostolic movement. Think for a moment about the six elements: if Jesus is genuinely the center (King) of the church, then you would expect that decision-making and programming would be based on a prayerful commitment to referring all things to him—ensuring consistency with his person, life, and commands. If disciple-making is part of our genetic code, you would expect that the culture would communicate that; you would expect lots of language, activities, and tools that ensure that outcome. Decision-making in a church that refers everything to Jesus ought to be markedly different from decision-making in one that doesn't, because the church that does is held by the primary commitment at the deepest possible level to becoming more and more like him. The mDNA, embedded in the heart of the community, sets the defaults of the church to discipleship and disciple-making. And so we can see this work with all six elements of mDNA and the paradigm as a whole.

Toward the end of this chapter, we will suggest many ways in which ethos grows out of the paradigm/systems story; for now, we need to recognize the *pivotal* (literally) importance of a consistent Verge ethos in developing a genuine Verge church. Ethos, you see, is the pivot around which the paradigm is converted into practice; it's the means by which the paradigm begins to take root and inform the culture of the organization. This is where the hard work of recovering the genetic basis of the church (mDNA) will begin to bear dividends; if the core of disciples and leaders are increasingly grounded in the Verge paradigm (the six elements of mDNA), then developing an appropriate ethos should be a relatively natural task.

Various Future Travelers churches have done different intentional things in order to transition into the Verge paradigm and create ethos. For instance, Kensington Community Church in Detroit, Michigan, radically reinterpreted my book *The Forgotten Ways* (a rather complex leadership-oriented book) into a more simplistic "dummy's version" and had all their small groups go through the series. At Mosaic Church of Central Arkansas (located in Little Rock), Pastor Mark DeYmaz did a long preaching series which intentionally reframed much of the language and structures of Mosaic in the process.

Recognizing the importance of shaping the imagination and thinking of leaders, Austin Stone Church started a whole missional leadership development system and process that eventually led to the church hosting one of the most missionally consistent, energetic conferences on the topic of apostolic movements. Now known as the Verge Network, it is itself the leading-edge movement cohosting the Exponential Conference in 2011.[5] The growth and interest in regard to their first Verge conference, in 2010, was remarkable. With no advertising, Austin Stone had over two thousand leaders come from all over the continent, and they were sold out three weeks before the conference — a rare event for any conference, even more so in the midst of a recession.

The Turning Point: Aligning Ethos with Paradigm

Next we will suggest examples and ways in which each mDNA in its own way can engender values, norms, and thinking that go together to form ethos. We in no way want to suggest that you simply adopt these (and certainly not that you do so without serious afore-thought and team reflection), because by their very nature, core beliefs and values must be *owned*—they must be *your* values. However, we do believe that some of the suggestions below would be authentic manifestations of mDNA becoming the ethos. Consider these manifestations and then use them as inspiration for your own.

Jesus Is Lord

Remember, this is about recognizing that the absolute centrality of Jesus—the incarnation, his life, his teachings, the cross, the resurrection, *parousia* (his second coming), and everything in between—becomes the spiritual center around which the church ethos (and culture) orients itself. For example:

- *Verge ethos = Jesus is ever-present King and Lord through the Spirit.* This will mean that Jesus must become the reference point for all decisions as well as for matters of spirituality and direction; he gets first say and the last word. Does it square with what Jesus said and who he is? If not, we don't do it. If Jesus says don't, then we won't; if Jesus says do it, we'll hop to it. He gets first say.

- *Verge ethos = Christocentric monotheism.* Monotheism is to theology what marriage is to relationships—you forgo all other options. Jesus is the *only* Lord. This will mean dismantling idolatry in all its forms—political, economic, domestic, sexual, relational, and so on. (Caution: watch for falling idols!)

- *Verge ethos = holistic worship.* This means broadening our notion of worship, getting beyond the over-romanticized "Jesus is my boyfriend" songs and seeing that anything and everything (including songs, friendships, business, play, and so on) can be worship, if directed toward God. Even sex can be true worship when it is so directed! When sex is undirected by holy intentions, it is a vile, enslaving idol. Worship is simply offering all that we have and do back to God through Jesus.

- *Verge ethos = nondualistic spirituality.* There is no compartmentalizing faith within a Verge culture. We must help people experience everyday things as filled with holy possibility. We have to stop doing church in such a way that it sets people up to experience life as a dance between the so-called sacred and secular. All of life can be made holy—get to it.[6]

How can "Jesus is Lord" become the center of your church ethos?

Disciple-Making

Disciple-making isn't a *peripheral* activity; it is *essential* activity. If you aren't inviting people to a consistent life-practice of yoking themselves to Jesus, you aren't doing what we're meant to be doing. Our job personally and corporately is to live in, out, and from God in Christ and to become more and more like him. With this in mind ...

- *Verge ethos = evaluating discipling reality.* You may want to do a constant mDNA checkup on this point. Do a discipleship audit, assessing all movement/church activities through the grid of discipleship and disciple-making. Ask, *does this hinder or help people becoming apprentices of Jesus?* Ask, *where and how exactly are disciples being formed in the way of Jesus?*

- *Verge ethos = everyone is a disciple.* With this ethos/value, the church commits itself to its core task. We don't seek to just convert people; we are committed to apprenticing them to the Master. This isn't for newbies only! Apprenticeship is "a long obedience in the same direction," as Eugene Peterson puts it, and this includes the leadership of the church. Only those who demonstrate ongoing discipleship to Christ should be put in positions of authority.

- *Verge ethos = helping people get back to God.* Discipleship takes place both *pre-* and *post-*conversion. When the mDNA discipleship informs ethos, it means that evangelism will be reframed in light of the Great Commission to disciple all nations. We begin discipling people, Christian or not, and see what God will do.[7] Share the gospel, to be sure, but don't just leave it there. We must commit ourselves to relationships and friendships, not *just* decisions for Christ.

- *Verge ethos = what would Jesus do?* This question wasn't just for youth groups in the nineties; it's for everyone. To be a disciple means becoming more and more and more like Jesus. To be his disciple, study the life and teachings of Jesus often and spend time directly with him in prayer.

- *Verge ethos = instruction-action-reflection (repeat).* When disciple-ship is actually ethos, then we are committed to lifelong, holistic learning, not just the transfer of information through doctrine done in the first thirteen weeks of membership classes. We need to be engaged in a cycle of instruction-action-reflection that doesn't end as long as we are breathing.

- *Verge ethos = mentoring mentors.* Everyone is in an apprentice-ship relationship, no matter who they are, how old they are, how mature they are, and so on. It's a lifelong process, and you never graduate this side of heaven. For instance, 3DM leaders commit themselves to what they call "8-6-4." A leader disciples eight people, those eight each disciple six, and each of those six commit to discipling four—which means one leader disciples over 250 people.

How can disciple-making and apprenticeship become essential to the ethos in your church?

Missional-Incarnational Impulse

This element of mDNA enshrines at our core consciousness a bonding with the theology of the missionary God *(Missio Dei)* and our calling to do likewise: "As the Father has sent me, I am sending you" (John 20:21).

As the Father: commits us to follow the logic of the incarnation of God in Christ.

Sent me: commits us to the idea that mission is rooted in the sent and sending God.

So I send you: commits us to follow in that way.

We are sent as the Father sent Jesus—to go deep among a group of people, to contextualize and personalize the gospel in ways that are meaningful. In other words, we are *designed* and *destined* to be a missional-incarnational people. It might look like this:

- *Verge ethos = going out. Sending* also means *going.* It means movement of some sort—if not geographical, at least into every sphere and domain of society and into every nook and cranny of culture. No one dodges this. There is no such thing as an unsent

Christian! We are *all* missionaries. It is not a profession; it's the calling of every disciple.

- *Verge ethos* = *going deep.* This means respecting people where *they* are at. Incarnational practice means being present, patient, humble, and respecting the humanity of people and people groups — their culture, their dignity, their current location in their journey toward God.

- *Verge ethos* = *church follows mission.* (And not the other way around.) Incarnational mission demands that the church be constantly adapting to suit the context. A missional church must be a culturally savvy church. We will constantly be inventing new ways to be the people of God in new and changing cultures.

- *Verge ethos* = *taking church to the people.* (And not just people to church.) This means that we actually have to spend time with the ones to whom we are sent: go into their worlds, inhabit their spaces, bring good news, and be the good news we proclaim.

- *Verge ethos* = *creativity and innovation in all things.* The contextualization (incarnation) of the gospel requires this. Innovation is implied in the foundational missionary calling of the church to incarnate the gospel wherever we are.

How can you contextualize a missional-incarnational impulse into the ethos of your church?

Apostolic Environment

This element of mDNA deals directly with the scope and potency of ministry that Jesus has deliberately laced throughout the church (Eph. 4:7 – 11). Here the ministry of Christ is being expressed through the body of Christ. As discussed previously, Jesus designed the church to have *at least a fivefold ministry* at its core. The current twofold version (shepherd and teacher only) violates the genetic coding of the church and creates a malformed *ecclesia.* It's time to repent, change, and mature up:

- *Verge ethos* = *ministry based on APEST callings.* All of God's people are vocationally empowered to do the work of the church. One of the core tasks of leadership, then, is helping people find and engage their God-given vocations as described in Ephesians 4 (see *www.apest.org*).[8]

- *Verge ethos = diversity of calling and gifting.* Clearly, if we're going to diversify our ministries into (at least) five forms, then we're going to have to value and manage diversity of thinking and approach, because each ministry style (APEST) is very different.
- *Verge ethos = every believer, a minister.* This ethos statement pops up all over because it's so much part of apostolic movement thinking and practice. Note that Ephesians 4 says, "To *each one of us* grace has been given as Christ apportioned it" (v. 7, emphasis added). Remember, this letter is addressed to the whole church — not a leadership conference or seminary — and the whole church includes men, women, different races and classes, and so on. It's radical but very powerful stuff.
- *Verge ethos = apostolic ministry for apostolic movement.* Apostolic movements are precisely that: *apostolic.* This means more than being missional; it also means that the organization ought to be focused in a distinctly apostolic way. This is a commitment to a certain *way* of doing church, and it differs greatly from nonapostolic forms.

How can your church recover an apostolic environment, as described in Ephesians 4?

Organic Systems

This element of mDNA determines the organizational shape that movements adopt to achieve spontaneous expansion and high impact. It is here where prevailing forms will possibly struggle the most to adopt/adapt, because it commits us to a more decentralized (chaordic) approach. Structures are hard to change, and they become more and more resistant over time. We have to encourage pliable structures or else suffer the consequences of religious institutionalism. Consider:

- *Verge ethos = both/and.* There are no points scored for trying to change the system overnight, and we certainly don't have to jettison perfectly good ways of doing church. The way forward for most churches is to embrace the idea of being a hybrid organization composed of some centralized and some decentralized practices and structures. Keep saying "and, and, and" to yourself and your team; it will help with the stress.

- *Verge ethos = adaptive leadership for adaptive structures.* A Verge church needs the kind of leadership that knows how to move a church and keep it moving. Once again, this highlights the apostolic and prophetic roles. The prophetic person will tend to call the status quo into question, while the apostolic leads with a positive vision of what can be.

- *Verge ethos = high accountability, low control.* This means that while there must be a strong permission-giving culture where people are encouraged to give it a go, there should be definite apprenticeship-based lines of accountability for actions. But, as leaders, we have to overcome our seemingly innate desire to control. The Holy Spirit can and does guide his people. Don't replace his work in the church with human power issues.

- *Verge ethos = ready-willing-able.* This recognizes that every unit/agency in the organization has everything it needs to get the job done. Jesus designed the church in precisely this way. Verge church organizations work to facilitate the inherent design of the church. Remember, Apostolic Genius is latent; it's all there. Seek to activate it.

- *Verge ethos = pushing out as far as possible.* In apostolic movements, both power and function need to be distributed as far out into the organization as possible. This needs to be an ethos issue, because it's going to have to direct your movemental practices.

- *Verge ethos = priesthood of all believers.* Verge churches recognize that movements require more than church planting and other "organized" activities. Every believer is an agent of the King in every arena of society and culture. The importance of this is largely missing in biblical teaching today.

How can you de-institutionalize your church to develop (verge into) a more organic system?

Communitas

The mDNA of *communitas* hardwires the church/organization to ongoing learning and adaptation, to engaging in the spiritual adventure of what God is doing in the global church, and to embracing risk-taking as a necessary aspect of life, mission, and creativity. A great example of *communitas* in organizations is suggested by Warren Bennis, the writer of the seminal book *Organizing Genius*. He says there are two essential traits of great teams: a compelling performance challenge or problem that unites the team in common purpose, and (of great importance) a sense of urgency. These are variables within the leadership mix and can be actively developed to create *communitas*:[9]

- *Verge ethos = risk-taking as spiritual discipline.* Risk-taking is tied directly to ongoing learning and is indispensable for any involvement in mission. The problem is, most churches (particularly middle-class ones) tend to be safety-minded and risk-averse. We need a good dose of theological teaching about missional adventure. It's a spiritual discipline, and it must become part of the ethos of a Verge church if movement is going to happen. I'm personally committed to doing something more risky every year I get older, just to exercise this muscle.

- *Verge ethos = managing from the future.* You can explore this in more detail in *The Forgotten Ways*, but effectively it is an approach to planning that starts from where you want to be and works backward.[10] This is what professional futurists call "back-casting," and they use it with some of the most powerful and influential organizations on earth. The reason why this is a possible approach here is that the future creates liminal (threshold) conditions out of which *communitas* emerges.

- *Verge ethos = mission as catalyzing principle.* When your groups are organized around ministry to other Christians, they will seldom, if ever, get to mission. If you organize the group around mission, you have to do ministry, because ministry is the means to do mission. Make sure groups are committed to something beyond their own selves and self-interests.

- *Verge ethos = cultivating urgency.* John Kotter, possibly the leading writer on organizational change, says that developing urgency is possibly the most important aspect of change.[11] Urgency, like the future, or a crisis of some kind, creates the conditions of learning and focuses the organization around essentials.

How can you develop *communitas* among the people of your movement?

Apostolic Genius

Finally, it's important to note again that while each of the six elements of mDNA codes or hardwires the church for apostolic movement, and that they are potent factors for change and mission, nonetheless it's vital to think of mDNA as producing a system: the much-discussed (but ever-crucial) Apostolic Genius. When you get past thinking in one-dimensional elements to thinking systemically, then you're really operating as a Verge church should.

- *It's the system, stoopid.* Systems-thinking is a habit of mind and a very important aspect of Verge church approach. Peter Senge calls systems-thinking the "Fifth Discipline" in a book by that name. At any point when you and others are tending to see things one-dimensionally and looking for a silver bullet, apply this discipline. Think of your own body as a system of systems (cardiovascular, nervous, digestive, and so on). It takes all to make it work. Discipline yourselves to always think of functioning wholes rather than reductionistically in disparate parts.

- *Living out of the center.* Again, this reiterates the importance of constantly educating yourselves, the leadership, staff, and the church in light of the apostolic movement paradigm. Paradigms take a long time to instill; as you move from unconscious incompetence to unconscious competence (via conscious incompetence and then conscious competence), you will need to really work hard at this. Make it a matter of ethos, guide to thinking, rule of thumb, and core value to live from the determinative center of the church—from the system of mDNA.

- *Thinking movements, not institution.* The apostolic movement paradigm takes a while to get into our heads—that's hard enough— but in doing that, it has to dislodge the deeply rooted institutional paradigm that has ruled our thinking for so long. Make it a discipline to think *movements*, not *institution*. If you identify yourself as a movement, and take this seriously, you will eventually start acting like one (the imperative is in the indicative).

All in all, this has been an exercise in what it means to develop ethos. When we apply it to our previous diagram, it might look like figure 17.

Example of Verge ethos

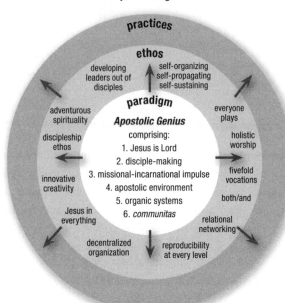

Figure 17

So now we have looked at the first two essential parts of the Verge church process. The first involves the embedding of the apostolic movement paradigm at the genetic center of the church. This revolves around the six elements of mDNA and the system that results. This chapter has explored the idea of developing an ethos that grows out of the reactivation of the paradigm. Ethos, as the effective operating system of the organization, has been about developing a language, formulating values, establishing guides to thinking, and generating a deliberate vibe that points to what is believed and valued in the organization. Now we turn to the issue of praxis, or practices.

Dave's Response to "Verge Vibe: The Operating System of Apostolic Movement"

Read the following and pay attention to your reaction: The setting is the beach. You have already arrived at the beach when a man and a woman show up together. They seem like a nice couple. They appear to be new but seem to be enjoying themselves and the surroundings.

They settle in, finding a seat, and get ready to take it all in. Before they sit down, the guy takes off his shirt, and the woman strips down to her bikini.

Now, let's try it again. The setting is your church. You have already arrived at church when a man and a woman show up together. They seem like a nice couple. They appear to be new but seem to be enjoying themselves and the surroundings. They settle in, finding a seat, and get ready to take it all in. Before they sit down, the guy takes off his shirt, and the woman strips down to her bikini.

What was your reaction this time? In the first setting (the beach), you probably didn't have much of a reaction. You may not have been at all surprised, and you probably didn't form any assumptions — especially about their mental stability.

> In the church that Jesus built, everyone gets to play.

But what was your reaction when the same scenario took place in church? You were probably taken off guard and a little shocked. If you'd had friends with you when it happened, you might have pointed out this odd behavior or nodded to them to "look over there." You probably would've begun to make negative assumptions about this couple, even questioning their mental stability.

Why do you have two different reactions to the exact same behavior when the only thing different is the setting? The reason is *ethos*, or culture. The beach has a culture all its own, and your church has its own unique culture. My favorite definition of ethos is this: *spontaneous repeated behaviors by a group of people.*

Taking off your shirt and wearing a swimsuit at the beach is a spontaneously repeated behavior every day! No one even questions it. That's what you do at the beach. But that's not a repeated behavior in a church.

Crazy Is As Crazy Does

In many churches, missional behavior would be as shocking and absurd as undressing in the sanctuary. While I was working on this, I received the following message through Facebook:

> I serve as a student ministry pastor.... God has been doing a huge
> work in me over the past six months and has brought me to a very

strong discontent to the way things are right now in church life. It all began when I heard Alan Hirsch at a church-planting conference. From that point, I began to study, pray, and read about the missional movement as well reread the New Testament with fresh eyes. I have tried to incorporate what I can into the ministry in which I am serving. I have also tried to challenge our senior leadership to come alongside me and learn more about what God is doing across the world. I have unfortunately got nothing but pushback and ridicule. It's crazy; I never would have thought that would be the case. I really believe that God is leading me to start an organic missional church that reproduces itself through the means of multiplication ... almost everyone thinks I am crazy.

You can just feel the church culture clash as this young leader writes to me! So how do we introduce ideas that currently sound crazy and make them mainstream? How do we make missional engagement the spontaneous repeated behavior of every church?

Click It or Ticket and Culture Shift

I remember hearing Erwin McManus talk about changing culture, when we were together for a leadership conference once. He explained it by talking about the mandatory seatbelt law in his state. He said, "Do you remember when seatbelt laws were implemented? If you were in any way like me, it was an absolute invasion of privacy! I didn't want to buckle up. It was uncomfortable, it was irritating; it wrinkled my clothes, and it hampered my dating style. But they passed the law anyway. So I would only buckle up when I saw police. They were smart, because for the first several months there was a grace period where the police would pull you over and give you a warning but not a ticket. Then, over time, that grace period expired, and you were required to buckle up at the risk of a penalty.

"Today, not only does it feel wrong if we don't put the seatbelt on, but if you see an unbuckled child in a car, your thoughts immediately turn to their negligent parents. Look how the world has changed. Our seatbelt experience as a society is an example of the successful transition in cul-

Every believer carries within himself the potential for world transformation.

ture. We once thought buckling was absurd and an invasion of privacy; now we do it because we believe it's the right thing to do. In fact, many of us don't even realize that we're buckling up. We just get in the car, strap the belt across us, and turn the key without a conscious thought."

McManus's story is a great example of culture shift and changing the spontaneous repeated behaviors of a group of people.

The New Normal

Here are the tools we've given you in this chapter: beliefs, values, vocabulary, hero-making, rewards, branding, and new measurements. All are great for giving your church the Verge vibe and shifting your ethos toward apostolic mission. These are the best of the best for creating a new normal. These tools in the hands of leadership can create a brand-new culture that would honor and encourage my Facebook friend in his desire to start a reproducing organic missional church. And in an mDNA culture, it would never occur to anyone that it was crazy, because all around them would be the same spontaneous repeated behavior by this group of missional folk called the church.

Getting a Handle on Ethos

I think that any church engaging the Verge church process needs to develop an evaluation tool/discussion guide around prevailing beliefs, values, vocabulary, hero-making, rewards, branding, and measurements of their movement. They will need to ruthlessly evaluate where their current context is at, what are the current beliefs, values, vocabulary, and so on, and then hold the results up against mDNA.

One useful process that can assist here is outlined in Will Mancini's book *Church Unique*.[12] One of the tools the book provides is called the Vision Frame, and it gives us a good handle on *how* to identify and organize the language guiding the actions and thinking of the church. To develop the language, Mancini walks through what he calls the five irreducible questions of clarity. These are:

1. *What are we doing?* In answering this question, the church formally articulates mission as its central organizing principle as *a missional mandate*. It's the golden thread that weaves through everything in the church. This asks questions of our

current paradigm, explores anomalies, and sets us on a search for answers that better fit who we are called to be.

2. *Why are we doing it?* The question defines values as *missional motives.* Here Mancini highlights that expressing no more than four to six of your core convictions is the best way for people to carry them consciously in shaping new patterns of thinking and acting. For a Verge church, this should take us back to the core codes—to Apostolic Genius—in the search for answers.

3. *How are we doing it?* The final "side" of the Vision Frame is the definition of a picture or process that shows how the church accomplishes the mission on the broadest level. This picture is called a *missional map.* This map, used in harness with the other sides of the frame, helps keep whatever methodology the church may be using the means of mission and not the end.

4. *When are we successful?* This question forces the issues of disciple-making mission in terms of how the church defines success. In answering this question, the church leadership articulates the *missional "life-marks,"* or practices, that define success. This begins to create substance around disciple-making as the core reason for being rather than the typical metrics that churches cling to in the North American context.

5. *Where is God taking us?* The final question of the Vision Frame is the middle of the frame, which answers the question, where is God taking us? As a tool for articulating vision, Mancini's model uniquely connects the practice and skill of communication to a missional reorientation on the paradigmatic level.

It can be viewed as in figure 18.

Be sure to measure the outcomes of the discussion against each of the six elements of Apostolic Genius, and this process will allow the church to develop a new operating system. The good thing that results from a process like this is that the church begins to use its own "love language," its natural language of the heart, to articulate its own vision and ethos.

Whatever tool you might use, keep this in mind: it's important for leadership to draw upon the prevailing sense of purpose and hopefully redeem and enrich the language already present in the church.

frame component	missional reorientation	answers	irreducible question of leadership
mission	ᵐMandate	question zero	What are we doing?
values	ᵐMotives	question hero	Why are we doing it?
strategy	ᵐMap	question how	How are we doing it?
measures	ᵐMarks	question now	When are we successful?
vision proper	ᵐMountaintop + Milestones	question wow	Where is God taking us?

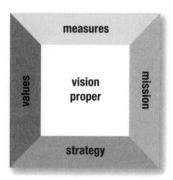

Figure 18

DISCUSSION QUESTIONS

Open

What company's branding, culture, or "vibe" do you admire? What do you like about them? Are there any learnings from them that you can apply to your church?

Explore

1. What announcements or accomplishments receive spontaneous applause at your church? What types of things do people typically celebrate?

2. Who are the heroes in your church, and why are they celebrated?

3. In the following verses, to whom is Jesus sent? (Pat answers are not allowed!) Cite examples from his life to back up your answers.

   As the Father has sent me, I am sending you.
   —John 20:21

   The Son of Man came to seek and to save what was lost.
   —Luke 19:10

4. What can we learn about Jesus' sentness that applies to how/where God is sending us? How can you help your church really grasp that as a theological truth?
5. Where has your church already answered the call to be sent? Do you see God making an impact through your church there? How are those stories being told?
6. How do the examples or manifestations of mDNA help your understanding of these elements? Which elements do you believe are most difficult to practice? Explain.

Move

1. Find at least two heroes over the next month who are living out Verge church mission and celebrate them publicly (weekend service, elder/leadership team meeting, all-church email, and so on).
2. Review the examples or manifestations of mDNA on pages 158 – 64. Choose one example from each one of the six elements that you can put into action in your current ministry environment.
3. Decide on at least two new metrics that you will start using to measure success.

Chapter 6

Embodying Movement-Programming Practices

ALAN

Without some sweat, the spirit ain't worth spit.

— CLINT EASTWOOD, *PALE RIDER*

Men acquire a particular quality by constantly acting in a particular way.... We are what we repeatedly do. Excellence then, is not an act, but a habit.

— ARISTOTLE, PHILOSOPHER

No! Try not. Do, or do not. There is no try.

— YODA, JEDI MASTER AND TEACHER

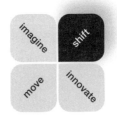

They say practice makes perfect.

While fundamental, systemic, and transformative sea change comes from the shifting of the paradigm (activating Apostolic Genius) and through the creation of an ethos consistent with the paradigm, there is one piece that still needs to be put in place for a Verge church to emerge: the formation of defining practices.

Practices are quite literally *embodiments of value*—especially when they are performed by disciples of Jesus. They require the living out of values in such a way as to be observable and experienced by others. As such, they testify to what we believe and what we think is important. In many ways, this is exactly what it means to bear witness to Jesus—to live lives observably consistent with his.

In many ways, when we are talking about developing core practices, we are really talking about a way in which the movement develops disciples *on the ground*. It is here where the paradigm gets to be actually lived out by adherents of the movement and/or members of the organization. This is really about active apprenticeship in the way of Jesus, but done in such a way as to express the uniqueness of any given community, movement, or organization. Discipleship will be nuanced through our distinctive ethos. Not all churches ought to be alike; each ought to be somewhat different and have a different personality, so to speak. It's here, where the mDNA elements of "Jesus is Lord," disciple-making, and even perhaps *communitas* will come to the fore. Right here, at the formation of core practices, you should experience the powerful influence of Apostolic Genius pulsing through the ethos, requiring conformity in practice to what is believed at the heart—practices are not formed in a vacuum.

Because the church Jesus designed is meant to be a disciple-making system, it should be *expected* that everyone in the movement has an active role to play. No one who claims faith in Jesus is exempt from the call to follow him. It should be an explicit expectation that when someone comes to faith, they immediately get involved in the church's practices—even before they might fully understand why they are important and how they express the ethos of the movement.

As is now generally admitted, Western churches have paid way too high a price for nondiscipleship of believers. By not being intentional about apprenticing people in the way of Jesus, we've handed people over to be formed and developed by the prevailing cultural forces that so deeply shape Western lifestyle. The net result is that biblical Christianity has been somewhat subverted by the powerful religion of consumerism—the search for identity, purpose, belonging, and meaning in what we purchase and consume. So raise the bar here, be unashamed about being disciples of Jesus, and expect—yes *expect*—everyone to participate. Don't reward mere spectatorship and attendance. *Require* active involvement in what it means to become like Jesus. Only in this way can we expect to create Jesus followers out of a church full of Jesus admirers.

Inside Out and Outside In

Change, when it comes, will come from both inside out (as we change the paradigm) and outside in (as we develop practices that shape who we're called to be). It's vital that leaders work hard at changing the frames of interpretation by recoding the paradigm and generating ethos, but for the most part change will come as people engage in sets of practices that will change their behaviors and thinking.

To return to the computer metaphor, with its three interactive levels, practices are the programs we get to use. Most of us are blissfully ignorant of the complexities underlying the computer programs we use—of the primary codes and operating systems—we just use them. But when we use them, we are changed. Imperceptibly at first, but irrevocably in the end. For instance, I'm so accustomed to using my computer and word-processing program, my handwriting has become barely legible—even to me. What's more, it's hard to even conceive of drafting a book without the aid of a word processor. (I'm genuinely amazed people could write books before personal computers!) The vast majority (85 percent?) of people in the church will be changed by acting their way into a new way of thinking. They don't need to know the internal process and ideas that leaders need to know.

In this chapter, we'll explore change from the outside in, but for now it's important to see the development of core practices as the natural end result to what has gone before in the Verge church process. What we do ultimately comes out of who we are and who Jesus designed us to be.

So developing core practices must be seen as the "business end" of the Verge church process. Change, particularly systemwide, *fundamental*, and lasting change, must come from deep inside: by displacing a non-missional paradigm with another, more missional one. Without this, there is unlikely to be any real and lasting change at all.

Verge Church Process Core Practices Level

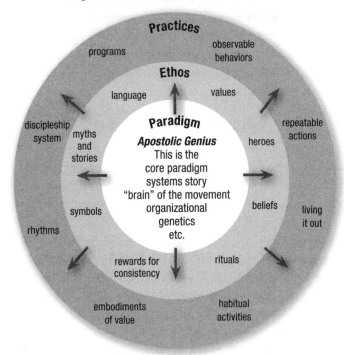

Figure 19

Acting Our Way into a New Way of Thinking (Outside-In Change)

We're all familiar with the gospel story, in which Jesus selected a ragtag band of disciples, lived and ministered with them, and mentored them on the road. It was this life-on-life phenomenon that facilitated the transfer of information and ideas into concrete situations. This is the way Jesus formed his apprentices, and we shouldn't think we can generate authentic Jesus followers in any other way.

So, guided by a core commitment to disciple-making, we will

encourage you to develop your core practices, consistent with the apostolic movement paradigm and ethos, as close as we can to the way Jesus seemed to do it with his disciples. Not only are we somehow obligated to Jesus' way of forming disciples; there are excellent reasons for adopting it in order to become a Verge church. We need to explain this in terms of worldview, but be patient because hopefully you're about to see why developing missional practices can be a very powerful tool in the hands of missional leaders.

The prevailing paradigm of church laced throughout the West has tended to try to make disciples primarily through the transfer (mainly) of doctrinal information about the Trinity, church, salvation, eschatology, and so on. Often, it has tried to track cultural trends and engage in apologetics and evangelism, but again it has done this mainly on an intellectual level, in classrooms and Sunday school sessions. Please don't misunderstand me here; we certainly do need serious intellectual engagement with the key ideas of our time. What is concerning, however, is that such engagement largely takes place in the disengaged and passive environment of the classroom. This is simply *not* the way Jesus taught us to develop disciples. And it isn't that Jesus lacked an appropriate model of the classroom — the Greeks had developed this hundreds of years before Christ, and it was well entrenched in the Greco-Roman world. The Hebrew worldview was a life-oriented one and was not primarily concerned with concepts and ideas *in themselves*. We simply don't believe we can continue to try to *think* our way into a new way of acting; rather we need to *act* our way into a new way of thinking.[1]

How did we move so far from the ethos of discipleship passed on to us by our Lord? Because Western Christianity has been so deeply influenced by Hellenistic, specifically Platonic, ideas of knowledge. By the fourth century, the Platonic worldview had almost triumphed over the Hebraic one in the church. Essentially, a Platonic view of knowledge is concerned about concepts, ideas, and the nature of being. The Hebraic, on the other hand, is primarily concerned with issues of concrete existence, obedience, life-oriented wisdom, and interrelationship of all things under God. It's quite clear that Jesus and most members of the early church, being primarily Jews, operated mostly from a Hebraic understanding rather than a Platonic one.

Action learning (discipleship) versus the academy

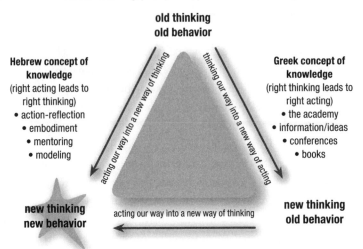

Figure 20

If our starting point is *old thinking* and *old behavior,* and we see it as our task to change that situation, taking the Hellenistic approach will mean that we provide information to get the person or church to a new way of thinking—and hopefully to a new way of acting. The problem is that by merely addressing intellectual aspects, we've failed to change behavior. The assumption in Hellenistic thinking is that if people get the right ideas, they will simply change their behavior. The Hellenistic approach therefore can be characterized as an attempt to try to *think our way into a new way of acting.* Both experience and history show the fallacy of this approach. And it certainly doesn't make disciples. All we do is change the way a person *thinks,* and their behavior remains largely unaffected. Even though gaining knowledge is essential to transformation, we soon discover it's going to take a whole lot more than new thinking to transform us.

So what is that better way? We mentioned it before. It's found in the ancient art of disciple-making, which operates best within the Hebrew understanding of knowledge. We need to take the whole person into account in seeking to transform an individual. We need to educate them in the context *of* life *for* life. The way we do this is the way Jesus asked his followers to do it: we act our way into a new way of thinking. So whether we find ourselves with old thinking and old behavior (or new thinking and old behavior), the way forward is to put actions into the equation.

The assumption is that we bring all these dynamic thinking processes with us into our actions. It's about context, not just content. We do not, as is supposed by the Hellenistic model, leave our thinking behind when we are acting. We think while we are acting, and act while we are thinking.

At Forge Mission Training Network, for instance, we have built our entire system around this concept of action-learning discipleship. Our twin aims are to develop missionaries to the West, along with a distinct pioneering missional mode of leadership. To do this, we host an internship where each intern is placed in an environment of mission. The vast majority of the intern's learning is by "having a go" at mission. They also meet regularly with a coach for reflection and goal-setting and attend inspiring intensives where they're exposed to a significant amount of theory. This information is communicated by those who have a demonstrated capacity to actually model and demonstrate what they are teaching — in other words, they are active practitioners in their own right. As interns engage in training this way, their ability to grasp the issues, to resolve and integrate them, is significantly increased.

> Even though gaining knowledge is essential to transformation, we soon discover it's going to take a whole lot more than new thinking to transform us.

From Core Values to Core Practices

Most organizations and churches have already identified what their core values are. They are then put on display on walls, in the literature, on the website, and so on. So far, so good. The problem arises in trying to actually live them out. The reason for this is partly because, as we saw in the previous section, we've mainly informed people's heads and not required anything of their behaviors; all we ask is that people passively believe and not act. But the problem is exacerbated by the confessional nature of the church: when we are talking about core values in a values-shaped community of believers, it's hard to disagree with them. Mainly because there is a Bible verse associated with each value (and who is going to argue with a verse?) but also because statements of values appeal to the head — to what we believe—and don't require much else. The common response for many would be: of course we believe in evangelism (though we hold back from it in most cases), and of course we care for the weak (even though we don't do much of it), and of course we confess to be monotheists (even though we are all practicing polytheists). You get the idea.

The problem in churches is that mere value statements can easily become "motherhood statements," which are preferred ideals and not lived-out values. If you don't develop practices based on the values, establishing core values simply becomes an intellectual process rather than a compelling way to live. It's very hard to change people's values by referring them to a new set of values on paper and asking them to believe in them and assimilate them into their lives. So rather than simply talk/teach/lecture about ethos and values, develop many common practices which will give people mechanisms by which they can act their way into a new way of thinking. You can do this in the way demonstrated by figure 21.

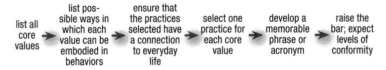

Figure 21

- If you haven't already got a list of values arising out of the development of ethos, we suggest you develop one (see previous chapter).
- Get people to list all the possible ways in which the value can be lived out and observed by others.
- Review the practices to make sure they have a connection to everyday life.
- Select just one (no more than two) practices which you feel best embody the associated core value. Try your best to ensure that these aren't seen as particularly religious or church-based terms and activities but are as close to everyday life as possible. So, for instance, if the core value is hospitality, then there are many ways in which hospitality can be lived out outside church walls (for example, eating meals together, visiting the sick, having a spare room).

- Develop an acronym that sums up your core values. (We'll give examples below.)
- Expect that members of the church/movement will somehow practice these.

Only by raising the bar on what we currently expect of people can we expect to transform them from being consumers to being disciples. By developing practices as a means of changing people, as well as engaging the Verge church process, you can expect change to come from both ends of the spectrum—systemic change from the Verge process (paradigm → ethos → practices), and local change from the discipleship process (practices → ethos → paradigm).[2] In other words, it becomes a self-reinforcing cycle. I believe that when practices are consistent with the genetic codes (Apostolic Genius) and vice versa, the apostolic movement is in full swing.

Getting Into the Swing of Things

Another important aspect of practice is the issue of rhythms. It isn't enough simply to have a list of preferred behaviors. If we are to generate a distinct and living Verge culture that will infuse the movement, it is vital that we become *practiced* in them and do this together as a community.

Actually, this idea of living according to a common rule is ancient; monastic orders have used rules for centuries. For instance, the Benedictine rule dates to the fifth century and has over ninety prescribed practices. So what is suggested here isn't inconsistent with the best processes of apprenticeship throughout the ages.

The difference in the Verge process is that we are seeking to apply a rule, or rhythm, not in ascetic withdrawal from others but missionally in the context of ordinary life. Jesus calls us to live out our discipleship in the context of where people live. The gospel, after all, is social force.

Furthermore, sociologists have long recognized the role that ritual plays in formation of identity, shaping thinking and dictating behaviors. For example, every Jew repeats the *Shema* (Deut. 6:4) at least three times a day, affirming that God is sovereign over all of life, and they always face east, toward Jerusalem, when they pray, thus physically acknowledging the role that the land has in their ongoing identity.

They always pray at sunrise, midday, and sunset, thus regulating their lives around predictable daily events. Also, Jewish liturgical life is built around Sabbath (the seven-day cycle) and around seasonal events. Jewish faith is thus a thoroughly rhythmic one built around events experienced in regular cycles. There is no doubt that this accounts, in part, for the capacity of the Jewish people to survive a two-thousand-year-old dispersion in the most hostile of cultures.[3] Simple rituals, redemptively constructed around natural life-rhythms and consistent with paradigm and ethos, can have profound consequences.

Perhaps the best way to illustrate what we're saying is to describe the way it's done by Small Boat Big Sea, the community founded by Australian missional leader Michael Frost.[4] This midsized community identified a set of rhythms called BELLS. It goes like this:

	Practice(s)	Description	Core Value Represented
B	Bless x Three	One act of blessing — small or big — one to someone inside the community of faith, one to someone outside, one spare to go either way.	Creative acts of goodness and kindness
E	Eat x Three	All members encouraged to share table fellowship three times a week — one with people inside the community of faith, one with folks outside, one spare to go either way.	Hospitality and openness with everything
L	Listen one hour a week	All are invited to spend at least one hour each week in contemplative prayer (knowing other forms of prayer will be practiced along the way).	Prayerful, God-attentive community
L	Learn	Everyone is expected to (1) constantly be reading and rereading the Gospels, (2) be reading another book of the Bible, Old or New Testament, (3) be reading the best books in any category (fiction or nonfiction, Christian or not — but only the good material). Everyone gives up trashy magazines.	Lifelong learning from the Bible and from other dimensions of life
S	Sent	Everyone experiences themselves as "sent" into every sphere and domain of society. At the end of each day, they keep a journal reflection answering two questions: (1) Where did I resist Jesus today? (2) Where did I work with Jesus today?	Missional calling (sentness) in every aspect of life. Everyone a commissioned agent of the King.

The power of nesting well-designed practices together—and calling for consistency in their use—becomes really evident when you begin to see the effect it has on the community. For one, a group of twenty-somethings are normally pretty difficult to organize (think about what it means to herd cats here), but when they all do the same practices week in, week out, a certain rhythm develops, and out of that rhythm a culture develops. While the bar of expectation has been raised, BELLS is by no means impossible to do. Consider this: if everyone in a community is doing three acts of blessing a week, eating together a whole lot (with all that goes on around tables), listening to God, learning a lot (not necessarily always needing to be taught), and experiencing their lives as filled with missional purpose, then I think all of us can agree we will have a pretty healthy community! The really wonderful thing about rhythms and regular practices is that you don't even have to teach about each value (you can, of course). People, together and corporately, will simply act their way into a new way of thinking. After just one year of this, they will be different people!

> The church has left the building. It's not so much about bringing people to church as it is about taking church to the people.

Note again, these are phrased not as core-values statements or ideas to be believed in (nouns) but rather as core practices (verbs), values that must be lived and embodied. Practices are what you see when a value is lived out by people. So when missionality is built into the practices that shape the very life of the church, it's hard to avoid becoming missional. The movement's heroes, like the martyrs of the early church, are those who have embodied these exceptionally well.

The best (and most comprehensive) example of practices that I have seen has been developed over many years by the ministry team of St. Thomas Crookes in Sheffield and now expounded on by 3D Ministries,[5] the training and resource arm of their international movement the Order of Mission.[6] These include, but go well beyond, personal discipleship to include missional, leadership, and organizational practices. They have cleverly ordered these practices around geometric shapes, each shape representing distinctive sets of practices. And while these don't directly address the issues of paradigm, the systematic and deliberate application of these practices will profoundly shape the systemic life of the movement. Consider figure 22.

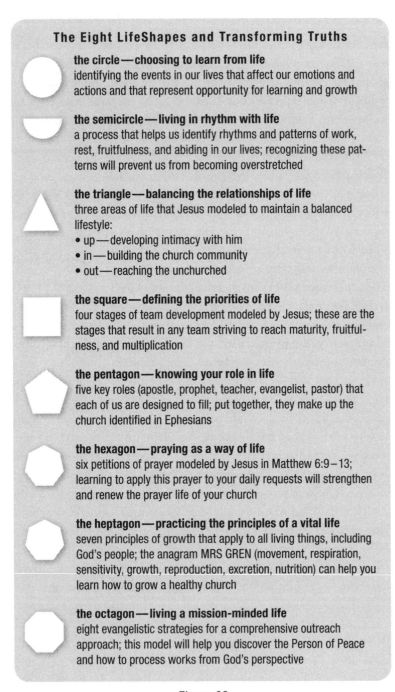

The Eight LifeShapes and Transforming Truths

the circle — choosing to learn from life
identifying the events in our lives that affect our emotions and
actions and that represent opportunity for learning and growth

the semicircle — living in rhythm with life
a process that helps us identify rhythms and patterns of work,
rest, fruitfulness, and abiding in our lives; recognizing these patterns will prevent us from becoming overstretched

the triangle — balancing the relationships of life
three areas of life that Jesus modeled to maintain a balanced
lifestyle:
• up — developing intimacy with him
• in — building the church community
• out — reaching the unchurched

the square — defining the priorities of life
four stages of team development modeled by Jesus; these are the
stages that result in any team striving to reach maturity, fruitfulness, and multiplication

the pentagon — knowing your role in life
five key roles (apostle, prophet, teacher, evangelist, pastor) that
each of us are designed to fill; put together, they make up the
church identified in Ephesians

the hexagon — praying as a way of life
six petitions of prayer modeled by Jesus in Matthew 6:9–13;
learning to apply this prayer to your daily requests will strengthen
and renew the prayer life of your church

the heptagon — practicing the principles of a vital life
seven principles of growth that apply to all living things, including
God's people; the anagram MRS GREN (movement, respiration,
sensitivity, growth, reproduction, excretion, nutrition) can help you
learn how to grow a healthy church

the octagon — living a mission-minded life
eight evangelistic strategies for a comprehensive outreach
approach; this model will help you discover the Person of Peace
and how to process works from God's perspective

Figure 22

In giving you these examples, I'm not suggesting you simply adopt them. That would violate the very necessary process of paradigm shifting and developing practices that arise from your distinctive ethos in the first place. However, if you were to simply adopt/adapt one of them, I would suggest 3DM's LifeShapes because these are definitely movemental in scope and nature. These *all* represent good examples of how regular, rhythmic practices can shape the life of a whole movement nearly effortlessly.

I suggest that in developing practices for your church, you should not only use them to shape discipleship and personal spirituality, but you should develop some to impact every aspect of the movemental organization — including leadership, ministry, mission, and so on. So, while the paradigm and ethos undergird everything, it is the practices that should be directly experienced by everyone — we should feel the visionary energy of Apostolic Genius and ethos, but we should see and experience the practices.

Examples of Verge Practices

Having mapped out the process, and having attempted to demonstrate that change comes from the inside (the paradigm) as well as from the outside (practices) and that the ethos (operating system) is the pivotal piece in the equation, we will now look at an example of a consistent application of the Verge process. Please keep in mind that the examples we give are just that: *examples.* The apostolic movement paradigm, because it's a deeply missional one and therefore driven to constant development and adaptation, will generate an immense amount of creativity and innovation in your thinking and acting. That is why we've presented an entire section on innovation — trust me, you're going to need to be innovative to keep up.

Also note, you don't have to have many practices to transform the way a community behaves. For instance, BELLS is only five practices combined in an intentional rhythm; allowing life to be shaped by them inevitably means the community *will* be changed. Develop sets of practices/rhythms for different arenas of the life of the movement. Leadership practices should define the life of leaders (that is, all should mentor others in a sustainable and reproducible ratio, all should model innovation). Apprenticing practices, as we've seen, should be designed to include everyone in the movement. But be willing to change and adapt throughout. Simplexity is the key!

Some Distinctly Disciple-Making Practices

Action Learning

Action learning is the commitment to learn from life and from events as they happen. It's focused on the present and bringing learning into the equation. It's a brilliant leadership tool, used extensively by Jesus, and ought to be in the fabric of church life.

A great example of teaching people the art of action learning and reflection comes from 3DM's LifeShapes, which we've already touched on. It's based on Mark 1:15, where Jesus says, "The time *[kairos]* has come ... the kingdom of God is near. Repent and believe the good news." Life is seen as a line from A to B (fig. 23); the *kairos* (the kingdom of God) happens in the midst of life and forces reflection.

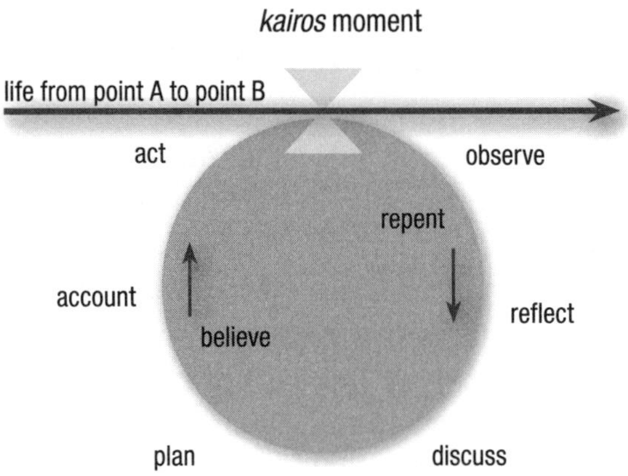

Figure 23

Here is what figure 23 looks like in your life:

- *Observe.* What happened, and how did you react/feel?
- *Reflect.* Reflect on your observations. Why did you feel the way you did? What does that say about you? Is there a pattern?
- *Discuss.* Seek the wisdom of others. Do your observations and reflections make sense? Do you discern an opportunity for growth?

- *Plan.* Figure out a practical way to grow.
- *Account.* Tell somebody about your plan and ask them to follow up with you on it. How successful will a diet be if you don't tell the people you eat with?
- *Act.* Do it![7]

Baptism Is Commission; Conversion Is Ordination

The core movemental idea that everyone is a minister of Jesus Christ has come up time and again. We suggest that one of the ways in which the unbiblical and missionally disastrous division between clergy and laity can be overcome is by recognizing that when someone becomes a follower of Jesus, they are commissioned into the ministry. It isn't an elitist profession. They might not all become "leaders" and work with other Christians, but it's vital for them to see themselves as players in the equation.[8]

APEST: Basing and Phasing

This phrase "basing and phasing" comes from 3DM's practice of Ephesians 4 ministry. Once the primary (or base) ministry is clear and on a pathway of development, disciples are encouraged to learn the dynamic of the other ministries by experiencing them (for a phase). So, for instance, if someone has a base ministry of teacher, they should deliberately learn the work of an evangelist, even though it will not likely become their main ministry. This way, disciples get to empathetically experience all aspects of the ministry of Christ through his body.

Some Distinctly Organizational Practices

Thinking Like a Beginner and Not an Expert

Stemming from the mDNA of *communitas*, and mediated through the ethos of adventurous spirituality, risky mission, learning organization, and the pressure of innovation, we should always be willing to put ourselves out of our comfort zones. All of us are masters of our current domain of knowledge, so we always approach issues like an expert. The trick is to learn to think like a beginner and not an expert.

The way we do this at Forge Mission Training Network, for instance, is to define the learning project for the year. Once this is clarified, we then suggest that people go to the edge of what they feel is comfortable — where they are 50 percent expert and 50 percent beginner. Then we say go another half step out of your comfort zone, where you are 75 percent beginner and only 25 percent expert. Now you are ready to really learn. It's an easy and excellent practice to keep people learning and adapting.

Multilevel, Multisize

As an outworking of the both/and (inclusive) nature of Apostolic Genius, a Verge church will practice church of all sizes (organic/simple, midsized, megachurch, multisite) and will seek to find a way to organize at every level.

Context-Based Learning and Training

One of the most powerful and simple practices is to apprentice people in their primary context, where they have to live the practice(s) out. Most of the learning we do is in the context of classroom-type environments or through sermons and books. Christianity can't avoid being conceived as being primarily theoretical when the primary way we teach is through books and study. When learning comes into my life-context, it changes everything. The simple rule should be that *context is everything.*

Innovate

In a Verge church, which is always seeking the new edge and is committed to being a learning community, innovation should become a core practice and not just a core value. This means that basic skills of innovation should be taught and that permission should be given to all to try new things. It should then be expected that when people propose new ideas and projects, they have more than one model of how they intend to do it, and don't simply do what others have done.

Multiply or Bust

The core value of multiplication, when it's embodied into practice, will mean there's a possibility of multiplication in everything we do. It means that if it can't be easily reproduced, it should be seriously questioned as a project/task. The questions that should constantly be asked as part of this practice are, can this be readily reproduced, and by whom? (And if not, why not?) As mentioned in chapter five, 3DM teaches what they call 8-6-4, in order to multiply mentoring (see p. 160). This is easily done and ensures that the commitment to mentoring and discipleship is written into everything. Organic church movement leader Neil Cole similarly teaches that inherent reproducibility is vital for movement, and he is right.[9] In Church Multiplication Associates, everything that cannot be easily reproduced is put on what they call "the shelf of shame."

Some Distinctly Missional Practices

Planting the Gospel

To help live out our paradigmatic commitment to incarnational mission (mDNA element: missional-incarnational impulse), a simple practice for people is to practice planting the gospel and not see what they do as planting "churches" per se. Questions that can be asked here are: What is good news for this person or people? What is going to sound like good news to him or her? This commits the planter to be very attentive to the Jesus factor, people's existential issues, and also the cultural situation of the people being reached. Missionaries first ask what is good news for a people group and then communicate the gospel of Jesus Christ in ways that fit.

Church Follows Mission

This practice flows directly from the one above. Because the church in the West is now in a context that demands a more distinctly missionary approach, we will have to learn the practice of starting with the gospel and not front-loading our idea of church in the equation. This takes practice and will require discipline, because we normally do church planting by placing a prefabricated model of church in the equation. Teach people to ask (and answer) this question in the context of mission: "What is church for this people group?"

Church in Third Places

A practice I have found very helpful is to try to get your groups and church-plants away from safe or sacred spaces and out into social zones, or the third place between workspace and home. One, it's very missional to be church in places where other people are, but it's also a good discipline because context forces contextualization. It's pretty hard to resort to default singing and mini-preaching in the middle of a café when others are around! The practice? Start groups in third places and not in homes.

Jesus for/with/of the Community

A good way to think of incarnational mission is to assess the depth of identification with the host community. Reflect on the depth of Jesus' care for people and on how we represent his love. See it as Jesus *for*, Jesus *with*, and Jesus *of* the community. The way love is shown is by full identification. Jesus is for, with, and of the community. Ask yourselves these same questions: Are you for, with, and of the community? Commit yourselves to be the Jesus of, for, and with the community people. The folks at RiverTree Christian Church take this very seriously.[10] So much so that Future Traveler Greg Nettle, the senior leader, moved out of the comfy suburbs and into the urban center of the church's community to demonstrate this! They also use this practice to guide all their mission efforts at home and overseas.

Mission As Organizing Principle

If evangelizing and discipling the nations lies at the heart of the church's purpose in the world, then it's mission (and not ministry) that's the true organizing principle of the church. The truth is that groups which come together around a nonmissional purpose (for example, prayer, worship, study) very seldom, if ever, end up becoming missional. It's only those groups that set out to be missional in the first place (while embracing prayer, worship, study, and so on in the process) that actually get to doing it.[11]

At South Melbourne Restoration Community, the church my wife, Debra, and I led for fifteen years, we developed a set of five discipling practices called TEMPT.[12] The *M* at the core stands for mission, and we maintained that unless the group had one, however they conceived it, it couldn't start. In fact, my general advice to what is called the emerging church is simply this: *don't emerge until you've got a mission.* If you take the mission out of the equation, all you get is a lot of talk about spirituality, theology, and worship.

Network Like Mad

This principle of church can become an extremely powerful practice. We know from networking theory that it not only bolsters the relational fabric of the church and forms the basis of decentralized movements but also is the source of much innovation and creativity. So the practice of networking — getting everyone connected, everyone commissioned, and everyone accountable — can be powerful if you can figure out ways to enshrine it in the rhythms of the church.[13]

Taking the whole process into account, an example (and not a prescriptive one) of a consistent Verge church might therefore look something like figure 24.

Example of Consistent Verge Church Processing

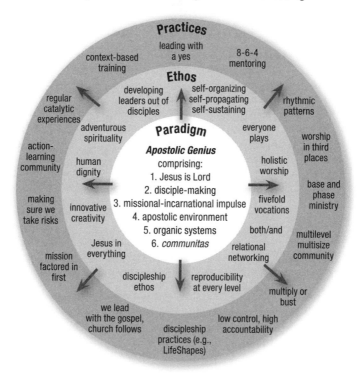

Figure 24

The process will require a constant return to the center and working through ethos to practices. But I believe that if this is done with passion and integrity, there will be significant movement.

When key leaders ensure that Apostolic Genius is (re)activated at the core, and all leaders collaborate in developing a Verge ethos consistent with it, then (inspired and informed from deep within) these leaders can go on to design powerful rhythms and practices that they can trust will profoundly shape the life of the emerging movement. Deep change therefore comes from the center (the paradigm) as well as the circumference (the practices).

Overview of Verge Process

Here is the entire shift process, looked at in a different way:

Level	Core Aims/Tasks	Responsibility Holders	Primary Recipients
Paradigm			
(highly conceptual, requiring a high-level engagement with theological ideas, myths, history, etc.)	To (re)activate Apostolic Genius, shifting paradigm from institutional to movemental, by: • Reimagining church • Embedding Apostolic Genius at the core • Ensuring buy-in by leaders • Reframing the systems story by telling an alternative story • Engaging anomalies to initiate deep learning • Identifying myths and metaphors and recoding	This shift is the responsibility of the highest level of leadership in the church/organization, but it involves recasting the vision (reframing reality) in light of the apostolic vision of the church, broadening from the more pastoral and didactic forms. Therefore: • Buy-in and stakeholding are important by all/most core team members. They must know and understand the paradigm and be able to articulate it.	Not all members of the church/organization need to understand the more conceptual aspects of the Apostolic Genius paradigm. However: • As Apostolic Genius begins to take root and is envisioned by the senior leaders, there should be high levels of discussion, integration, and comprehension by midlevel leadership, staff, and any other interested parties, as they have to embody it as well as interpret it to the rest of the church.

Level	Core Aims/Tasks	Responsibility Holders	Primary Recipients
Ethos			
(conceptual but expressed through symbols, ideas, and popular culture)	To create a Verge culture and so shape the spirit of the organization, by: • Identifying and realigning core values and beliefs • Developing new language consistent with Apostolic Genius • Developing a new hero system with rewards for consistency • Branding consistency	Ethos is the pivotal level as the interface between the Apostolic Genius paradigm and the members of the church. This is very important work. • Responsibility for constructing a fully consistent Verge ethos in the church is the work of midlevel leadership as they drive change, but it must be guided by senior leaders for a consistency to the vision.	Ethos creates the atmosphere of the organization. It's pervasive, and everyone should feel it. Thus: • All leaders should become culture creators, using art, metaphor, story, website, whatever to ensure that the ethos informs every level of organization.
Practices			
(concrete embodiments of value and belief, highly accessible to the people they're aimed at)	To create a comprehensive discipling/apprenticing system based on practices, actions, and rhythms at every level of the organization, by: • Developing core practices from core values • Developing rhythms out of practices • Expecting and rewarding compliancy with practices (raising the bar)	Practices take their cue from the ethos. This really is how ministry is experienced in the church. • Hence, all leaders and staff can be engaged in the development of good practices. • It's wise to seek advice and input from anyone wishing to offer it. The more buy-in from everyone, the more likely they are to do the practices.	Various organizational practices should be aimed at every sphere and department of the church. Which means: • Basic discipling practices will be engaged in by everyone in the church/movement.

Dave's Response to "Embodying Movement-Programming Practices"

I can tell you from personal experience that practices are vital to shaping and informing the culture of a movement. With about ten thousand people considering Community Christian Church, which I pastor, to be their church, the burning question that keeps repeating itself over and over in my mind as we Verge is, how do you mobilize ten thousand people for mission?

The idea of movement is not new to us. Our dream since the very beginning was to be a "catalyst for a movement of reproducing churches." And, indeed, we are a church that reproduces Christ followers, groups, teams, campuses, churches, and even networks, but we have not always been deploying all of God's people for mission. At one point, we realized there were literally thousands of people who were a part of Community who weren't missionally engaged. We now know that if we want a different outcome, it requires change.

We are at the humble beginning stages of engaging in the very process that was laid out in this chapter. If we at Community are going to change our paradigm, it will require a change in culture, and for that to be sustainable, it will need to infiltrate the everyday practices of our people.

The current established cultural practices at Community came from our study of Scripture and the early church over a decade ago. We concluded that there were three relational experiences that were primary to followers of Jesus. Those three relationships could be summarized in these experiences:

> *Celebrate: the relationship between God and us.* The first experience of the early church community is "celebrate" and is described in Acts 2:46–47 (NLT): "They worshipped together ... each day ... [they] shared their meals with great joy and generosity—all the while praising God." The celebration between God and his people was a gathering to worship but was also an everyday part of community life. We encourage all people to celebrate their relationship with God when they come together and every day in Scripture.

Connect: the relationship between the church and us. The second experience that characterizes the kind of community God longs for in his people is found in the word *connect.* The first church community was unequivocally and tightly connected to one another and to God. So connected, the Bible says, they were together every day: "Every day they continued to meet together" (Acts 2:46).

Contribute: the relationship between the world and us. The third experience that characterizes this community is "contribute." Acts 2:44 (NLT) says they "shared everything they had." Verse 45 adds, "They sold their property and possessions and shared the money with those in need." This was a group of people who could stand up and say, "If you've got a genuine need, we will help you."

If you've ever been to Community, there are a couple things you will come away knowing for sure. The first is our mission, which is helping people find their way back to God. The second is the challenge for every person to become what we call a "3C" Christ follower. We say it with clarity and we say it often: we want every person to become a 3C Christ follower. We even created our own data management system, called 3CMS, that tracks if someone is a 1C or 2C or 3C Christ follower. On a weekly basis, a dashboard tells us how every campus is doing (and how we as a church are doing) in regard to the three experiences: <u>celebrating, connecting, and contributing.</u>

While these practices had been tremendously helpful to date, we knew that in order to shift to a more grassroots movemental paradigm, we had to make changes to these expected practices of a Christ follower, community groups, and campuses.

Christ Follower Practices

The challenge we had given to be a 3C Christ follower was measured solely on participation within the realm of Community Christian Church programming. You might be reading this and thinking, "Seriously? You guys are stupid!" And you're right!

We did have a business owner who'd relocated a significant part of his business into a third world country to do economic development, but that didn't count. We had a mom who started a backyard Bible club with fifty neighbor kids, but that didn't count under the measurements of the paradigm we had at that point.

With a new passion to mobilize people for mission in every domain of life, we knew that had to change. We made a subtle (but important) shift and began to affirm and count the contribution of that business owner, the stay-at-home mom, and many others who were being intentionally missional outside our church campuses and programming.

Communal Practices

We wanted our communal practices to be consistent with the individual practices, so we recast the vision for our small groups. In the past, we were content if these small groups became cul-de-sacs of assimilation. Again, it was our passion to mobilize all people for mission, so we challenged every small group to fall into one of two categories:

1. *A group on mission.* These groups would come together around a missional cause. One group we have is called the Hammerhead. This is a group of guys who gather primarily on the weekends and help people in need with home repairs. What draws this group together is the missional cause of using their handyman skills to make a difference in Jesus' name.

2. *A group of missionaries.* These groups would come together around an affinity for each other. This could be a moms' group or parents-of-teens group or a support or a recovery group. We've had lots of these groups for many years, but the big adjustment was that they could still gather based on affinity; they simply had to covenant to hold one another accountable to engage in mission *outside* the group.

It was our intention, through these new categories, that we would establish new practices in our small groups and thus develop a new missional culture. To ensure that *groups of missionaries* were establishing new practices, we asked those affinity groups to follow this monthly rhythm:

- Week 1: Connect with each other
- Week 2: Mission to the 67 percent of the world who are far from God
- Week 3: Connect with each other
- Week 4: Mission to the 20 percent of the world who live on less than a dollar a day

We are still in the process of experimenting with this monthly rhythm, but early indications are that these practices are helping us in making this shift to mobilizing all God's people for mission.

We seriously contemplated a name change for our small groups, to call them missional communities. We decided against that for a couple reasons: First, the name "missional community" sounded too much like insider talk to an average non–church attender, and we've always been able to reach lots of people far from God through our small groups. (We definitely didn't want a name that was a turnoff.) Second, we were reticent to just declare that all our small groups were now communities with a mission, if in fact they were not! We wanted to make sure that the groups *made* that shift and that we didn't just *rename* them as they were.

> Mission is worship and worship is mission.

Campus Practices

A third change we made regarding practices was in regard to what we expected from each of our campuses. For the last several years, we had laid out annual expectations for each campus, which involved setting actual and specific percentages — much like a budget — of church attenders we expected to celebrate, connect, and contribute individually (our 3Cs). We in fact laid out an annual expectation that only 50 percent of our church would be involved in contributing.

But with a new understanding that contributing could (and should) happen in all domains of life and not just within church-related programs, we are shifting the expectation of contribution to 100 percent. Anything less seems foolish.

It's still too early to know the outcome of these changes. My gut and my experience tell me these will produce gains, but not enough. We will need to make other shifts. But I am sure of this: we aren't content with 50 percent of our people engaged in Community Christian Church programming; we want 100 percent engaged in mission.

We will only let our hearts rest when we meet the vision that Jesus had for his church: a genuine move of the Spirit mobilizing every follower into every domain of life for the sake of the mission.

DISCUSSION QUESTIONS

Open

What is one practice you are thankful you added to your life? What is one practice you want to eliminate?

Explore

1. Does your church typically carry out change from the inside out (paradigm shifting) or the outside in (changing practices)? Or in some other way?

2. "Go and make disciples of all nations, baptizing them in the name of the Father and of the Son and of the Holy Spirit, and teaching them to obey everything I have commanded you. And surely I am with you always, to the very end of the age" (Matt. 28:19 – 20).

   Which of the practices Jesus used in developing disciples are you currently applying in your church? What's missing?

3. What are three common practices of discipleship/mission in your church right now? Are there any you need to let go of, that aren't contributing to producing the kind of disciples you're desiring? Any you need to add?

4. "Baptism is commission; conversion is ordination." What do you think of this idea? Do you think your attenders believe it? Why or why not?

5. Assess where you're at on incarnational mission. Do you think people in your community see Jesus as being *for* them, *with* them, or *of* them?

Move

1. On page 180 Alan challenges us to create a list of values that arise from the development of ethos, or culture. He then suggests a series of steps to develop practices that reflect these values. Take sixty minutes and walk through these steps in rapid-fire fashion as a way to get you started. Then, when you have more time, work with a leadership team and follow this plan to bring about lasting change in your current ministry.

2. If you haven't yet, have your team take the APEST test *(www. apest.org)*. Then, as Alan suggests, find practices to help you grow in the roles of fivefold ministry that don't represent your main role.

Part 3

Innovate

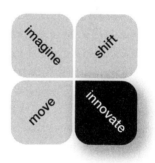

Chapter 7

Innovate or Die

DAVE

The Japanese character for "crisis" is a combination of the characters for "danger" and "opportunity" (or promise); crisis is therefore not an end of opportunity but in reality only its beginning; the point where danger and opportunity meet; where the future is in the balance and where events can go either way.   — DAVID BOSCH, MISSIOLOGIST

Thus far, we've laid out the foundations for the Verge church by describing the vision (imagine) for what the church must become to survive, exploring the core transition process (shift), suggesting that we refound the church based on Apostolic Genius, developing the ethos (or operating system), and developing practices that are consistent with the whole system.

So far, so good. But this all begs the question of *how*. As has been hinted at all along: to become apostolic in nature, the church will simply have to learn how to innovate.

Crisis Is the Birthplace of Innovation

If you really want to see innovation happen, find a crisis. It's in the middle of a crisis that we come to the realization that either the end is near or a new future is being born. On the verge of a crisis, we are also on the verge of our greatest moment. It's at that moment that we must decide: innovate or die.

There's no doubt anymore that the church of the West is clearly in some form of long-term, trended decline that is now reaching critical level—witness the demise of Christianity in Europe and Australia, for instance. Furthermore, the number of people who will be in a church in the United States has shrunk to just more than 18 percent, the lowest level in the history of a once very religious country. And if that isn't alarming enough, we need only look to the major cities of the U.S., where leading cultural indicators are birthed. In these, only 10 percent of the population attends church. This is just a precursor to what has already taken place in Australia, where less than 10 percent attend church, and Europe, where no more than 2 percent of the population will participate in church life this weekend. We have a crisis, which is going to necessitate something very drastic.

Necessity, the Mother of Innovation

The leadership at Community Christian Church knew they had a crisis. They also recognized that this was going to necessitate something very drastic. Community had seen nineteen consecutive years of growth, and for the majority of those years it was double-digit growth. So when we projected an 18 percent increase in income for the coming year, it was nothing out of the ordinary. But then it happened: the bottom fell out of the economy. Week after week there was a shortfall—first thousands of dollars, then tens of thousands.

The bigger the plane, the bigger the hole it makes when it crashes, and Community was now a very big plane with a financial hole that was getting bigger every month. Over the next several weeks, budgets were slashed and we were forced to let staff go. Six months into the new fiscal year, we were five hundred thousand dollars short of our projections. This called for something drastic!

In the middle of this brutal situation, we decided as a staff to spend a day in prayer and fasting, asking God what to do. We were a church used to moving at full speed ahead, and we really weren't sure what came next. We wondered, "Do we slow way down? Should we back off the vision? Should we flatline the budget?" On Tuesday we fasted, and on Wednesday we regrouped over a meal and debriefed what we had heard from God. I stood in front of my team, reexplained the crisis, thanked everyone for fasting and praying, and then asked, "So what do you think God is telling us?"

There was a lot of silence.

Then more silence.

Finally Steve, an IT specialist, spoke up and said, "I know we are in a crisis, and I know this won't make sense in our current economic climate, but I don't think God is calling us to shrink the vision; I think God is calling us to expand the vision."

What Steve said was not what I expected. It wasn't what most of us were thinking. But God was doing a new thing, and we decided to move forward in faith. So in the middle of this crisis, we did something everyone thought was crazy: rather than shrink the vision, we expanded the vision. This new vision was not about the shortfall or just the ministries behind the walls of a Community campus. The new vision was a dramatic missional shift toward what we called the Sixty-seven and the Twenty. If the world were a village of one hundred people, sixty-seven of those would be far from God, and twenty of those would live in extreme poverty. How could we be more attentive to people who were even worse off than we were, spiritually and/or materially? With this shift in direction, we challenged all of Community to a weekend where rather than keep the money that was so desperately needed for the budgetary life of our church, we would give away everything that came in to four outside causes: a ministry that saved kids living on the streets of San Pablo in the Philippines; a ministry that worked to eradicate poverty in a Ugandan village; a local effort to bring community transformation to an underresourced community; and the support of new churches being planted in the United States.

The result? When we finished counting the offering, it was by far the largest offering ever. (It was almost double the highest giving up to that date!) In the middle of a financial crisis, Community gave away $250,000!

My first reaction was, we just gave away $250,000 ... awesome! But my second reaction was, we're way behind in our budget and just gave away a quarter of a million dollars ... that kind of stinks! But God knew what he was doing. Not only did Community give away $250,000 that year; the following year we gave away $490,000, and the year after that nearly $600,000 on a single weekend! *And* in the three years since that crisis, our generosity has exploded! In the middle of what appeared to be our most desperate hour, God was doing something new to advance his mission! Innovation gave birth to God's purposes in our church.

Innovation: Most Risky or *Least* Risky?

Before innovation can take place, we must have a clear understanding of what we are discussing. Most of us think of innovation as the introduction of something new or different, requiring a great amount of courage and risk. While that is partly true, Peter Drucker offers some contrarian thinking in his classic *Innovation and Entrepreneurship*: "Innovation is the least risky rather than the most risky course."

> "Innovation is the least risky rather than the most risky course."
>
> —Peter Drucker

And he is right. If Community had not gone through a paradigmatic shift that expanded our vision to include the 67 percent and the 20 percent outside its walls, this missed opportunity could have been the first of a series of organizational heart attacks leading to complete cardiac arrest. It seemed risky. It sounded crazy to give away the entire weekend's offering when there was no human way we could afford it. But looking back on it now, it was the *least* risky course. We had to listen to the Spirit's prompting: it was innovate or die.

Drucker also gives us this ho-hum definition of innovation that sucks most of the fear out of innovating: "The shifting of resources from areas of low productivity and yield to areas of higher productivity and yield." That is why innovation is so important for the mission of Jesus. It isn't just so we can be on the cutting edge or part of the next cool thing. Innovation is critical for the mission because it allows us to steward our resources, our people, and our very lives away from low-yield kingdom activities to high-yield kingdom productivity.

Imagination × Implementation = Innovation

Innovation isn't synonymous with imagination, nor should it be confused with creativity. In the last couple years, some creative new ideas have been introduced in the marketplace under the banner of innovation, but I'm not buying it. Let me give you some examples. There is the inflatable dartboard (very creative, but it's hard to imagine it working well after the first dart is thrown).[1] Or how about airbag underwear? It's underwear that can sense when you're about to fall and automatically inflates.[2] It sounds ridiculous. (I'd rather have a Clapper installed to turn my appliances on or off with a simple clap of my hands.) Or how about lawn mowing shoes?[3] Sounds too dangerous to me! These products are creative but not innovative.

While the starting point for any Verge church is the missional imagination of the community, that alone will not accomplish the mission. Innovation is what happens when a Verge church moves from imagination and makes the shift toward apostolic movement. Innovation is imagination put to work. Imagination is all about ideas and dreaming, but innovation is about implementing the ideas and beginning to live out the dream. Scott Belsky's presentation from his bestselling book *Making Ideas Happen* inspired the equation in figure 25.[4]

imagination × implementation = innovation
$$5 \times 0 = 0$$
$$100 \times 0 = 0$$
$$3 \times 2 = 6$$

Figure 25

Think about innovation in terms of a math equation. No matter how great the imagination, if it doesn't bring with it implementation, it is ultimately of no value. When even a small amount of implementation is put alongside imagination, you will see great gains! A good example is James Patterson, who has more bestsellers than any published author and claims to work on seven novels at once. Critics suggest that many of his plots are very similar and he needs a greater imagination, but his background as a CEO of a company has taught him that the value isn't just in imagination but also in the implementation of a good idea. The solution isn't to lower the level of creativity but instead to be sure we're as passionate about implementation as we are about imagination. Implementation happens when we do the hard work of restoring the mDNA into our church culture and practices. In the same way that faith without works is dead, missional imagination without implementation has no redemptive value.

Lars Kolind, in *Second Cycle*, tells us that organizations fifty years ago could have one good innovation and milk it for decades. Today, with the exponential increase of technology and information, he suggests that the life cycle of new innovations is typically six to twelve months. Then it becomes necessary to adapt and innovate on the previous innovation. So we need to switch from a battleship mentality of holding our ground in the ever-changing tides and waves to a surfing mentality. We have to be catching waves all the time. And, as much as we might resist it, that wave we catch will die rather quickly. So we need to paddle out and find the next wave to ride. A Verge church recognizes that our era is not just a time of crisis but also a season of unprecedented opportunity. An apostolic movement thrives on innovation, knowing that God is doing a new thing. When this new thing comes to fruition, it is first and foremost because it's being guided by a leadership that values and practices innovation.

Leadership That Values and Practices Innovation

"If this church disappeared tomorrow, I wonder if anyone in the community would even notice?"

All the other church leaders around the table were silent as they pondered the question. Conviction had walked in on the noontime meeting. It was a question they had all heard asked rhetorically in sermons, but they'd never heard the question asked sincerely by one of their own. This pastor was in a crisis. The church he was leading was in a crisis. And this was not the kind of crisis that comes from too few nickels in the offering plate or too few noses showing up on Sunday.

The pastor, the asker of the profound question, had planted this church several years earlier, and all the graphs were up and to the right. It was not that kind of crisis. It was instead a crisis of mission. Despite the brand-new building and all the new attenders, the pastor said out loud what many wondered deep within: if my church disappeared tomorrow, would anyone even notice?

> "If this church disappeared tomorrow, I wonder if anyone in the community would even notice?"

About twelve months later he resigned as senior pastor of the church he'd founded twenty years before. A couple months after that he started working in sales, and a few months after that he and his wife divorced.

I guess he answered the question.

The church itself may have been healthy according to institutional standards, but the question of whether anyone would notice betrayed the lack of connection between what was going on in the world and what was going on inside the church walls. The pastor made a choice to abandon his work to irrelevance rather than try to change the answer.

Innovate or die—it isn't just an ecclesiological issue; this is a very personal issue for every leader. Verge churches will be led by leaders who settle for nothing less than trading their lives for missional impact. These leaders know the importance of not only engaging every follower's missional imagination but also putting that imagination to work through innovation that changes lives and leaves a lasting impact on a community.

How about you? Will you dare to ask and answer the question, if this church you are a part of disappeared tomorrow, would anyone in the community even notice?

Don't fear the crisis. It is in the midst of crisis that we are on the verge of something grand and brand-new. It's at that moment that we must decide: innovate or die.

There are three key descriptors of a leader on the verge.

1. A Verge Leader Leads from the Front, Not the Back

There is a saying in the military that generals who lead troops from the safety of the rear should have to take it in the rear. Jim Kouzes says it this way in *The Leadership Challenge*: "Only those leaders who act boldly in times of crisis and change are willingly followed."

One of the best generals I know is my brother, Jon Ferguson. Jon and I launched Community together and have seen it grow from a few friends to thousands at eleven locations all over Chicago. Jon is also the strategic mind behind NewThing, a reproducing church movement which now has more than one hundred churches and sites around the world. It would be easy for him to feel a sense of accomplishment and decide to take some time off and kick back a little. He could rationalize that he has done his part and it's somebody else's turn to step up, so he can back off. Heck, he could call it a sabbatical! But Jon is the kind of general who is leading the missional charge from the front. Rather than settle into a nice suburban home and spend his time telling old stories at workshops and conferences, he and his wife, Lisa—along with their two kids—recently moved into the city of Chicago to start a network of new sites for Community. He is leading the charge with dozens of others who are moving from the safety of the suburbs into the adventure of urban life. He is leading the way and asking others to support this important initiative by either moving with him or helping out with their finances. He's recruiting a team of leaders to bring what he imagined to life. Jon is the kind of innovative leader people want to follow and imitate.

This kind of leadership isn't restricted to vocational ministry, nor is it isolated to the church building. These leaders pull others through this shift with them to the front lines rather than pushing from the back office. These leaders will emerge in every domain of society: economics, health, science, journalism, communications, the arts, agriculture, government, and finance. They'll do the good work that God has prepared in advance for them to do in all walks of life, giving leadership to a missional movement. We're seeing the firstfruits already.

Perry Bigelow, president of Bigelow Homes, isn't the kind of CEO to just sit behind his desk and bark out orders to his people. Perry is a missional leader who leads from the front, not the back.

When Bigelow Homes built HomeTown, his vision was to build neighborhoods of genuine community, where kids are safe to play, the environment is honored, and a church would be present to serve the people. He described his intentions like this: "I want to build a community the way the Master Carpenter would build it." Perry not only shared that vision with his company and challenged them to complete it; he moved into one of the HomeTown neighborhoods himself and works every day to see that vision fulfilled. In addition, from the profits of HomeTown, Bigelow Homes makes very generous donations to HomeAid and Hope International. As a result of Perry's leadership, Bigleow Homes was named Builder of the Year by *Professional Builder* magazine. The cover story read, "Doing Good by Doing Right."[5]

This wasn't surprising to anyone who knows Perry. He's always been someone who leads by example, not vague dictates. When he saw a need for quality housing for single moms in the city of Chicago, he started a nonprofit company that built condos specifically for single working moms with school-age children. He not only built these condos but moved out of his suburban home and into one of the condos for seven years.

Do *you* lead from the front? When you lead from the front, every decision you make and action you take is for the sake of the mission. For too many of us, ministry has become a job and not our life's mission! When your ministry becomes a means to get what you want instead of a means to accomplish what God wants, there's no way the mission will be accomplished. Too many leaders are looking for a fatter paycheck, a bigger church, and early retirement in a better climate.

The apostle Paul led from the front. That's why he could say, "I urge you to imitate me. For this reason I am sending to you Timothy, my son whom I love, who is faithful in the Lord. He will remind you of my way of life in Christ Jesus, which agrees with what I teach everywhere in every church" (1 Cor. 4:16–17). He felt confident enough in the mission that if others would just follow his lead, the mission would be accomplished. In fact, Paul felt confident enough that he was sending Timothy to lead them, because he knew that he had apprenticed Timothy and that if they just imitated Timothy's life, they could accomplish the mission.

I think every leader should answer this question: if the people who follow you just imitated you, would they accomplish God's mission?

2. A Verge Leader Leads with Curiosity, Not with Certainty

Albert Einstein was such a genius that when he died, Thomas Harvey, the coroner who did his autopsy, stole his brain, reasoning that it needed to be put into the hands of experts who could figure out the key to Einstein's brilliance.[6] But Einstein's brilliance wasn't to be found in his brain. Before Einstein died, he left behind his own understanding to the secret of his genius, saying, "I have no special talent. I am only passionately curious." We believe the same secret is true of innovative leaders: they are passionately curious people.

There is no doubt that vision is essential to leadership and that "a leader cannot blow an uncertain trumpet."[7] A clear and certain vision is a given, but what makes a leader special is an accompanying unquenchable curiosity. The one who can lead with the crystal-clear vision of a general and still maintain the curiosity of a child is a special leader and will foster innovation in the people around him or her.

But beware. It's often our successes that cause cataracts to develop over our curiosity and eventually blind us to future successes. It's often the very thing that made us successful that later causes us to stumble and fall. The more successful a church is, the happier they are with the way they are currently doing things. So the megachurch which is growing can feel sure that what they are doing is the real recipe for success and just increase what they are doing in hopes of continued success. Success can be built from even one unique innovation, or just a small number of them, within a church, and a church's monopoly on those innovations can give them that sense of having an edge. The contemporary/mega/multisite church has been that innovation which has created successful growth within that 40 percent "market." But our very success in those areas can blind us to the possibility of movement that is waiting for us beyond the scope of those particular innovations.

So be curious. Pursue your questions. If we have the faith of a child, shouldn't that include a wonder about where God is working in our world? Go on a God hunt. Snoop. Hunt. Probe. Certainty about the vision is not enough for the innovative leader; it requires a constant questioning and curiosity about what new thing God is doing next.

Few contemporary leaders have been as innovative or curious as Peter Drucker, known as the father of modern management. Drucker spent thirty years studying innovation in both the for-profit and not-for-profit sectors, and he tells us where not to look and where to look for innovation. He says, "Do not just look for the biggie, the innovation that will revolutionize the industry."[8] When you think of innovation, don't think of yourself as trying to be the Wright brothers, discovering flight. Instead look for changes right around you that have already occurred and are under way. Drucker identifies several sources for innovative opportunities around every one of us. Here's where a curious leader should begin to look:

Unexpected Success

The Austin Stone Church grew rapidly in the first several years of its existence and created small groups in which the focus was on creating community to get the growing number of people connected to one other. But they struggled getting people connected, and it seemed the more they focused on community, the less genuine community people actually experienced. Yet when they put out the challenge for serving, people would show up in droves. They couldn't explain this unexpected success, but over time it started to make sense.

> Change the metaphor, and you change the imagination.

Matt Carter, lead pastor of the Austin Stone Church, describes the surprising discovery they made about small groups: "When we aimed simply for community, we got neither community nor mission. But when we aimed for mission, we got both community and mission almost every single time." Michael Stewart, who oversees their missional communities, explains: "We told people, 'If you aim for Acts 2 community, you will experience real community,' but what we discovered was that Acts 2 community only came as a result of Acts 1 mission. It was this unexpected success that set this church in a whole new missional direction." The Austin Stone Church now has more than three hundred missional communities, and they are just getting started.

Where are you seeing unexpected and unanticipated successes in the life of your church? What leaders, groups, or events seem to succeed despite very little funding or attention from staff? As you look to the fringe and rogue efforts on the periphery of your community, who is making an impact and seeing changed lives? Those are the places a curious leader will investigate to discover what God is doing next.

Incongruity

A friend of ours was working with a church in the Atlanta area, helping them on a plan to reach young adults. The assumption was that people's entry point into the life of that church was through a weekend worship experience. When they did interviews with the young adults in that church, they discovered a big surprise: a huge percentage of the young adults first became aware of the church through their participation with a local chapter of Habitat for Humanity. There was an incongruity between what the leadership perceived to be true and what actually was. They believed that young adults would need to be a part of the community (weekend worship services) before they would join the cause (service through the church), but instead they discovered just the opposite: being part of the cause brought them into the community.

Have you discovered any inconsistencies in how things *are* versus how you *perceived* them to be in your ministry? Have you noticed blips on the screen of your own observations that are incompatible with how it "ought to be"? If the answer to either question is yes, you may be on the verge of a tremendous advancement—the perfect place to pry and snoop for innovation.

Need

The needs are there. Hugh Halter and Matt Smay remind us in *AND: The Gathered and Scattered Church*, "Understand that God has been at work weaving together Spirit-led thoughts, dreams and kingdom innovations in a city, in a neighborhood and in the life of every person you'll meet."[9]

Before Matt and Hugh started their church, Adullam, they made it their simple goal to make fifty friends. They discovered what we all discover when we become a real friend: real needs. They found people who need help getting (and keeping) jobs. People who need help with their marriages and their kids. People with drug dependencies and codependencies. Since then, Matt and Hugh have launched Missio,[10] a training network to apprentice others to engage with their own unique context and find needs that can be met.

Where are the needs in *your* community? Can't answer that? Take a look at your local paper over the last month, and the needs will be revealed to you in black and white. Compassion by Design[11] works with curious leaders and churches by showing them how to conduct a needs assessment of any community. Curious leaders will find needs in the arts community, the public school system, the local government, or the parks and recreation department. The next innovation can be as easy as finding a need and meeting it.

Opportunity

Bill Barton of the Institute for Community[12] heard opportunity knocking on the door of apartment communities. They realized that apartment communities have a goal of about 95 percent occupancy and that retention (getting renters to renew their contract for another year) was the key to their financial success. It caused Bill to put together a kingdom-minded mission called Community Life. Bill asked apartment managers for one of their already-vacant apartments, where he would place a Community Life Architect in exchange for the promise of increased retention rates. The Community Life Architect, motivated by the gospel, would work to create genuine community that accomplished not only the mission of Jesus but also the goals of the apartment manager. Marquette Properties agreed to pilot this program, and the first apartment community not only saw increased retention rates but also had higher rates than any of the other twenty-six properties within the company's portfolio. In the next three years, the Community Life program expanded to ten apartment communities, with a goal of one hundred by 2015.

Opportunity is similar to need, but the motivation is not desperation, abandonment, or lack of resources. Opportunity knocks because a unique partnership can emerge, or the gifts and skill set of a group or individual are needed to bring improvement. Curious leaders will sniff out opportunities, and when they follow the scent, it leads to innovation.

Changing Demographics

For some leaders, a changing demographic is a sure sign to relocate or to move out of the neighborhood to a more familiar setting. For the curious leader, a change in demographics is a signal to begin probing for innovative opportunities. To Rick and Desiree Guzman, the influx of new refugees into their neighborhood brought about Bryan House,[13] a mission to bring community transformation through home ownership. Through the generosity of Bryan House, supporters' funds are raised to purchase homes where refugee families, who can't afford a home, will pay rent for eighteen months. During that time, the rental money is put into an account and returned after one and half years to the family so they can make a down payment on their first home.

When new artists start moving into a depressed community, this is the first sign that economic redevelopment is coming. Curious leaders coming alongside those artists can help in the redemption of that neighborhood. Running or retreating from change is like pretending tomorrow will be 1980. It won't. The curious leader knows that tomorrow will be different from today and that difference will providentially bring the opportunity for innovation.

Changes in Perception

A mathematician would tell you there's no difference between the glass being half full or half empty. But a curious leader knows there is a difference in these two ways of thinking, and the difference is found in their consequences. If a general perception shifts from seeing the glass a certain way to seeing it another, a major innovative opportunity presents itself.

September 11, 2001, was a day that dramatically changed people's perception of their personal security. On September twelfth of that year, people felt scared, angry, vengeful, and afraid. Just two days before, on September tenth, they had very few of those feelings. What changed? A single catastrophic event.

Were we really less safe on September twelfth than on the tenth? Probably not. In fact, because of heightened attention to national security, we were actually safer on the twelfth. What happened was a change in perception. With that change in perception regarding personal security, there came a tidal wave of spiritual searching and a huge influx of people into churches—often people who hadn't been in church in years. That change brought about an innovative opportunity to help people see that the only lasting peace and security is found in Jesus. Unfortunately, most churches missed that opportunity.

There are constant shifts in mood regarding the economy, political landscapes, and perceptions about the future. Peter Drucker tells us, "Whether sociologists or economists can explain the perceptional phenomenon is irrelevant. It remains a fact. It is concrete; it can be defined, tested and above all exploited."[14] The curious leader isn't as concerned about whether the glass is half full or half empty as about the perception of others about the glass and the innovative opportunities it brings.

When we think of a curious leader and innovation, we might imagine him or her with *Wired* magazine in one hand and the Bible in the other, discovering some new technology that revolutionizes how church is done in the future. That's how we might imagine it, but it's seldom how innovation actually happens. The curious leader should recognize that very few will ever be the Wright brothers, but lots of us can be right when it comes to seeing the next innovation, if we look at what God is already doing right around us. So snoop. Hunt. Probe. Above all, remain curious.

3. A Verge Leader Leads with a Yes and Asks How Later

Time magazine compiled a list of the ten best commencement addresses ever.[15] This list included speeches by Winston Churchill (Harrow College, 1941), John F. Kennedy (American University, 1963), and even Steve Jobs (Stanford, 2005). Also on the list was Stephen Colbert (yes, *that* Stephen Colbert!) and his 2006 commencement address at little Knox College in Galesburg, Illinois.[16]

Colbert, whom Knox had just awarded the honorary degree of doctor of fine arts, closed his address with a challenge about the power of saying yes:

> When I was starting out in Chicago, doing improvisational theatre with Second City, there was really only one rule ... When you improvise a scene with no script ... you have to accept what the other improviser initiates ... Well, you are about to start the greatest improvisation of all. With no script. No idea what's going to happen, often with people and places you have never seen before. And you are not in control. So say yes. And if you're lucky, you'll find people who will say yes back. Now will saying

yes get you in trouble at times? Will saying yes lead you to doing some foolish things? Yes it will. But don't be afraid to be a fool. Remember, you cannot be both young and wise. Young people who pretend to be wise to the ways of the world are mostly just cynics. Cynicism masquerades as wisdom, but it is the farthest thing from it. Because cynics don't learn anything. Because cynicism is a self-imposed blindness, a rejection of the world because we are afraid it will hurt us or disappoint us. Cynics always say no. But saying yes begins things. Saying yes is how things grow. Saying yes leads to knowledge. Yes is for young people. So for as long as you have the strength to, say yes.

You may or may not like Colbert's politics, but either way, if you want to be an innovative leader, you'd better listen to his words of wisdom. Innovative leaders will lead with a *yes* and ask *how* later.

Yes Reflex

The one thing every leader possesses (that every follower needs to make his or her own missional shift) is *permission*. And permission always comes in the form of a *yes*. Leaders, if you want to see missional engagement in your churches and ultimately a movement, you must lead with a yes. If your followers can't get permission from you, they will never be engaged in the mission. The great temptation is to respond with questions of how. But questions of how need to wait. If we respond with, "How could you do that?" we immediately begin to sow seeds of doubt by responding to the individual's vision with a question about strategy. If we ask, "How much would that cost?" we are responding to their vision with a question of tactics. The questions about how will come later, but the reflex of an innovative leader needs to be *yes*.

Jordon Prosapio, seventeen years old, and John Macikas, eighteen, were both totally fired up after the winter Blast retreat. The challenge was given to them at a student ministry retreat from the life of Peter to "step out of the safety of the boat" and, in faith, engage in the mission of Jesus. They heard it and began to imagine the difference they could make. As high school students, they came to the leadership of their church with the idea of a Food Fight. *What?* Food Fight: Students Fighting World Hunger.[17] What a great tagline! But what could two high school students really do? What could two kids accomplish in the global battle of hunger relief? Rather than asking how, their leadership responded with a yes. That yes led to people of influence and affluence getting behind Food Fight. The yes led to a great marketing campaign donated by the premier ad agency in Chicago. The yes led to civic leaders getting behind this initiative. And what has transpired since getting a yes to this totally student-led nonprofit over the first two years has been absolutely amazing! The first year, they enrolled 1,200 students at two high schools to raise $17,000 and pack almost 100,000 meals for the hungry. In the second year, 3,000 students at five high schools raised $30,000 and packed nearly 200,000 meals for people in Haiti.

> God is already involved in mission to his lost world; you can join him.

The old paradigm many churches are built upon was borrowed from the business world, and it says you need to know your target group, understand the niche of your brand, and say no to anything that isn't within that clear focus. This is a great business strategy for developing a high-quality brand with deep penetration into a specific market segment. It's a money maker. But it's not a movement maker! A movement requires a clear set of core values and a leadership with a yes reflex to many different kinds of ideas and to many different kinds of people in many different disciplines, all moving forward for the same cause!

Furthermore, if the church is genuinely informed/propelled by the mDNA of missional-incarnational impulse, it means we'll feel the deep drive to keep searching for new opportunities to plant the gospel and integrate new groups into the broader movement. While local expressions of *ecclesia* can and should be focused on certain groups, given the multicultural context we all live in, we cannot remain monocultural in the movement and be true to the church Jesus wants us to be.

Democratize Innovation

Let me be clear: Yes doesn't mean you will fund the idea. And in most cases, you absolutely shouldn't fund the missional ideas of others. You may do more harm than good. Yes also doesn't mean you'll assign a staff person to oversee it. Sometimes that makes sense, but often it will not. Yes doesn't mean it gets announced at a weekend celebration service. Yes doesn't mean it gets space on the website. Verge churches know that ministry doesn't have to happen "on campus" or be announced on Sunday to have tremendous missional value. Yes simply means you really do believe that what they are describing is needed, and by using their giftedness with God's help, it could be accomplished for the good of the Jesus mission.

We need to develop a yes reflex. If someone comes to you and says, "I got this idea about reaching kids through sports." What do you say? "Yes." If someone says, "I want to care for HIV patients." What do you say? "Yes." If someone says, "I want to help provide support for single moms." What do you say? "Yes."

A yes reflex leads a *coup d'etat* against the clergy-only, campus-based form of ministry and ushers in the democratization of innovation and creativity for the kingdom of God. A yes reflex acknowledges that God may use even kids like Jordan or John or a boy named David from the Old Testament. A yes reflex is verbal manifesto that says to every follower of Jesus that they have a much-needed role to play in the mission of Jesus.

At the risk of sounding like a street evangelist, all signs are telling the church in the West that the end is near. A Verge church knows they must choose between ongoing innovation or ultimate death/demise. Innovation is the byproduct of leaders who personally set the pace, are chronically curious, and give permission to all God's people to play a part in God's great mission. While we are on the verge of a great crisis, we are also on the verge of our greatest moment. So it is right now that we must decide to either innovate or die!

Alan's Response to "Innovate or Die"

Pastor and innovator Erwin McManus had an interesting experience while being interviewed on the radio. It was a major show with a large Christian leadership audience, and the subject was on innovation. He was second in line to be interviewed. The person being interviewed before him was an extremely influential leader, and his advice to the listeners was that they shouldn't attempt to be innovators, that innovation itself was too risky and the odds are stacked against people who try out new ideas. Instead his advice was that they should be early adopters. They should take the innovators' ideas and improve on them.[18]

This placed Erwin, who clearly belongs to that more creatively restless 2 percent of the population called the innovators, in a very difficult situation: what could he now say without directly contradicting this senior leader? So when the interviewer turned to him and asked what he thought of the issue, taking a deep breath, Erwin asked what would happen if everyone took Pastor X's advice to avoid the risk of innovation and opt to be good early adopters instead.

Well, the answer is obvious, isn't it? We would have no innovation! And without innovation, we're unable to advance our cause or create new possibilities. In other words, without innovation, as Dave has noted, we die. And this is a poignantly real truth at the dawn of the twenty-first century, when Christianity faces decline in every Western context.

> Paul goes into Thessalonica, gets kicked out nine days later, and he still calls them an *ecclesia* of God. Now *that's* church planting!

In *The Forgotten Ways*, I suggested we face today what is called an adaptive challenge. There are basically two times when adaptation and innovation are appropriate: in the face of a threat or in the face of compelling opportunity. In other words, one is an adapt-or-die scenario, and the other is "change because it really benefits you to do so."[19] The adaptive challenges we face are in many ways real opportunities to rediscover some world-changing potentials lying mostly dormant in God's people. In fact, feeling a real threat or engaging new opportunities are the sweets spots for innovation. They are the "burning platform" out of which much learning emerges. When productive agitation runs high, innovation thrives and startling breakthroughs can come about.[20] Disruption can be a blessing.[21]

Movement theorist Steve Addison notes that in order to fulfill their mission, the most effective Christian movements in history are prepared to change everything about themselves except their core beliefs. Unencumbered by tradition, movements feel the freedom to experiment with new forms and strategies. Hence they are natural innovators. Movements pursue their mission with methods that are effective, flexible, and reproducible, outlasting and even surpassing the influence of the first generation of leaders. Furthermore, he notes that innovation enables a movement to function in ways that suit its changing environment and its expansion into new fields. Following Collins and Porras *(Built to Last)*, he notes that "a movement's commitment to both its core ideology *and* to its own expansion provides the catalyst for continual learning, renewal and growth." And importantly, he goes on to say, "Dying institutions display the opposite characteristics—willing to sacrifice their unique identity, conservative in setting goals, and unable to face the reality of their mediocre performance."[22]

I doubt that churches who find themselves in such situations like the state of affairs very much, but they should take the advice General Eric Shinseki gave to Donald Rumsfeld: "If you don't like change, you're going to like irrelevance even less."[23] "Change before you have to," Jack Welch, one-time CEO of General Electric, tells us. We have to *feel* the need before we will change.

The truth is, learning and innovation actually work hand in hand. It's foolish, indeed dangerous to the missional cause, to think that what was successful yesterday will be sufficient for tomorrow. If we engage in a blue ocean strategy—and I believe we have to if we are to engage the 60 percent of the population that is increasingly alienated from our prevailing expressions of church—then we simply have to innovate. This doesn't mean we should abandon what we're doing now, but it does mean we must learn what we don't know now and not just use the same tools, approaches, and methods that work in the red ocean. What got us *here* is unlikely to lead us *there*. In other words, we need to learn to fish in the blue ocean. It is patently clear that what works in and among the 40 percent of those reached by conventional church forms won't work for the 60 percent of those unreached. Respond, innovate, adapt, learn! Innovation will lead you into the new (and blue) waters. Innovation, inspired by the internalized fires of Apostolic Genius, is a precondition for growth.

DISCUSSION QUESTIONS

Open

When have you been the most innovative? What was the crisis that preceded it, and what was the outcome?

Explore

1. Opportunity abounds in crisis through the power of imagination. What was the crisis in the following passage, and how did the early church use imagination to solve it?

> The congregation in Antioch was blessed with a number of prophet-preachers and teachers:
> Barnabas,
> Simon, nicknamed Niger,
> Lucius the Cyrenian,
> Manaen, an advisor to the ruler Herod,
> Saul.
> One day as they were worshiping God — they were also fasting as they waited for guidance — the Holy Spirit spoke: "Take Barnabas and Saul and commission them for the work I have called them to do."
> So they commissioned them. In that circle of intensity and obedience, of fasting and praying, they laid hands on their heads and sent them off.
>
> —Acts 13:1–3 MSG

2. What are other examples of innovation in Scripture?
3. If your church disappeared tomorrow, what kind of impact would that have on the rest of your community?
4. "And so this is good-bye. You're not going to see me again, nor I you, you whom I have gone among for so long proclaiming the news of God's inaugurated kingdom. I've done my best for you, given you my all, held back nothing of God's will for you. Now it's up to you" (Acts 20:25–28 MSG).

   In Paul's final moments with the church of Ephesus, he boldly proclaims that he has given them his all and that he is worthy of being imitated. If those you lead simply imitated you, would God's mission get accomplished? What would get accomplished? What wouldn't?

5. Are you a curious leader? Using the list on pages 213–17, how might your community be primed to innovate?

6. What was your response to the concept of leading with a yes? What obstacles might you face if you developed a yes reflex? How can you implement this type of leadership immediately?

Move

1. Based on your answers to question 3, who do you need to meet with to learn more about how God is moving in your organization/church? Schedule a meeting with that person.

2. Lead with a yes today! Take the first step and release someone with your verbal affirmation. If it's hard, do it again and again until you get the hang of it!

Chapter 8

Out-of-the-Box
Innovation

DAVE

At first, the new thing is rarely as good as the old thing was.
But if you need the alternative to be better than the status quo
from the very start, you'll never begin.

— SETH GODIN, MARKETING GURU

W e are going to end our church service early today."

Very seldom had I heard those words come out of the mouth of a pastor. And what I was about to hear next I had never heard before: "I'm kicking you all out!" Now he really had my attention.

He continued, "There is a big citywide festival starting this morning in our town, and I want you to get out of this church building so we join the rest of our friends and neighbors." A concluding prayer was said, and the next thing I knew, we all quickly exited the doors of the church facility and were listening to good music, eating great food, and enjoying ourselves with several thousand neighbors on a gorgeous sunny day.

As I look back on that experience, I'm struck by how a simple act by that leader could feel so remarkably radical. Why did it feel that way? It goes back to our understanding of innovation. How many times have you heard a leader say something about needing to get people out of the church's four walls and into the community? While having these thoughts are good signs that the missional imagination is at work, imagination isn't enough. Imagination is only the first step. We have to take our churches through the shift process that begins with imagination and results in innovation.

And remember, the equation that gets us innovation is: imagination x implementation = innovation. That's what happened when the pastor kicked us out of church — and thus out of the box — that Sunday. He made a decision that the church would no longer just talk about living beyond the four walls but would get their butts out of the sanctuary seats and into the city square. That seemingly simple act was radical because it gave us all a glimpse of an out-of-the-box culture and what it would look like to make the shift from imagination to innovation.

The shift in ethos and practice toward out-of-the-box innovation had been in the making for some time in this church. Over the last several years, this pastor had already begun to reorient what happened inside the church "box" for their neighbors and mission. They hired two part-time chefs on their staff, not to serve them but to make eight hundred meals every week for the homeless in their community. They opened up their facility to be used as a gallery where artists could display their crafts. I was there on a weekend that a young artist in his late teens sold his very first painting. You think he'll ever forget where he sold his first painting? No. He will always remember that church. They also used their box as an upscale concert venue and the home of several twelve-step recovery groups open to the entire community.

And before the pastor ever kicked his church out of the building, he gave himself the boot. After preaching on Sunday mornings, he would spend time with his family in the afternoon and then hang out at the local pub on Sunday nights. It was there that he got a chance to talk to guys about life, work, and spiritual things; these were guys he never got to talk to on Sunday morning. So he went to the owner and told him he had an idea for bringing in a few more customers: Pub Church. The owner said that if it brought in more business, great. So the pastor began to put posters up all over the neighborhood. The tagline in the middle cracks me up: "Two Beer Service Every Sunday." This pastor's Pub Church led the way in out-of-the-box innovation.

During 2007 and 2008, my friends at *Outreach* magazine published a list of the twenty-five most innovative churches. Because Community Christian Church is a multisite church, uses a lot of creativity in the weekend celebration services, and loves technology, we would frequently be on this list of churches. Now, you might be thinking it didn't hurt that I was also a part of the panel that helped select the most innovative churches, but I couldn't nominate my own church! While serving on that panel, it was my observation that much of what was considered innovative was actually in-the-box innovation.

Let me explain. Much of what was identified as innovation was literally happening within the four-walled boxes of the church facilities. In 2009, at the encouragement of pastor and author Tony Morgan, who spearheaded this project, they quit listing innovative churches and started focusing more on particular innovations. When I asked *Outreach* magazine's editor Lindy Lowry for her observations, she said, "Having worked on the 'Twenty-Five Most Innovative Churches' list, it does seem that a high degree of the innovation is happening within the walls of the church. Of course, we have discovered and highlighted churches that are thinking creatively about what it takes to reach people outside the walls, but we definitely need more churches with that mindset, more churches that will take risk and ask, 'What is good news for this community, and how can we bring it to them?'"

To successfully make this paradigmatic shift to become a Verge church, it requires a leadership willing to kick people out of their steepled boxes. It requires leadership that pushes others beyond discussion about mission to actually doing mission. These leaders refuse to make mission merely an academic interest; instead it becomes their first thought every morning. That is the type of leadership it takes to create an out-of-the-box innovative culture.

Darrin Patrick, lead pastor at Journey Church, has a bias for action and is moving his people out of their multiple boxes in the St. Louis area. Journey Church was not started with the intention of being a megachurch; it was started in Darrin's home to reach the people around him. As he began to reach people in his neighborhood, this new church established three values: mission, community, and beauty. Over the next ten years, the church grew at a very rapid pace.

This was good news and bad news. The good news was, they were now reaching about three thousand people every week at four different locations. But the bad news was, approximately 60 percent of those people were from other churches in the St. Louis metro area. It was time for them to return to where they started: reaching their neighborhoods, and the core value of mission. As Darrin and his staff team led this back-to-the-future shift, the result was out-of-the-box innovation.

In a nearby Bellville neighborhood, a Journey member opened a thrift shop in a storefront, with the support of two community groups, to help serve indigent people in that community. Then there was Josh Willis and his wife, who led the way by getting out of their box and moving their family into an underresourced neighborhood in Forest Park. The Willises established a house church and began to volunteer in the local daycare center that supports a lot of single moms. Because

> Make contact: relationships are critical to mission. We need to ensure the good disciples have meaningful contact with non-Christians and don't spend all their time *organizing* the bad disciples.

of their leadership, others began to move to the neighborhood, and a couple hundred people began volunteering to do repairs on workdays for the local daycare. Meanwhile, another Journey attender, named Joe, didn't feel the need to move to a new place but was called to the people right around him. Joe owns a used-car lot and is using it as a gathering place on Wednesday nights to bring together a very diverse group of about thirty people from his neighborhood who are all taking next steps on their way back to God.

Once a church makes the shift of recognizing their Apostolic Genius and allowing it to permeate their ethos and practice, it's in a place where constant and ongoing out-of-the-box innovation is very possible. But establishing this out-of-the-box culture takes time and care. There are no instant cultures. New churches don't have a culture. Culture is the byproduct of consistent behaviors.

Nine Characteristics of Out-of-the-Box Cultures

1. Beta, Not Better

Arguably two of the most innovative companies around today are Apple and Google. Both are exceptional brands and extremely smart companies, but they innovate in distinctly different ways. Let's compare: Apple gets a product 100 percent complete before they drop it into the market. Steve Jobs gets up and announces the new thing and bam! It hits the market and is ready for consumption. If they talk about it, it's ready to be consumed. Google, on the other hand, drops a beta into the world. It's an unfinished product, with all kinds of improvements needed to make it a success.

Apple innovates entirely in secret. Its innovation is pioneered in a closed system and done behind closed doors. Google still pioneers, but it only comes up with the prototype. The users actually help Google finish the product by their use and feedback. Google listens to the people as they are innovating and refining the product. It is an open system — crowd sourcing, if you like. Apple rarely has failures, but they have a very limited product line compared with Google's. Google has more failures than Apple, but they have a lot more diversity in their scope of innovation.

These are two very different approaches to innovation. The point here is that Google is not afraid to put an incomplete product out there and ask people to help them improve it. They are saying, "We don't know what will work best until you tell us." They are telling us they want to listen. There is a lot of risk out there too when you do this. Some products don't fly; they don't even crawl. And failure is very public in this model. However, they have made incredibly successful products as well, like Google Search, Books, and Gmail.

Verge churches have used the Apple approach in the past to get better and better. However, these churches aren't content with a better version of church; they want to see a movement. And movement requires that you're constantly engaging new cultural contexts with the gospel and seeing new innovative forms of mission emerge. One of the ways many Verge churches sustain innovative cultures is through pilots.

The Austin Stone Church periodically brings people together to simply ask them this question in a variety of ways: "What would it look like for you to incarnate the gospel where you live and work?" Then they ask them to dream without any fear of failure. Next they ask them to not just imagine but implement, with complete understanding that some of the pilot projects will work and some won't.

Verge churches look more like Google than Apple. Verge churches understand it's not just about a "better" innovation; it's about many "beta" innovations.

2. Trusting and Trustworthy

Verge churches are often recognized for their willingness to take risks and for the speed at which they make changes. We seldom get beyond our awe for their swiftness and fearlessness. The reason why Verge churches can go so fast is because all their energy is full-speed toward the goal of the mission, and there is very little sideways energy spent checking up on each other. Why? Verge churches are composed of teams of people that are trusting and trustworthy. The people on these teams assume the best of one another and move forward with complete confidence in each other. The trust is so high that even when someone breaks the rules, the first assumption about that teammate is that they have only done so for the good of the mission. The reason why the trust is so high on these teams is that on a daily basis they demonstrate to one another that they are trustworthy. This is accomplished through their tireless work ethic, their uncompromising commitment to their shared values, and a shared belief that together they will accomplish the vision.

3. Permission Is Assumed and Forgiveness Is Expected

The general reaction after spending some time in and around a Verge church is something like this: "These people get away with murder ... they get to do whatever they want! If I was here, I would be unstoppable too!" You're right, and that is what God wants for you and your church — to be an unstoppable movement. These churches have created cultures where the staff has permission to spend money, allocate resources, make decisions, and schedule their own time — it is all assumed to be okay. If staff were to ask permission, the reaction would either be a look of shock or laughing out loud. They don't ask for permission; it is assumed. When too much money is spent, a decision oversteps the boundaries, or protocol is not followed, forgiveness is expected. For those who have never been in a Verge church culture, it is like a trip to a foreign country.

The culture that is created by the staff is a microcosm of the rest of the church. The rest of the church feels free to initiate new endeavors at work or in their neighborhood. Every person knows there is a people group or a place they're called to reach. It never occurs to them that ministry or mission is something that needs to get approval. And when they make mistakes and can't figure out what to do next, the staff is a safe place to get resourcing and encouragement. If you asked the average member of a Verge church, "Do you need to get permission to do that?" they would respond with a raised eyebrow and a turned head and say, "Why?" In Verge churches, permission is assumed and forgiveness expected.

4. Hurry Up ... Wait

Verge churches go fast. Real fast. Faster than you think. But they also know how to go slow. Real slow. Grinding-to-a-halt slow. It's this hurry-up-and-wait culture that cultivates the two most important habits for sustaining an innovative culture.

First, creative cultures place a high value on accomplishment through collaboration. When they see opportunity, they sprint as a team toward the finish line. *Balance* is not a word that would describe the lifestyle of a Verge church, but *mission accomplished* is!

Second, creative cultures also find ways to make time for solitude. The great artist Pablo Picasso told us, "Without great solitude no serious work is possible." So while they move together at breakneck speed, they also find time in the daily, monthly, and annual rhythms to "be still, and know that I am God" (Ps. 46:10). These times of solitude and silence aren't just a backdrop or an empty cup waiting to be filled. Silence is its own kind of perception and receptivity. This more subtle sense of perception can only be clarified when the noisier perceptions fall silent. It's a lot like learning to see in the dark. At first everything appears totally black. But if you're patient, you can, little by little, begin to see shapes. Silence and solitude allow us to see, in new ways, things that were hidden from us before.

If you look at the rhythm of Verge community life, it is filled with the practice of high-energy celebration as well as the practice of retreat into solitude and silence. The routine of hurry up and wait is what nurtures their innovative culture.

5. Fail Forward Fast

Verge churches have cultures in which the heroes are not just those who are successful in the mission but also those who take great risks for the mission. These churches are far from risk-adverse; instead they have created cultures with a new hero system that honors those who risk the most. In that kind of environment there is no fear of failure, only the fear of not having risked. John Wooden, arguably the greatest college basketball coach of all time, said, "When you punish your people for making a mistake or falling short of a goal, you create an environment of extreme caution, even fearfulness. In sports it's called 'playing not to lose'—a formula that often brings on defeat." These churches are always on the offensive and playing to win. Verge churches celebrate failure knowing that if a few things are not failing, they have not risked enough. And when they do fail, they bring the people back into the community with an ovation that acknowledges their faithfulness and willingness to risk it all for the cause.

> Verge churches celebrate failure knowing that if a few things are not failing, they have not risked enough.

The ethos and risk-taking spirit of Verge churches is exemplified in a story that takes place toward the end of Paul's life, in Acts 21. He was at sea and landed in Tyre, where prophets in a local *ecclesia* had for Paul a dire warning: don't go to Jerusalem!

In Ptolemais, Philip the evangelist's four daughters prophesied and Agabus the prophet corroborated: "Coming over to us, he took Paul's belt, tied his own hands and feet with it and said, 'The Holy Spirit says, "In this way the [Jewish leaders in] Jerusalem will bind the owner of this belt and will hand him over to the Gentiles."' When we heard this, we and the people there pleaded with Paul not to go up to Jerusalem" (Acts 21:11–12).

What do you suppose Paul did? It seemed the *Holy Spirit* was the author of this warning after all! "Paul answered, 'Why are you weeping and breaking my heart? I am ready not only to be bound, but also to die in Jerusalem for the name of the Lord Jesus'" (Acts 21:13).

Verge churches are not afraid to fail. They fail falling forward. And they fail forward fast!

6. Love the Edge

If home is where the heart is, then the home of a Verge church is on the edge. The edge is the point of the next and newest missional engagement; this is where Verge churches feel the most comfortable. Most churches prefer the safety of the center and the comfort of their steepled facilities, but the people in Verge churches resent the thought that they might get left behind at the old, the familiar, or the established. They are passionate about church planting. They are addicted to entrepreneurial endeavors. They have a bias toward new things. Both the staff and the people who make up Verge churches would rather go and start the next new thing (missional community, campus, or church-plant) than be a part of the existing larger and more successful thing. They have created cultures that love the edge, and it's on the edge that innovation occurs. If for no other reason than their preferred proximity to the edge, they are always in the middle of the latest innovation.

7. They Put Their Money Where Your Mouth Is!

The stuff that other leaders and churches only talk about, Verge churches will invest resources into. They put dollars, time, and people behind making things happen. They aren't naive enough to think that throwing money at something will bring it to life. But they also apply stakeholding principles and invest their best people and assets in their greatest opportunities.

In an effort to sustain an out-of-the-box culture, RiverTree Christian Church in Massillon, Ohio, doesn't just talk about it; they budget it! This church offers a financial grant to incentivize communities of people to meet in off-site spaces with the mission of reaching out in that context. The elders of the church enter into a "memorandum of understanding" with the leader of that missional community to determine how much funding is needed and how it will be spent. Perhaps the most successful example from RiverTree was Jason Lantz, who served on their staff in the area of college and career groups. Jason lived in Canton, about eight miles away from RiverTree's first site in Massillon. Consequently, all of the eleven missional communities he started were in Canton. These communities started working together under the banner of "Love Canton," with a vision of bringing transformation to community. The leadership of RiverTree saw the potential in Jason and his passion for Canton, so they gave him complete autonomy and funded his salary, just as they do in overseas missions.

While other churches are still talking about it, Verge churches are putting their money behind it!

8. Everyone Gets to Play

Many churches have created a missional apartheid—we allow the professionals and a few of the very gifted amateurs to participate in the mission, and the rest have to stay on the outskirts of missional engagement. Verge churches have cultures in which the next great idea can come from anyone! Verge churches believe that God has a great idea about how to use everyone! We are all born with a craving for mission and "good works, which God prepared in advance for us to do" (Eph. 2:10).

The remarkable story of Monroe Circle Community Center started when two women from Granger Community Church, Jody and Sarah, went on a mission trip to Cabrini Green, a public housing development on the near north side of Chicago, to do a vacation Bible school. They just fell in love with the kids. On their way back to Indiana, they realized there were kids they could serve in very similar conditions but much closer to home in South Bend, Indiana. The two women went to their pastor, Rob Wegner, and asked how they could get involved. Rob sent them to the Housing Authority to find out what was happening in South Bend. It turned out that no one was doing anything there, and many of the churches that had been involved in the past would briefly do something and then leave. Jody and Sarah began meeting with seven kids around a picnic table, and after eighteen months they were serving and loving more than one hundred kids a week. Other ladies got involved and started meeting with moms to build into them as well.

In the same area where Jody and Sarah were meeting with the children, there was a food pantry run by some elderly people. Volunteers from Granger Community Church rebooted the food pantry, so that it was built around values of community and connection. The older people who ran the food pantry were so impressed with the volunteers, they sold them the large building for a single dollar. The whole team from Granger went to work rehabbing the facility that now houses the food pantry, space for kids programs, a stage with room for celebration services, and much more. Thus the birth of Monroe Circle Community Center, which is now under the leadership of LeRoy King, who grew up across the street. What is emerging is a new monastic model in which church is fused with every aspect of life (education, health care, commerce, and so on). Granger Community Church is committed to the people of Monroe Circle for the long term, and over the next decade is dreaming about entire family legacies being transformed. I believe it's going to happen! It's already begun. It started as a grassroots initiative led by two women with a passionate love for God's kids. Jesus said his kingdom is like yeast in the dough; a little bit of leaven is an unstoppable force that raises the whole loaf. That chemical reaction is happening at Monroe Circle.

Apostolic movements not only support the priesthood of every believer but actively practice that belief. Verge churches don't just celebrate the big wins led by paid staff; they also celebrate the smaller stories of innovative missional gains by passionate followers. Verge churches have created cultures that are intentional about commissioning the artist who plays in the pub in front of five people, as well as the church planter starting the next new site with five hundred people. A Verge church celebrates a mom who starts a postabortion recovery group in her home as much as the missionary team returning home from a third world country. These cultures recognize that everyone is needed and that everyone gets to play in the kingdom of God.

9. No R&D Department

In larger churches, the temptation will be to create a department and silo the research and development regarding missional engagement. In smaller churches, when people want to experiment, it will be tempting for the leadership to turn their heads the other way and ignore it until they hear about the outcome. While individual experimentation or the creation of a taskforce may be a good short-term strategy for making the shift to movemental thinking and behaving, it doesn't reflect the innovative culture of a Verge church.

Acts 2 describes the first apostolic movement: "They devoted themselves to the apostles' teaching and to the fellowship, to the breaking of bread and to prayer. Everyone was filled with awe, and many wonders and miraculous signs were done by the apostles. All the believers were together and had everything in common. Selling their possessions and goods, they gave to anyone as he had need. Every day they continued to meet together in the temple courts. They broke bread in their homes and ate together with glad and sincere hearts, praising God and enjoying the favor of all the people. And the Lord added to their number daily those who were being saved" (Acts 2:42–47).

I can't help but notice two words in that section of Scripture: *everyone* and *all*. It wasn't just a small percentage of the church engaged and living out mission. It was enough that it appeared to the writer Luke that everyone was in on it; they were all a part of God's holy experiment.

Verge churches don't have a department set aside for research and development. Instead these churches consider *themselves* the research and development department of the kingdom of God. They don't mind saying, "Let's give it a go." Some say they have no sense of responsibility, but Verge church leaders would say they are permission-giving and aren't afraid to get it wrong. Getting it wrong means they are one experiment closer to getting it right.

In order to sustain an innovative culture that consistently mobilizes people for mission, it will take these kinds of behaviors on the part of the leadership. And remember why all this talk about innovation. It isn't about being cool, trendy, or new! It's about getting the church out of the box of its building and into the fabric of the community and the life of its neighbors. The point of the whole shift process that starts with reimagining the church as an apostolic movement and then creates a culture with routine missional practices is to get the church going and not just coming!

Once you're successful in creating a culture of innovation where God has a dream for every life and where the next great idea can come from anyone, you're on the verge of great momentum and, in time, an apostolic movement. To mobilize people into existing missional ministry opportunities requires a simple infrastructure of relational care with proper spans of control. However, when people come with new and creative ideas to accomplish the mission, you will need a repeatable process so you don't overwhelm the leadership and you honor those people who are presenting the new ideas.

Process for Creating Out-of-the-Box Culture

Ten million people tuned in to watch *Nightline* introduce the world to a company called IDEO, one of the leading design and innovation firms in the world. *Nightline* had agreed to feature IDEO, if they could show their viewers how to do innovation. IDEO founder David Kelley agreed. Their assignment: "Take something old and familiar and completely redesign it in just five days." They chose a shopping cart as their project. The whole world got to see their innovative process for creating a new kind of shopping cart (which took just five days) in that thirty-minute show. The process for innovation was amazing!

IDEO's assignment, taking something old and familiar and completely redesigning it, sounds like a very familiar challenge to every church leader. But in a recent survey, less than 20 percent of church leaders said that their church was one that could foster innovation. We are convinced that if churches have a leadership that values and practices innovation and helps create a culture that fosters innovation, there is still one missing piece: churches need a process that creates a clear path for missional ideas to be implemented and lived out. With a clear innovative process, you can train ordinary people to be extraordinary innovators. Without a clear innovative process, you will end up with incremental change or fantasy ideas that are never implemented.

Turning Ideas Into I.D.E.A.s

Kim and Maria Hammond, along with their three boys, just moved into a new development with lots of young families, many of whom were lower-income. Kim is a big guy with a huge heart for mission, and Maria is a beautiful mother with a tender heart for people far from God. A quick study of their neighborhood and a nearby park revealed that kids had to travel outside their neighborhood to play Little League baseball, and many couldn't afford it. This got Kim and Maria's missional imagination working. Their idea: what if we started a baseball league for elementary-age kids? It was an idea they believed would be good news to the neighborhood, and a way to build redemptive relationships.

So how do we help Kim and Maria take that idea and implement it? The following is a time-tested, simple, and reproducible process for turning an idea into an I.D.E.A. It's a handy acronym, but it's important to realize that these steps are carried out in reiterating loops. Even though the terms are fairly self-explanatory, a little explanation is in order. Each step is focused on answering a few key questions.

Step 1: Investigate

The first step is to investigate and conduct the fact-finding needed to fully assess if this idea is something that would be considered good news in that context. In our case study with Kim and Maria, the very first task would be to gain a good understanding of where they now live and if a baseball league is something that would be received as good news in that neighborhood. Here are some of the questions we would ask in coaching them:

"I" Questions
- What does your current context look like—what do we know, what don't we know?
- What are the needs in this context?
- What are the strengths of this context?
- What does it look like to be good news in that setting?

Step 2: Design

Once we've done our investigation and believe that the idea is good news for that context, the second step is to design it for implementation. Once Kim and Maria's investigation proved there were many young families with children in their neighborhood who would welcome and contribute to a baseball league, the next step would be to help them think through how to get it started. Together we would paint a mental picture of how to implement this idea and what the future would look like when this idea was successfully working. The coaching conversation would include the following questions:

"D" Questions
- What does the future look like if the problem is solved or this strength is accentuated?
- What other ideas like this exist that we can learn from?

- What is the best way to do this?
- What can we pilot quickly, with little risk, to test our idea?

Step 3: Experiment

Once we've done our homework on contextualization and have designed what we believe to be ministry with the potential for transformation, it's time to experiment. The third step is experimentation and selecting the option or solution that holds the greatest promise, by conducting a pilot project to test the idea. Knowing that the community is supportive of a baseball league, Kim and Maria can design a pilot project that allows them to experiment and learn how to make this idea even better. They decided to host a half-day baseball camp where they would teach kids some fundamentals, followed by a pickup game. In a coaching conversation with them, we would ask these types of questions:

"E" Questions
- How will you test the idea?
- What do you expect will happen during that experiment?
- What is the scope of impact, and how will you measure it?
- How will you know if your idea is successful?

Step 4: Adjust

After the experiment, you will take the fourth step in the I.D.E.A. process: making adjustments. This is the step where you assess and tweak and where results are compared with expected outcomes. Once the necessary adjustments are made, you follow up with a redesign to improve the original idea. After the half-day baseball camp, Kim and Maria had learned a lot. They still believed that a baseball league would work, but now they had a better idea about how to make it work. Here are some questions we would work through in helping them adjust their original ministry idea:

"A" Questions
- What worked and why?
- What didn't work and why?
- What adjustments must be made?
- What is the plan for redesigning?

Investigate, design, experiment, and adjust are the universal common denominators to successful innovation. The beauty of the I.D.E.A. loop is that it can apply to any context and any church, thus opening up everyday innovation to every person.

Kim and Maria not only started a baseball league that in the first summer included fifty-plus kids and parents, but they also started several other community events. The result? Lost people are finding their way back to God, and the neighborhood is being transformed. The mission of Jesus is being accomplished. None of this occurred in a steepled box on a Sunday morning. It is out-of-the-box innovation!

Alan's Response to "Out-of-the-Box Innovation"

Recently Dave and I were in conversation with some key denominational leaders. We talked about the need for innovation in the church, much as we have in the chapters you're reading at the moment. At one point, one of the execs said that not all people can be innovators. To which I answered, "They could, if their lives depended on it."

The truth is, human beings are incredibly creative. Given the right conditions, even the most seemingly ordinary person can come up with bright solutions. One could even read history as a series of events initiated and directed by certain innovations that shape social patterns, influence decisions, and so change the course of human history. The invention of the printing press is one such example. It's not too much to suggest that both the Renaissance and the Reformation were initiated by the availability of mass printing.[1] And we all know how personal computing, the ubiquity of the internet, and the social media revolution are changing everything. Philosopher and communications theorist Marshall McLuhan was right: we invent our tools, and then our tools reinvent us.[2]

Sneezing the gospel: the gospel is an idea virus; it must be sneezed to become a contagion.

But innovation is as much science as it is art. It is not always dependent on the genius. To say this differently: what goes by the name of "genius" can be traced down to some common factors and understood in terms of networking and chaos theory. It can be learned, studied, and it certainly can be prompted by the right conditions.[3] As we have seen in the previous chapter ("Innovate or Die"), these conditions are upon us.

Most innovation theorists now understand that innovation doesn't necessarily mean concocting something radically new, seemingly out of nowhere, but that new ideas and products arise out of combining different ideas from seemingly disparate areas of concern. The real key to innovation, then, comes from combining ideas drawn from a tumult of already existing, if separate, developments and ideas. Researchers Francis Crick and James Watson cracked the DNA code by bringing together the sciences of genetics, physical chemistry, X-ray crystallography, and mathematics. Trying to unlock it from within the narrow scientific discipline of genetics *alone* produced no results — it could not; the answer had to come from outside the discipline.[4]

The printing press came about from combining the dissimilar technologies of the wine press and the coin punch! But it was precipitated by the sponsorship (and money) of the Catholic Church, who wanted to standardize some theological ideas in order to control free-thinking![5] Who would have guessed how *that* would backfire! Cirque du Soleil opened up an entirely new market space (blue ocean) by blending opera and ballet with the circus format while eliminating star performers and animals.

The principle? Look near and far for possible answers, bring seemingly disparate things together, be playful and imaginative, look for answers outside your specialist interests, and think outside your overly developed institutional/Christendom box.

In *Built to Last*, James C. Collins and Jerry I. Porras offer some more ways to stimulate creativity and movement:[6]

- *Good enough never is.* Encourage a continual process of relentless self-improvement with the aim of doing better and better, forever into the future.
- *Try a lot of stuff and keep what works.* Try to develop high levels of action and experimentation — often unplanned and undirected — that produce new and unexpected paths of progress and enable visionary companies to adapt and develop.

As Dave has indicated, a climate of change can be promoted by a preparedness to act outside the box. In *The Shaping of Things to*

Come, Mike Frost and I suggested that you try some of the following challenges:[7]

- *Ask a jester.* That's what kings did to break out of the dead-end environment of their yes-men. The jester's job was to parody any proposal, make it appear in a fresh light.
- *Learn from mistakes.* Before Thomas Edison invented the light-bulb, he discovered 1,800 ways not to make it. Columbus was looking for India. Errors are natural—one of life's primary vehicles of learning.
- *Try a different approach.* Most of our advances have occurred because someone challenged the rules and tried a different approach. What rules should you challenge here and now?
- *Break out.* The more you do something the same way, the more difficult it is to think about doing it in another way. Eat ice cream for breakfast. See a film you wouldn't normally see. Take a different route to work.
- *Get out of your box.* Anyone can look for fashion in a boutique. Anyone can look for history in a museum. Explore. Look for fashion in a hardware store or an airport.
- *Dig deeper.* Nothing is more dangerous than an idea when it's the only one you have. The best way to get a great idea is to have lots of ideas.
- *Adopt a genius.* You can benefit by learning from the lives, ideas, and actions of the great geniuses of history. You can probably tell by now that my heroes include Einstein, Kierkegaard, and Buber. But you could easily pick Van Gogh, Leonardo da Vinci, Picasso, T. S. Eliot, Thomas Edison, or Hannibal (not Lecter!).
- *Brainstorm.* If properly carried out, brainstorming can help you not only come up with sackfuls of new ideas but also decide which is best.[8]

Some great—and seemingly small—ways I have found to spur creativity and innovation:

- *Take notes.* Always carry a small notebook and a pen or pencil with you. That way, if you're struck by an idea, you can quickly note it. (You can use an audio-recording device as well, but I find the visual aspect of writing helpful.) Upon rereading your notes, you may discover that about 90 percent of your ideas are nutty. Don't worry, that's normal. What is important is the 10 percent that are brilliant.

- *Use charts and diagrams.* I'm a right-brained person, so this helps me immensely. All who know me know I find it helpful to put my ideas into graphic form. In fact, I would say that almost all my best thinking is done with diagrams first and articulated afterward.[9]

- *Use words.* If you're stuck for an idea, open a dictionary, randomly select a word, and then try to formulate ideas incorporating this word. You'd be surprised how well this works. The concept is based on a simple but little-known truth: freedom sometimes inhibits creativity. There's nothing like restriction to get you thinking.

- *Define your problem.* Grab a sheet of paper, electronic notebook, computer, or whatever you use to make notes, and define your problem in detail. You'll probably find ideas positively spewing out once you've done this.

We can and must be innovative. This means fostering the environment where creativity and innovation is encouraged, acknowledged, and rewarded. To do this, we need to promote a culture of creative and holy dissatisfaction. Onward and upward!

DISCUSSION QUESTIONS

Open

Have you ever been kicked out of anything? A club? A school? A church? A dorm? Was it deserved? Explain.

Explore

1. What would happen if your pastor were to kick your church out of the building? Seriously, what would happen to your church? How would it function?

2. In the following Scripture passage, what impresses you most about this new and innovative community of Christ followers?

They devoted themselves to the apostles' teaching and to the fellowship, to the breaking of bread and to prayer. Everyone was filled with awe, and many wonders and miraculous signs were done by the apostles. All the believers were together and had everything in common. Selling their possessions and goods, they gave to anyone as he had need. Every day they continued to meet together in the temple courts. They broke bread in their homes and ate together with glad and sincere hearts, praising God and enjoying the favor of all the people. And the Lord added to their number daily those who were being saved.

—Acts 2:42–47

3. This description of the early church indicates that there was a high level of participation in missional engagement. Notice the words *everyone* and *all*. Why is it so difficult today to move Christ followers toward engaging in mission like the members of the early church did in the first century?

4. Take a second look at the nine characteristics of out-of-the box cultures. How would you evaluate your church, based on these characteristics? Put an *S* next to the characteristics in which your church is *strong*, and a *D* next to the characteristics in which your church needs *development*.

   1. Beta, not better
   2. Trusting and trustworthy
   3. Permission is assumed and forgiveness is expected
   4. Hurry up … wait
   5. Fail forward fast
   6. Love the edge
   7. They put their money where your mouth is
   8. Everyone gets to play
   9. No R&D department

5. Pick a couple of characteristics in which your church needs development. What are some steps you and your leadership team can take to grow your church in these areas?

Move

1. Pair up with someone. You have fifteen minutes to walk through the I.D.E.A. process and come up with a new and innovative approach to bringing the good news to a community or neighborhood near you. Use the I.D.E.A. outline/process to present your new approach to the rest of the group.

   Step 1: Investigate
   Step 2: Design
   Step 3: Experiment
   Step 4: Adjust

Part 4
Move

Chapter 9

Gaining Missional Momentum

DAVE

In building a great institution, there is no single defining action, no grand program, no one killer innovation, no solitary lucky break, no miracle moment. Rather our research showed that it feels like turning a giant, heavy flywheel. Pushing with great effort—days, weeks and months of work, with almost imperceptible progress—you finally get the flywheel to inch forward.... You keep pushing, and with persistent effort, you eventually get the flywheel to complete one entire turn.... You keep pushing, in an intelligent and consistent direction, and the flywheel moves a bit faster. It builds more momentum ... then, at some point—breakthrough! Each turn builds upon previous work, compounding your investment of effort. The flywheel flies forward with almost unstoppable momentum. This is how you build greatness.

— JIM COLLINS, BUSINESS STRATEGIST

The Apollo 13 mission may have been famous for its difficulties — immortalized forever in the words "Houston, we have a problem" — but it is just as renowned for its innovative solution. Midway to the moon, an oxygen tank internally combusted on Apollo 13, ruining the mission and jeopardizing the crew. The spacecraft circled the moon to turn itself around, and the crew had to shut down the command module and use the lunar module *Aquarius* as a lifeboat. Carbon dioxide levels were rising, but the air filtering canisters from the command module were square and wouldn't fit the *Aquarius*'s round openings. While Apollo 13 threatened to be lost forever, the NASA team back in Houston scrambled to put together a solution to save the ship, using only parts from that spacecraft. NASA's mission control engineers used duct tape to alter a square canister so it would fit a round hole. They called this contraption a "mailbox" and instructed the astronauts on how to alter theirs. The innovative problem solving of NASA's astronauts and engineers saved Apollo 13's mission from complete disaster and their crew from death.

The church in the United States is also facing a life-threatening problem. Without innovative problem solving using all God has given us, the church will flame out in its generation. As by now you're no doubt aware, we believe that the solution lies in reactivating the church as an apostolic movement. And to do this, we have suggested a distinct, somewhat unique process. It's important to see this process as a self-reinforcing system, like the flywheel described by Collins in the quote on p. 249: turn it over and over and over again, and finally you can develop the kind of unstoppable momentum that will lead to apostolic movement.

In chapter 1, we addressed the twofold issue facing the church: a strategic problem and a missionary problem. To review:

- *Strategic problem.* The majority of churches in the U.S. are using a model of church designed to reach 40 percent (and declining) of the American population. This leaves around 60 percent (and climbing) of the American population outside the reach of the local church.

- *Missionary problem.* The church of Jesus in America has forgotten its call to be a "sent" people. Without a sending competency and capacity, the mission will never be accomplished. If we are going to reach that 60 percent segment of the population, it means that every Christ follower is a "sent" person with a missionary call on his or her life.

The Solution: Apostolic Movement

Now that we know the problem, what's the solution? Apostolic movement. Figure 26 succinctly illustrates the solution needed by the church in the West, and also our understanding of apostolic movement. It's going to take a *missional church* plus *missional people* to make a *missional movement.*

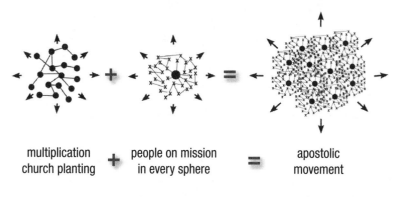

| multiplication church planting | + | people on mission in every sphere | = | apostolic movement |

Figure 26

A missional church will always express itself as a reproducing church that multiplies new sites and churches. A missional people involves Christ followers sent as agents of good news in every sphere and domain of life (work, play, politics, economics, education, and so on). When you add those two together, you have the missional equation of an apostolic movement. Let's take a look at why those two parts of the equation are so important in creating movement.

Multiplying Churches

Dave Olson, director of the American Church Research Project and author of *American Church in Crisis*, conducted groundbreaking research from over two hundred thousand churches in the United

States. His research compared the impact of new churches with that of existing churches. Figure 27 shows the percentage of yearly growth based on the decade in which a church was started. His data goes back over two hundred years.

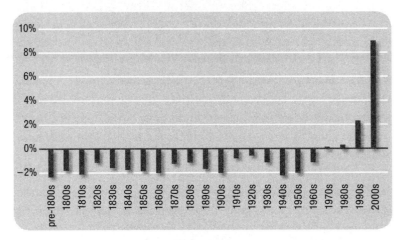

Figure 27

Let's make a few observations showing the clear need for church multiplication:

- First, eighteen out of twenty-two decades show negative growth.
- Two out of those twenty-two decades indicate less than 1 percent growth or a plateau.
- Only two decades indicate a positive growth rate, and the first positive indicator is among churches started in the last ten to twenty years (at a little more than 2 percent growth rate).
- However, new churches started in the last ten years grew on the average by 9 percent.

It's only as we began to take church planting seriously that we begin to see a change in growth patterns! Here's why: according to Olson and others, new churches have three to four times as many conversions as do established churches. That means that if an established church of five hundred people helped ten people become Christ followers, a new church of five hundred would likely help thirty to forty people in that same time frame. And in the first ten years, new churches grow twenty-three times faster than churches over ten years old. Is there any doubt that new churches and church multiplication are a crucial part of the equation leading to apostolic movement? I think not![1]

People on Mission in Every Sphere

In this case, rather than persuade you with stats, let me tell you about Kathy, who convinced me of the need to see all of God's people mobilized for mission into every domain of life.

I was surprised when Kathy told me, "Dave, I'm not sure I can get them to come to church with me." The reason why I was surprised was because nearly every week, she brought people who are far from God to Community. I told the first part of this story in *Exponential*, but now there is even more to this story. The reason why her statement surprised me was because I would often look out into the crowd at a weekend service and see an entire row of people sitting next to Kathy, and I knew those were people early on in their spiritual search. Kathy is as passionate about helping people find their way back to God as I am. So when Kathy described these young ladies in an eating disorder group she was leading and said, "I'm not sure I can get them to come to church with me," I had to listen.

> The real revolution in China was not the Communist revolution; it was the fact that the people of God recovered Apostolic Genius.

She went on to tell me the girls were overwhelmed and terrified to come into a room with several hundred people. It was too intimidating. She said some of the girls would get into the building but would stay out in the café and lobby area the whole time. Then Kathy asked me, "Could we start something for people who won't come to church?"

That was one of the conversations that forced me to grapple with the change that needed to be made at Community if we wanted to see an apostolic movement. We were seeing church multiplication happening through starting new sites at Community and new churches through NewThing, but we were not seeing all the people of God on mission. We had thousands of people who were sitting on the sidelines and needed to be mobilized for mission, just like Kathy was requesting. Without this change, a true apostolic movement wouldn't occur.

Kathy's question challenged me: "Could we start something for people who won't come to church?" And the answer—remember that yes reflex—absolutely had to be yes.

Kathy was working at a local hospital and had a genuine love for young women with eating disorders. One of the girls in Kathy's eating disorder group was Kristin, a very bright young adult and avid reader who was spiritually curious but not yet a believer. Kathy and Kristin became friends and talked about everything. One day Kristin was particularly scared as her struggle grew dangerously close to death, and she asked Kathy to pray for her. This was the beginning of her journey back to God.

It was a long and hard journey for Kristin, as she would spiral down into depression and even attempt suicide—overdosing on drugs and finding herself hospitalized again. As Kathy visited Kristin after one overdose, she'd just received the news that her liver was shutting down and ceasing to function. Kathy prayed for Kristin's liver to start working again, and that prayer was answered almost immediately. It was huge for Kristin, and her faith soared. Eventually Kristin was released to Arabella House, a house for girls with eating disorders to continue in their recovery process. It was at Arabella that Kristin met Allyson as they were both going through their recovery, and they started attending Community.

Soon both girls were released from Arabella and continued their friendship and joined a small group together. One weekend in February, we had a celebration service in which we challenged everyone to take their faith public in baptism. Kristin was at Community on Saturday night and went forward to be baptized by Kathy. Then on Sunday, Kristin was working her new part-time job as a barista at Community's café when her friend Allyson came up to her saying she wanted to get baptized. Allyson pulled Kristin out from behind the counter to go with her and baptize her. I saved Kristin's Facebook message to me: "This baptism weekend was absolutely incredible! I made my public declaration of acceptance of Jesus as my Savior on Saturday night and then had the honor of baptizing one of my best friends this morning—she grabbed me right from the café!"

Kathy is simply one example of someone living out the missional strategy that Jesus gave to his disciples in John 20:21: "As the Father has sent me, I am sending you." Now multiply Kathy thousands and millions of times over. As Christ followers engage in mission and begin to move into every sphere of life, momentum builds, and in time an apostolic movement will burst into full force. To miss this part of the movemental equation is to make a big blunder. In my opinion, this is the mistake most church leaders make. They forget the sheer missional power of the people of God.

Looking for the equation for missional momentum? Do the math. When you add church-planting multiplication with people on mission in every sphere of life, it equates to apostolic movement: *movementum*.

On the Verge of Movementum

Movementum, when we are operating from the right paradigm of church, should be entirely natural; it's what happens in all exponential movements everywhere. It is, we suggest, the church's deepest design. It is what happens when *ecclesia* is being what *ecclesia* is meant to be: an expansive, high-impact, transformative people-movement. Remember, we all have within us the full coding and potential of Apostolic Genius, and so with the Spirit's guidance, at any time we can become the people we were designed to be. Recall the metaphor of the spark and the seed used earlier by Alan: in the same way that a seed has the full potential of a forest, so too the spark contains the full potential of a forest fire. What is needed is (re)activation of Apostolic Genius, not an imposition of some trendy new organizational concept from the business world. This is liberating, because it means becoming what we were originally designed to be — it should feel right.

We know the problem. And although we find it hard to get there, we really do know the solution. So now let's turn our attention to the very practical question of how. How do I conceive of, communicate, and apply the process outlined in this book?

Previously Alan indicated the shift processes of embedding Apostolic Genius, developing ethos, and shaping practices needed to activate and maintain a consistent apostolic movement. How do imagining, shifting, and innovating contribute to movement and momentum?

The simple diagram in figure 28 shows us that movementum occurs via a continuous cycling of the church through the three-dimensional process: imagine, shift, and innovate.

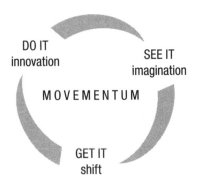

Figure 28

These phases aren't three steps you take and then you have arrived, nor are they three boxes you check off as accomplished. This is a journey of movement with the Spirit of the living God. Your church will have to imagine and reimagine itself as a movement for every time and every context you find yourselves in. In relationship with others and by the leading of the Spirit, your church will make the shift to integrate the right practices that create a culture of mission in your community. Once those practices are identified, they will become part of the routine and rhythms of life that allow you to gain missional momentum.

As the wheel turns over, time and time again, you'll find that the momentum continues to gain traction. And remember, in the way that momentum works, with every rotation of the flywheel, the church gains greater and greater momentum, until it finds itself accelerating at a pace that can only be called an apostolic movement.

A Categorization of Movement

Before we rush into the future and take you through the exciting process of gaining missional momentum, it would be wise for us to pause and do some serious reflection on where your church is right now. In many ways, where you are determines what you see, and also will determine the approach you might take to ignite movement in your midst. In other words, approach and strategy are likely to change depending on where your church is in the continuum. The following are five major categories of churches:

1. sacramental/high church
2. traditional/mainline Protestant or conservative evangelical
3. contemporary/church-growth model
4. micro-missional/incarnational
5. apostolic movement

Understanding that all churches are hybrids of various forms, we can say there is some overlap between the different categories. However, all churches that are interested in the Verge approach will fit somewhere on this Verge process continuum. Because of the latent Apostolic Genius, we believe that each category of church can generate movement, but that it would be harder depending on the existing church system. The highly institutional forms (on the left side of the diagram) are likely to find it harder, because of entrenched thinking and paradigm.

So perhaps we can represent this as in figure 29.

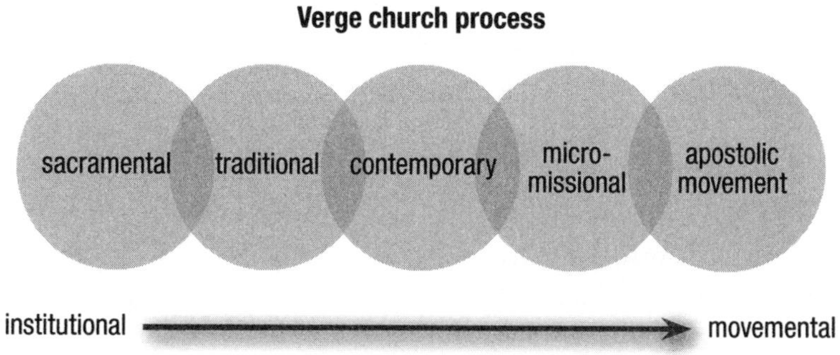

Verge church process

institutional ⟶ movemental

Figure 29

It's a very useful exercise to see our churches somewhere on this continuum between institutional and movemental forms; this is because identifying our current organizational style situation will affect the way we determine strategy and advancement in the Verge process. With the appropriate disclaimers in mind about the particulars (and recognizing that there are usually a few exceptions to all generalizations), let's consider each type of church and the unique challenges and opportunities of moving each through the change process toward apostolic movement. Why? Because it's important to acknowledge that some church forms are going to struggle harder and longer to get through the Verge church process, depending upon where they are at right now. Know where you are, and you will have an easier time getting where you need to be.

Sacramental Churches

Historically, Catholic, Orthodox, and Anglican churches draw upon ancient liturgy, prayers, and music in worship and gathering. Sacramental churches at their best are excellent at evoking a sense of awe and the grandeur of God, as well as the high calling of the church throughout different ages and cultures. It's always a challenge, however, for sacramental churches not to miss the "forest" of God's movemental mission for the "trees" of centuries of accumulated tradition.[2]

Historically, sacramental churches have been the most resistant to the more movemental forms, because of the deep entrenchment of the institutional paradigm. The most significant challenge will come here, in the ecclesiological self-understanding. Missiologically, they'll need a lot of convincing, because they are built squarely on the Christendom assumptions of church and society.

Traditional Churches

Traditional churches include most historic mainline Protestant churches, Baptist churches, some of the mainstream Pentecostal churches, and Brethren congregations. Traditional churches can offer a real sense of warmth, hospitality, and — for those who are successfully acculturated into their congregations — belonging. Historically, these churches have tended to be the most supportive of world missions. Perhaps more than any other model, however, traditional churches face the challenge of not becoming victims of their own past success by continuing to pursue the dwindling 40 percent of the population at the expense of the growing 60 percent. Furthermore, the mainline Protestant churches, which form part of this grouping, have become bastions of liberal theology, which by its nature cannot fund (theologically or morally) apostolic movements.

The issues faced by traditional churches therefore will be largely missiological, as they are geared mainly for a Christendom approach to mission, both structurally and ideologically.

Contemporary Churches

Some of the first churches to become aware of shifting population trends were the church-growth movement, a trans-denominational phenomenon beginning at Fuller Seminary in the sixties with voices like Donald McGavran and C. Peter Wagner. Church-growth congregations tend to possess an amazing capacity for incubating vision and carrying out this vision. This skill set is invaluable for movemental growth. The Achilles' heel for church-growth churches is becoming calcified in one way of being missional. The adage is true: those married to the spirit of this age are vulnerable to becoming widows in the next. Baby boomer generations that were faithful in pioneering authentic expressions of church for their culture need to become champions of today's apostolic movement.

Micro-Missional Churches

Seeded in the Jesus movement of the 1970s, house churches began proliferating in the eighties and really came into their own in the nineties with the advent of the internet. People burned out and left more institutional forms of church and began to find the intimacy and community they craved in smaller, home-based gatherings. In the past decade, micro-missional communities (these days called simple or organic churches) have come into the Christian mainstream, many laying aside past animosities born of reaction toward authoritarian or abusive institutional models. The great virtue of micro-missional churches is their small, portable, multipliable size.

Their peculiar vulnerabilities include the ever-constant danger of becoming insular. In addition, more organic forms are suspicious and resistant to any form of organization and therefore find it hard to act collectively.

Apostolic Movement

The fulfillment of our missional God's dream for redeeming his world and his beloved people is an apostolic movement. Having rediscovered its Apostolic Genius, it leaves behind the institutional form of church and becomes a viral, highly transformative, gospel movement. It's a reproducing church whose sole focus is the mission of Jesus filled with people who are engaged in mission in every sphere of life.

At this point, it would be helpful to discuss the Future Travelers church cohort and how they fall into this continuum, as many started out in a very different place.

Future Travelers Churches

In our work with the Future Travelers churches, we notice a pattern which is depicted by figure 30.

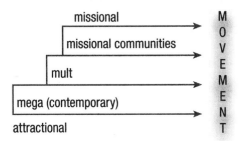

Figure 30

The majority of the churches in Future Travelers were started with the vision of being a contemporary church that would attract the unchurched. In a relatively short period of time, these churches grew into megachurches, reaching thousands of those who were far from God.

Having developed the proficiency for reproducing large, the next step was to go to multiple sites and/or church planting. They began efforts toward reproducing small through missional communities. From that platform and experience, they are using all their resources for missional movement. It's the conviction of this group now that over the next decade, all of these expressions, both large and small, will reproduce and exist simultaneously inside the movement. That's what we are seeing in other parts of the world that are experiencing apostolic movement.

Every Church Has Movement Potential

Each type of church has its own unique challenges in shifting toward an apostolic movement, but because of the mDNA that resides within each of us and each of our communities, every form has movemental potential. The intention of the above diagram isn't to discourage but instead to take a candid look at the challenges of each expression of the body of Christ. If you are willing to take an honest look at your community, any expression has possibility of movement. Furthermore, in coming years, we expect that all forms will be included inside the movement.

Gaining Missional Momentum through the Verge Process

The Verge process is a change strategy for any church to use to move from a more institutional paradigm to a more movemental way of believing and behaving. And before there can be movement, there must be momentum, and that takes time.

Jim Collins describes it this way:

> Picture an egg. Day after day, it sits there. No one pays attention to it. No one notices it. Certainly no one takes a picture of it or puts it on the cover of a celebrity-focused business magazine. Then one day, the shell cracks and out jumps a chicken. All of a sudden, the major magazines and newspapers jump on the story: "Stunning Turnaround at Egg!" and "The Chick Who Led the Breakthrough at Egg!" From the outside, the story always reads like an overnight sensation — as if the egg had suddenly and radically altered itself into a chicken.
>
> Now picture the egg from the chicken's point of view. While the outside world was ignoring this seemingly dormant egg, the chicken within was evolving, growing, developing — changing. From the chicken's point of view, the moment of breakthrough, of cracking the egg, was simply one more step in a long chain of steps that had led to that moment. Granted, it was a big step — but it was hardly the radical transformation that it looked like from the outside. It's a silly analogy, but then our conventional way of looking at change is no less silly. Everyone looks for the "miracle moment" when "change happens."

Change doesn't happen that way, not for chickens and not for churches. Using the Verge process as a guide for gaining missional momentum, let's journey together through this three-move change process.

1. Imagine (See It)

The first priority in mobilizing for mission has to be the redemption of the imagination. We must help people think creatively about how to accomplish the mission of Jesus. There are many well-meaning followers who are stuck in existing paradigms and don't know what they don't know. If people can't see it, they can't believe it, and if they can't believe it, they will never do it! What they need is imagination.

Four Ways of Engaging Imagination

The Austin Stone Church is having success in helping their people see it. They are using at least four ways to engage and inform the imagination of their people:

Modeling. Michael Stewart, director of missional communities, started his own missional community in an at-risk neighborhood that reproduced into three new missional communities, including a house church. The best way for people to see it is for leaders to be it!

Pilots. Periodically, they will bring together groups of people and encourage them to pilot new missional endeavors. By piloting first with risk-takers before going into a churchwide transition, you get all the benefit without the responsibility. Pilot projects allow you to experiment without fallout and give you your early stories to tell.

Stories. Tell stories of success in missional community. Stories have embedded within them training and vision. Stories give people a picture of what could be. They are little doses of hope. Stories should always precede the actual churchwide transition process. Start good rumors.

Heroes. Create new heroes. Point to Jesus first, then to the folks who are early adopters and are willing to take risks and step out into missional engagement. Heroes are just stories with faces. Make heroes!

"Real Talk"

One of the best ideas for mobilizing people is also the simplest: one-to-one coaching conversations. Reggie McNeal, in *Missional*

Renaissance, describes the process used by Peninsula Covenant Church in Redwood City, California, called "Real Talk." The following five questions can be used between friends, between staff and volunteers, or between a mentor and the person being mentored, to spark the imagination of others toward mission.

Heroes are just stories with faces. Make heroes!

1. *What do you enjoy doing?* Since most of us like to talk about ourselves, this is a great first question. This question is an eye-opener because many have never made the connection that what they love may be a clue to their life mission. In Richard Bolles' words, "Your mission in life is to be in the place where your deep gladness and the world's great hunger meet."[3]

2. *Where do you see God at work right now?* This question is designed to help people see that God is already at work in their lives. Many of us only look for God at church; this question helps people discover that God is at work in their family, in their neighborhood, and in the place where they work.

3. *What would you like to see God do in your life over the next six to twelve months? How can we help?* This question is important for the relationship and for missional imagination. This question tells people that you aren't merely interested in them to fill a slot in a church program; you are genuinely interested in helping them serve in a meaningful way.

4. *How would you like to serve other people? How can we help?* This question helps people focus their service in a particular direction and offers ongoing help toward that end. This question also implicitly reminds people of the truth that spiritual growth occurs most through service.

5. *How can we pray for you?* The conversation ends by taking this all to God. I'd encourage you to ask God for courage to act and for continued direction on this journey, as both are essential for next steps.

A Crazy Thought

When the Holy Spirit comes within us, he prompts us to move. Those first promptings cause us to think and want to behave in ways

that were previously unthinkable. The reason why we've often credited
new believers with being on fire is because this is their first experience
of the missionary Spirit at work in their imagination to advance the
cause of Jesus.

I recently received a Facebook message from a young adult who is
a new believer at Community. She's never read anything Alan Hirsch
or Neil Cole have ever written. If I said something about Forge or
NewThing, she might think I was talking about iTunes' new music

Tuesday. She still has huge sin hang-ups that would

The risk of learning:
disqualify her in most churches, but inside her heart

sometimes to grasp
is the beating of the Spirit's missional impulse dying

the new, you have to
to get out. She sent the following message to me:

let go of the old.
"Just a crazy idea, but wouldn't it be cool if there
could be church in random places that wouldn't be
the place you thought of as a traditional place to worship ... bars,
beaches, and so on ... places nonbelievers frequent a little more
and feel a little more comfortable. Crazy thought, I know, but you
wouldn't believe how lonely people are in some places like that ...
maybe its something to pray about. Thanks!"

Did you notice how she said, "Crazy thought ..."? God is placing
those kinds of crazy thoughts in all his believers. We need to get inside
their heads and activate the potential that lies within their missional
imagination. When that happens, people will make the shift from
seeing it to really getting it.

2. Shift (Get It)

Once the people in a church are able to see it in their mind's eye, we
need them to get it in their head and heart. You know that people are
starting to get it when they understand God has sent them. While making this shift, they will begin demonstrating they get it by living it out.
They aren't yet integrating mission into everyday rhythms and routines
of life, but it is showing up from time to time in their life. When this
happens, they are making the shift toward the sent life, and the mission
of Jesus is on the move! If your people are getting it, their felt experience
of the living Christ will be enlarged; mission will beat in their chests,
and they will find new missional articulation in word and deed.

Embedding mDNA (Apostolic Genius)

As leaders, we are responsible for creating cultures where all six elements ("Jesus is Lord," disciple-making, missional-incarnational impulse, apostolic environment, organic systems, *communitas*) of the mDNA are present and thriving. We went into quite a bit of detail about each of those elements in the previous chapters and about how to accentuate the strengths and overcome the weaknesses in a variety of types of churches, from sacramental to micro-missional.

One of the very best things you can do for gaining missional momentum is to have your church go through the mPULSE assessment.[4] This is a unique online tool that measures the missional nature of your church. It's specifically designed to assist in applying concepts unique to the Verge process. The mPULSE assessment will identify the missional strengths and weaknesses of a church, church-plant, missional movement, or organization. It also provides you with a report, and a suggested action plan to aid strategic planning and implementation. All critical for gaining momentum.

Cultivating Ethos

Once the six elements of mDNA have been fully released within a faith community, they have tremendous influence over the behavior and practices of each individual in that faith community, because they permanently shift the culture. There is nothing more powerful for mobilizing people for movement than a strong missional ethos or culture. When a faith community has a missional culture that expects every person to be a sent person, all who assimilate into that church or group will likely behave as sent people. Why? Either because that is what attracted them to the group in the first place or because they simply don't know any other way. Those who aren't engaged in the mission will feel the dissonance and will often self-select out.

Once the mDNA has been released and informs the ethos of a group of people, it is critical to keep the culture strong. If ethos and culture are the spontaneous patterns of repeated behaviors, we must find ways to reinforce those positive patterns of behavior.

Here are some proven important approaches for gaining missional momentum and keeping the ethos of movement strong:

1. Ordain Every Christ Follower

Challenge leaders to ordain every Christ follower. I once stood in front of all our volunteer leaders and gave them our blessing to go and plant churches in a variety of expressions. I left that experience with two feelings: first, an overwhelming sense of God's approval, and second, a sense that God wanted me to offer that same blessing to our entire church and not just those in lay leadership. That led to the weekend where we ordained more than two thousand adults with the blessing of our church to go to the people and places God had sent them.

Since then, I have given this same challenge at several conferences, and I'm surprised at how much pushback I've received. Some is out of fear. Some of this is deserved, since in a nondenominational church like Community it's much easier to put this into practice than in most denominational churches. No matter what your tribe, if you can find creative ways to give your people language and license, they will sense the approval and commissioning to go. They need biblical language that affirms their calling and empowers them on their mission. And they need license in the form of full permission from the leadership to whom they have submitted.

So be creative and find a way in your context to affirm the sentness of every Christ follower. Ask them to name out loud the particular people or place to which they feel called. Commission them with your blessing.

2. Utilize Symbols

Symbols can also be powerful devices for keeping a culture of movement strong. When David Cho gave the women of Yoido Full Gospel Church head coverings as a symbol of his blessing and permission to lead cell groups, the church experienced exponential growth! This church now has the reputation of being the largest church in the history of Christianity, where women today lead more than 80 percent of the fifty thousand cell groups. The backstory is that as a young pastor, Cho was so driven, he literally went to the largest church building in Seoul, South Korea, and walked it off — all to determine how big it was. He then determined he would build an even bigger church. Cho did build a bigger church building, but in the process he worked so hard, he literally collapsed in the pulpit, which left him flat on his back for much of the next ten years. While he was disabled, he gave head coverings to women and gave them permission to lead and reproduce small cell groups. It was during that decade of ministry that the Full Gospel church exploded! There are at least two takeaways from this remarkable testimony:

1. The clergy had to get out of the way before the church could experience apostolic movement.
2. The whole people of God—men and women alike—had to be given permission to serve to their fullest capability for the church to reach its full God-given potential.

The catalytic event in this story was giving head coverings to women. This was a powerful permission-giving symbol. Whether we use head coverings, a certificate on a piece of paper, a title given, or prayer of public commissioning, symbols and symbolic actions are powerful ethos builders. The symbolic act of the first apostolic movement was baptism, and it should be the goal of every church to restore that symbol to its full meaning.

3. Standing Ovations

If you want to know what a group values, notice what gets spontaneous applause. At Community, whenever we announce the launch of a new site or a new church, it not only gets spontaneous applause but also gets a standing ovation! As we made the shift to not only reproduce the macro (sites and churches) but also reproduce the micro (missional expressions), we had to teach our people to applaud for the small works of God and not just the big. As a part of our culture shift, we began to intentionally put people on stage who could tell their stories of how God had sent them and was using them to make an impact in their neighborhood, workplace, and third places of life. As they would leave the stage, the campus pastor would begin the applause, and the rest of the congregation would follow. What gets applause is often what gets done.

The nurturing of a strong missional culture will create momentum through church multiplication and the continuous mobilization of Christ followers into all domains of life. As the momentum grows, an apostolic movement will burst forth.

Developing Practices

The goal for every believer is to move from missional imagination to missional innovation, from creatively being able to see it to having the courage to do it. But in between they must get it; they have to understand it and desire to make the shift to being a sent people. There is nothing more powerful in making the shift or in reinforcing a movement culture than the ongoing practices that are a part of the daily routine and rhythm of the church. These practices are consistent with Apostolic Genius/mDNA and take their cue from the ethos of the community. These routine and rhythmic practices are what create the momentum in individual believers and entire churches that is so essential to movement making.

Great examples of missional practices are what the Soma Communities call their "rhythms." Highly reminiscent of the BELLS practices of Small Boat Big Sea, described in chapter 6, the following rhythms are lived out routinely in the life of the community.

- *Story-formed.* We know and submit our lives to the story of God while also becoming familiar with each other's stories and the stories of our culture.
- *Listen.* We submit to God through consistent backward and forward listening. We also listen to others, our culture/community, and ourselves.
- *Celebrate.* We gather together as a community to celebrate God's extravagant blessings in Jesus.
- *Bless.* We intentionally bless others through words, gifts, or actions.
- *Eat.* We regularly eat meals with others to invite them into a gospel community.
- *Recreate.* We take time to rest, play, create, and restore beauty in ways that reflect God and the work of the gospel to others.

Again, these specific practices of other apostolic movements are not shared in order for you to adopt them indiscriminately. Rather we hope these will inspire you to come up with your own unique practices that are consistent with your own cultural expression of the mDNA God has put within you. But for these practices to create missional momentum in every follower of Jesus, you should keep these two guidelines in mind:

1. *Routine.* Make sure these practices can fit into the daily routine of life. These practices should be applicable to all people in your context and work into the routine of life. This isn't because you're trying to make it easy and accommodate the mission to a certain lifestyle; instead you're trying to make the mission a part of everyday life.
2. *Rhythm.* There should also be a rhythm to these practices. It's ideal if these practices can be lived out in some daily expression as individuals and in weekly expression as a community.

As these practices are being lived out routinely and rhythmically by individual people, you will be able to feel the growing missional momentum and know that apostolic movement is just ahead.

3. Innovate (Do It)

The third phase moves a church beyond imagining or understanding toward every believer living out the dream God has for his or her life. Each person is now, on a daily basis, thinking and behaving like one sent by God. When they are challenged with being a part of a missional movement, they can honestly say, "I'm doing it."

Mark Dwyer, a real estate broker from Plainfield, Illinois, noticed that churches don't always do a great job of reaching men. But he knew who did: golf courses. He couldn't always get guys to come to church, but they would always go golfing with him. So he started intentionally taking guys golfing and talking to them about life, family, and spiritual stuff. Pretty soon he had so many guys golfing with him that he bought a membership at a local course. The process gave him the idea for the Divine Back Nine.[5]

He negotiated a deal with a golf course to rent the back nine during the early morning hours. He then got other guys to invite their friends, and as of last year he has had more than 250 different golfers participate. They golf in the morning, and a bunch of the guys stick around in the "members-only lounge" to talk about life, family, and spiritual stuff and sometimes study the Bible together. The results? Unemployed men were reenergized and finding purpose in their lonely days. Workaholics were challenged to put life in perspective. Depressed men were finding excitement and joy. And guys were finding their way back to God. When it comes to missional engagement, Mark is doing it.

The Flywheel

Before there is the rush of momentum, these three phases will be experienced over and over again. A follower of Jesus will be inspired by the creativity of the Holy Spirit to reimagine the call of their mission. They will grow in their love and understanding of who Jesus is and what it means to be an apprentice of Christ. A follower will be diligent about the daily practices of followership but will continually be called to deeper levels of commitment. These aren't three steps a Christ follower takes and then gets an A in discipleship class. This is a journey of apprenticeship with Jesus, guided by his missionary Spirit. This is a process that takes time for a church and the people of that church and must be nurtured with patience before something new is born.

The Verge process is the flywheel that turns again and again. With every rotation of the see it, get it, do it Verge process, believers see the mission of Jesus move forward with greater and greater force until the cumulative force of their momentum is an exponential apostolic movement (fig. 31).

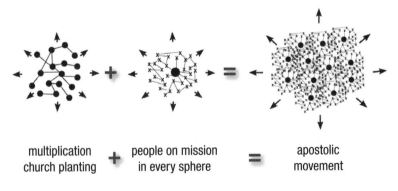

multiplication church planting **+** people on mission in every sphere **=** apostolic movement

Figure 31

When every church is on mission multiplying other life-giving churches, and every follower of Jesus is on mission catalyzing difference-making ministry in all spheres of life, we will have a genuine apostolic movement!

Alan's Response to "Gaining Missional Momentum"

It's critical to remember at this point that Apostolic Genius not only describes the elements that come together to make up the phenomenon of exponential Jesus movements. As a dynamic paradigm, it also provides leaders with an interpretive grid, a working framework, for determining how we see things. As a distinct paradigm, it's a way of looking at all aspects of church through the highly distinctive lens of apostolic movement. I want to limit my response to Dave's chapter here by showing how leaders can use the Apostolic Genius paradigm both as a *diagnostic tool* as well as a means of *developing strategy*.

Taking Your mPULSE

To assist in this, I have been involved in developing the online instrument Dave has already mentioned called mPULSE, which helps determine the relative strengths and weaknesses of any given system.[6] The mPULSE assessment is a thoroughly accessible diagnostic tool designed to help move churches to the Verge. Designed to work with this book as well as with the very practical workbook *The Forgotten Ways Handbook*, it assesses the presence and strengths of each of the six elements of mDNA. It then provides the respondents with a report, and a suggested action plan to aid the strategic planning and implementation Dave suggests in this chapter.

The Systems Approach

Remember, Verge church thinking is a form of systems-thinking. To assess the strengths and weaknesses of your organization in relation to Apostolic Genius, it is critical to engage a systems-thinking approach. A system is always made up of a series of interdependent and interrelating parts; if you change one element in the system, you will indirectly impact the whole system — for good or ill. Because everything is interconnected, it isn't good enough to simply focus on one part as if it were a silver bullet, a prepackaged answer to all our problems. All elements, both individually and as a whole, have to be factored into our thinking. And because this is a system, you can use any element of mDNA as an entry point, a lens into the organization that allows you to see the other elements in its light.

Furthermore, in systems-thinking, weaknesses will always tend to undermine the whole system. As Peter Senge, the master of organizational development, taught us, systems approaches are sometimes counterintuitive; the aim is largely to identify and remove obstacles and not necessarily bolster the apparent strengths.[7] While we need to use our strengths, we definitely have to see the weaknesses in the system as the primary focus of *strategic* activity.

A leading application of strategic systems-thinking in church-growth circles is given to us by Christian Schwarz, founder of Natural Church Development (NCD).[8] NCD talks about identifying the church's "quality factors." Furthermore, Schwarz believes that a church could only grow as far as its "minimum factor." To illustrate this, he compared his (eight) quality factors principles to the individual pieces (staves) of wood that are combined to make a barrel. If in a barrel (picture one without a top on it) one stave is shorter than the rest, then the volume/capacity of the barrel to carry water is limited to the shortest stave. To increase the volume capacity of the barrel, one has to increase the length of the shortest stave. Likewise, by measuring the strongest and weakest of the six mDNA elements, mPULSE identifies relative weaknesses and strengths in the system.

Because Apostolic Genius (like biological DNA in your own body) resides in the smallest part and is laced throughout the system, the mPULSE can be taken at any level of the organization. You can use it to assess the organization as a whole, a new church-plant, or something as small and organic as a house church. And I suggest that it be done on regular occasions. This will allow for adjustments of strategy as weaknesses and strengths shift. Furthermore, I suggest that you always identify the two weakest elements and work on them.

Diagnosis and Strategy

Now, you *don't* have to take the mPULSE test to be able to detect your weaknesses and strengths, but it ought to take a lot of time and guesswork out of the equation. It can be found at *www.theforgottenways .org/mpulse*.[9] But if you should chose to bypass the test, then I suggest that together you prayerfully discuss the six elements and discern which ones are your strengths and why, and which ones are your weaknesses and why. Certainly, you should get feedback from three levels: key leaders, staff, and other stakeholders in the organization. Once you've identified the relative weaknesses and strengths (diagnosis), focus your strategic effort on how you're going to develop the weakest ones so as to strengthen the whole. Use this book and *The Forgotten Ways Handbook* when you need to problem solve, innovate, and develop strategy.

Often the other elements of mDNA can provide the solution. Focusing on the weakest element will bring the other elements in to bear. Remember, God has already given each church everything it needs to get the job done! It's *there*; you just have to look for it and activate it. The solution to your problem is already present in your inherent coding, in Apostolic Genius itself.

For instance, if discipleship turns up as the lowest minimum factor, you will want to identify what exactly is inhibiting Christlike development. What activities are you doing to create dependencies? What tools might you use or develop to enhance disciple-making and apprenticeship? How might you get the maximum people on the journey?

Clearly, developing a set of practices will be vital here as well. But remember, the other elements contain part of the answer. One way in which discipleship might be enhanced is through cultivating *communitas* experiences, helping the church experience the thrill of encountering each other, and finding God again, in missional experiences. Another way might be to connect each believer with his or her God-given vocation from Ephesians 4, and so on. When people operate within their calling/gifting, they will come alive in ways they haven't before.

Another example: If organic systems is your weakest mDNA, then look at places where power and function can be effectively decentralized. Discern what factors in the system inhibit the movement vibe. Watch for control issues, as movements are by nature low-control but high-accountability. Also, the church that Jesus designed is built for reproduction; do an assessment on why you are not reproducing. Don't start new projects that cannot be easily reproduced by nonprofessionals! And remember the both/and equation — in all likelihood, there is going to be some form of hybrid. Nonetheless, identify the organizational hindrances to growth, and as far as is possible remove them without damaging the integrity of the whole.

Not Losing Our First/Primary Love

The only other qualification that ought to be made is about the central defining element in Apostolic Genius: Jesus is Lord. I would suggest that this always remains the number one issue. Everything must be constantly referenced against him. And even though the mPULSE test does probe the church's Christological awareness, you should just assume that this is an invariable constant and you should always be developing your understanding and experience of God in Jesus.

Let me illustrate. Recently I was engaging with a group of Anabaptist seminarians. As many readers know, Anabaptism has always taken the Gospels seriously and Jesus as the focal point of their spirituality. On the whole, Anabaptism is pacifist in theology and orientation; their view of Jesus as peacemaker makes them committed to nonviolent action and witness. Wanting to probe their Christology a bit further, I applauded their commitment to this clear aspect of Jesus' teachings, and then I asked them the question, "What do Anabaptists do with the distinctive image of Jesus revealed in the book of Revelation?"

In Revelation, we are presented with a picture of an altogether warrior-like Christ figure, who has a burning sword coming out of his mouth and is opening up divine seals that unleash judgment, with all its associated violence, on the earth. My question caused a big stir because it challenged their prescribed view of Jesus and begged the question as to how they might have simply co-opted Jesus to be an idealization of their vision of the world — the über-Anabaptist of all time, but still an Anabaptist. But surely Jesus is much more than that. We never reach the end of our comprehension of him, our experience of him, and our becoming like him.

In other words, all lovers of Jesus need their Christology to expand and perhaps need to be less ideological in their interpretation of the gospel. And if the Anabaptists, who have so lovingly centered on the life and teachings of Jesus, have troubles integrating him, then how much more the Reformed tradition (for instance), with its deeply ingrained historical tendency to short-circuit around Jesus and focus on Paul? To what degree do Reformed churches need a thorough reJesusing, a recalibration of theology and practice around the life and teachings of Jesus? What about the more fundamentalist traditions that so easily become belligerent and legalistic? The high church traditions that tend to lose the simplicity of Jesus' way in the complexities of high, sacerdotal religion? The point of all this? We *all* need to be reJesused. All the time. This is the central lesson of the letters to the seven churches in Revelation 1–3: Jesus is Lord, and we all have issues to deal with in relating to him.

So let Jesus be Lord, and in our submission to the whole Christ let us lovingly, prayerfully, and strategically lead the church onto the Verge. Put on the mind of Christ. Think with the genius of Apostolic Genius—it belongs to your church.

DISCUSSION QUESTIONS

Open

If you could go to any particular place or visit any particular people in the world, where would you go or who would you visit?

Explore

1. The chapter begins with the story of Kathy, who reached out to young ladies in an eating disorder group. Before reading this book, how would you have responded to Kathy if she were in your church and said to you, "I'm not sure I can get them to come to church with me"?

2. Look at the continuum on page 257. Where do you see your church on this continuum? What advantages and challenges are inherent with each form of church as it advances toward apostolic movement?

3. "You are a chosen people. You are royal priests, a holy nation, God's very own possession. As a result, you can show others the goodness of God, for he called you out of the darkness into his wonderful light" (1 Peter 2:9 NLT).

   Think about a particular group of people: people who live near you, people with whom you work, or a specific neighborhood or community organization with which you are involved. What would it look like for you to show the goodness of God to them?

4. Take a second look at the journey of an apprenticeship with Jesus:

   • To see (imagination) what Jesus wants you to see
   • To fully get (shift) what Jesus wants you to understand
   • To obey and do (innovation) what Jesus wants you to do

   Let's get personal: Where are you on this journey? What do you need to do in order to take the next step forward?

Move

1. "As the Father has sent me, I am sending you" (John 20:21). Who are the people and where are the places God is sending you to in order to accomplish his mission?
2. On page 263 is a set of questions called "Real Talk" from Peninsula Covenant Church in Redwood City, California. They are designed to spark the imagination toward mission. Set up a time with a friend and have a conversation with him or her based on these questions.
3. Report back to the team about how this dialogue sparked missional imagination.

Chapter 10

The Making of an Apostolic Movement

DAVE

The great Christian revolutions come not by the discovery of
something that was not known before. They happen when
someone takes radically something that was always there.

— H. RICHARD NIEBUHR,
THEOLOGICAL ETHICIST

Our God has always been on the move. Even from the very start, God has existed in movement. Genesis tells us, "In the beginning God created the heavens and the earth. The earth was barren, with no form of life; it was under a roaring ocean covered with darkness. But the *Spirit of God was moving* over the water" (Gen. 1:1 – 2 CEV, emphasis added). From the birth of time, God has been moving. And just as God has been on the move, his people have been on the move with him. When the Gentiles were without knowledge of the one true God, God sent Abram, telling him to go to a foreign land: "Leave your country, your people and your father's household and go to the land I will show you. I will make you into a great nation and I will bless you" (Gen. 12:1 – 2).

When we read about the incarnation in John 1:14 — "The Word became flesh and blood, and moved into the neighborhood" (MSG) — the text is describing God moving from his own time and space continuum into ours. And when the Spirit of God comes within his followers, they also begin to move: "The wind blows wherever it pleases. You hear its sound, but you cannot tell where it comes from or where it is going. So it is with everyone born of the Spirit" (John 3:8).

If you're a lover of God and a follower of Jesus, you will be moved.

A young man named Patrick was once sold into Irish slavery after being kidnapped from his native Britain. After he escaped and returned home, he was moved one night by a vision of an Irishman who handed him a letter titled "The Voice of the Irish." As he read the letter, he heard the voices of those he knew in Ireland crying out, "We beg you, come and walk with us again." Patrick recalled he "was stung intensely in my heart so that I could read no more and thus I awoke."

The year was AD 405, and Patrick became the first missionary to move outside the Roman Empire with the good news of Jesus. It took six years of hunger, loneliness, and cold for God to move Patrick from a teenager with an inherited nominal faith to an apostle to Ireland. Once God moved Patrick, his mission met with great success. He baptized thousands, influenced the halt of the Irish slave trade, and fueled a missionary movement through the Celtic church that lasted the next five hundred years.

God was on the move and continued to move.

It was 1755, in rural North Carolina, when God moved Pastor Shubal Stearns and the Sandy Creek Baptist Church. Historians describe this movement: "In seventeen years [this church] has spread branches westward as far as the great river Mississippi; southward as far as Georgia; eastward to the sea and Chesapeake Bay; and northward to the waters of the Potomac; it, in seventeen years, is the mother, grandmother and great-grandmother to forty-two churches, from which sprang 125 ministers." And more than 250 years later, the people of Sandy Creek Baptist Church who moved with God are still being held up as an example.[1]

God is still on the move today. Over the last sixty years, the Chinese church has moved with the Spirit and seen the number of Christ followers grow from about 2 million to more than 130 million! Roland Allen, a missionary to China, explains how he saw the Spirit of God move in the Chinese people:

> If we seek for the cause which produces rapid expansion when a new faith seizes hold of men who feel able and free to propagate it spontaneously of their own initiative, we find its roots in a certain natural instinct.... This instinctive force which drives men even at the risk of life itself to impart to others a new-found joy.... But in Christians there is more than this natural instinct. The Spirit of Christ is a Spirit who longs for, and strives after, the salvation of the souls of men, and that Spirit dwells in them. That Spirit converts the natural instinct into a longing for the conversion of others which is indeed divine in its source and character.[2]

There is something moving inside each of us and inside every community of faith — and it is our God who is always in motion. Movement isn't new. Movement is God at work. Movement is the way God has always worked. Movement is how Jesus' mission will be accomplished.

Movement Blink

We've spent the breadth of this book challenging you with a change process that can restore the primal apostolic mission that was meant to be the driving force of every church and follower of Jesus. To fully implement the process of imagine, shift, and innovate, resulting in missional *move*mentum, will take months and probably years. And it well should. But for those of you who are less patient, like me, let's try a blink test.

Malcolm Gladwell's bestseller *Blink* introduced us to a psychologist who learned to predict whether a marriage would last based on a few minutes of observing a couple. He also told about a tennis coach who knew when a player would double-fault before the racket even made contact with the ball. The point is that often our first intuitions are right, and first impressions are lasting ones.

Gladwell describes the main subject of his book as "thin-slicing" our ability to gauge what is really important from a very narrow period of experience. In other words, this is an idea that spontaneous decisions are often as good as — or even better than — carefully planned and considered ones. What follows is a blink test for your church to determine if you currently have movement momentum. Read each question to determine if you're moving in the right direction. Don't think too long. Just blink.

Blink: Is your church more interested in quality programs or quality people? What is the blink on your church in regard to spiritual formation? The promise that church programming alone will make your life better has been exposed. It doesn't work. Everyday living is where spiritual development is worked out. Loving God and loving our neighbors cannot be fulfilled in a church building. Ask yourself, is your church propagating an implicit assumption that you can live out your entire spiritual journey as a part of a church-sponsored or church-operated activity? Or is the emphasis more on the discovery of every person's unique call and the good work that God has prepared for them to do? Is the emphasis at your church on recruiting and finding a person to fill every slot or on the notion that every person has a mission and we need to help them discover it?

If the blink on your church is that it is more concerned about quality programs, then there is no movement momentum. But if they are willing to kill a program and put life-on-life relationships and the development of people first, there is movementum.

Blink: Is your church as passionate about sending people out as they are about bringing people in? "Now that was church!" was my friend's reaction as we got back into the car around noon on Sunday and headed back home together. Where had we been? 329 North Dearborn in Chicago, home of the House of Blues. I wasn't teaching that weekend, so we went to one of our Saturday night services and then on Sunday morning headed to the House of Blues for their Gospel Brunch. It was an amazing experience! They had a buffet that included a place to create your own omelet, fresh made-to-order waffles, a salad station, a seafood station, and a carving station with every kind of meat. In addition, they brought in the best gospel music in the entire city. They even had a quick devotional that mentioned Jesus. And all of it was in a world-class venue with great lighting and sound. We got all that for $37.50 per person—far less than a tithe! And my friend half joked, "Now that was church!"

If you want to create a great place to bring people to, then the House of Blues Gospel Brunch is the best model! That is what they do. They provide the best music, best entertainment, and best food in a world-class venue. Why? Simple: to attract you and your money. Yes, they did mention Jesus, and they challenged us to be a friend to somebody today, but that was only to make the experience more authentic. There was no interest in mobilizing people for mission in the neighborhoods that surround North Dearborn.

If the blink on your church is that they are only interested in creating a place to bring people and are not equally passionate about sending people, then there is no movementum. If the communal conversation is all about nickels and noses (offering and attendance), there is not movementum. But if the blink is that you see a growing interest in church planting, reproducing new outwardly focused groups and teams, the birth of missional communities, causes of restorative justice and citywide transformation, then you have movementum.

Blink: Is your church content with addition, or does it long to see exponential reproduction? What is your blink on your church's strategy for growth and expansion? Addition is a good thing, but exponential reproduction is the stuff of movements. Addition provides incremental growth, but multiplication produces exponential growth. Addition often relies on the pull of event-based ministry, while multiplication comes through life-on-life apprenticeships at every level: Christ followers, leaders, and church planters.

Neil Cole, who has dedicated his life to trying to discover the secret of starting spontaneous church multiplication movements, reminds us,

> Because addition is faster in the beginning and multiplication takes time, we are often content with growth through addition. We are easily seduced by the more immediate success and instant gratification of addition instead of waiting for the momentum that can build with multiplying. The success promised to addition is hard to turn down. It is so rare to have a church ministry grow at all that one growing fast with addition is desirable enough. It is hard to turn away from the glamour of potentially being labeled the fastest-growing church. It is difficult as well for leaders to turn away from the crowds and invest in the few, but Jesus Himself did exactly that.[3]

The question of incremental addition versus exponential reproduction applies to everything: new converts, Christ followers, small groups or teams, campuses and churches. If your church has the heart for the long view of exponential reproduction and not the immediacy of addition, then movement momentum is coming.

Blink: Is your church holding on to control, or are they leading with a harmonious blend of order and chaos? Control or an intermingling orderly chaos—what's your blink? As a church invests in people and sends them out on mission over and over again with the dream of an exponential movement, things will get out of control. The question is not if it is out of control but what is the reflex of the church? Will they have done the hard work of people development and then embrace them with trust because of what they have invested in them, or will they fall back on policymaking and pull in the reigns? Control is an illusion: it's never something you grab; it can only be granted to you by others. This does not mean that the leadership of a church should surrender to anarchy. Not at all. Rather than trying to lead by grasping at control, they must move forward with shared values that align people and communities of great diversity to bring about catalytic movements. If your church is courageous enough to not try to control but trust and nurture what they have given life to, then movementum is the reward.

If in a blink you can see a growing momentum of movement within your church, that is great news. If you came away from the blink saying either "not much momentum here" or "I can't tell for sure," then there is work to do. Out of my own commitment to lead into a missional movement, and my role as an apostolic leader, I am constantly doing a movement blink. From experience, there are two tasks leaders must steward with all their might if they want to see the making of a movement: first, a vision that is vivid, and second, values that are equally vivid.

Vivid Vision

While in college, a friend of mine challenged me, "What if your church never has a thousand people in it?" I remember thinking her notion seemed ridiculous. I couldn't imagine it, and I walked away very content with my vision for the church I would plant one day. Yes, I was very naive and extremely green, but in my own mind I could clearly see a thousand people and felt like I had a plan that could make it happen. It was after we planted Community Christian Church that I was challenged again — this time by a respected leader — to reevaluate my vision: "Take your ministry goals and multiply them by one million." He continued, "If your vision is to reach one hundred people, try multiplying it by one million. Now ask yourself, what do you have to do differently to fulfill that vision?" This was stretching my imagination. If I multiplied one thousand by one million, that would be one billion people. How could we ever reach one billion people? That was about one-sixth of the world population. I certainly couldn't do it through one church, on one campus in one city. I would need to mobilize every person into every realm of life. Everything about the way I would see the future of this church and the people who made it up had to be drastically altered!

Ever since then, when we huddle with our team at Community or NewThing, we begin with the end in mind: imagining a movement of one billion people finding their way back to God. Outrageous? Yes! Have we seen that vision fulfilled? Definitely not. Not even close. But God has used this vision to build a church of not just one thousand but thousands, and networks of tens of thousands. And we are just getting started!

A vivid vision for a movement has to be far more than quantitative; it must also have a creative quality to it that captures not only the imagination of the leader but also the imagination of others. Matt Carter, the lead pastor of the Austin Stone Church, was given a vivid vision from God that took hold of the hearts of people in his church. The church had outgrown the suburban high school they were meeting in, and the leadership began to ask if it was time to build a permanent facility. They hired a broker to help them locate a piece of property and started looking everywhere, in the nearby suburbs and in the city of Austin. At the same time, Matt was taking a sabbatical. During a time of prayer, Matt was reading a passage of Scripture from which God spoke to him: Amos 5. The passage was all about God's disdain for the way Israel had been blessed but refused to be a blessing to the poor and oppressed. Then he read verse 23: "Away with the noise of your songs! I will not listen to the music of your harps."

His church was known for their great worship, and the verse and passage stuck in his mind, causing him to reflect and pray on what it might look like to move the church into one of the poorest communities in Austin, St. John.

Three days later, while Mark was still on sabbatical, his phone rang, and it was a call from the church's Realtor. He said, "Matt, I've found fifteen acres; the price is great, but I'm sure you won't want it."

Matt asked, "Why?"

Then the Realtor said, "Well, it's in St. John." There was silence on both ends of the phone.

Matt finally spoke. "I think we are supposed to buy that property."

Right now they are in the process of moving this Caucasian, twentysomething, upwardly mobile church into their first permanent facility, in one of the most underresourced neighborhoods in Austin.

Matt admits, "I know the problems we could bring to this neighborhood; I've read the books and I know we could really mess things up. We aren't the great white hope. We are coming in with open hearts and open hands, saying *how can we serve you?* We just believe this is what God is telling us to do next."

The crystal-clear vision for a missional movement is birthed in and of the imagination of an apostolic leader. When the leadership allows God's creative Spirit to captivate their mind's eye, they begin to see a whole new future for the people they are leading. They see changed lives. They see transformed communities. They begin to see the world as God sees it. And together they move forward into that and the making of an apostolic movement.

Vivid Values

Then there are those seasons when the vision is not seen with 20/20 vision, and as a leader, you find yourself asking, "God, where are you taking us next?" It is during those times that the values of the movement will sustain you. As important as it is to have a vivid vision, it is even more important to have vivid values. It is the values that remind you of who you are as you move from point A to point B of a vision. It is the values that provide a compass for those times when you are walking in a fog.

Dee Hock, who is the founder and CEO emeritus of the Visa Corporation and now a legendary organizational guru, knows the power of values to a movement. One of his favorite tricks to play on an audience is to ask, "How many of you recognize this?" while holding out his own Visa card. Every hand in the room goes up.

Next Hock asks, "How many of you can tell me who owns this multitrillion dollar corporation?"

Silence.

Then he asks, "Who knows where it is headquartered?"

More silence.

"Can anyone tell me how it's governed?"

Even more confused silence. No one has the slightest idea, because no one has ever thought about it, even though they use Visa services almost every day. And that, says Hock, is exactly how it ought to be. "The better an organization is, the less obvious it is," he says.

In *Birth of the Chaordic Age*, Hock tells about the rise of Visa and the creation of the word *chaordic*. The chaordic infrastructure of Visa was designed to encourage as much competition and initiative as possible—in other words, *chaos*—while building in values that held the organization together—or in *order*. With that structure, he built a multitrillion dollar global corporation that has no visible headquarters. Hock explains the power of a chaordic organization: "Purpose [vision] and principle [values], clearly understood and articulated, and commonly shared, are the genetic code of any healthy organization. To the degree that you hold purpose and principles in common among you, you can dispense with command and control. People will know how to behave in accordance with them, and they'll do it in thousands of unimaginable, creative ways. The organization will become a vital, living set of beliefs."

The challenge Hock gives to every organization is to marry a solid core with a changing periphery.

Chaordic is a perfect description of the organization behind an apostolic movement. It encourages dreaming and initiative by all of God's people (chaos), while also establishing a clear set of values that align everyone for the greater kingdom good (order). A vivid set of values everyone buys into is what allows you and your community to move through the stages of imagination, paradigm shifting, and innovation unencumbered toward a true missional movementum. Without those vivid values, you will not have a chaordic community; you will have only chaos, because it is the values that provide the order.

Eight Movement Rules

As we think about the vision and values that make an apostolic movement, it's also wise to lean into those who have gone before us and those who have more experience than us. The good news is, there is more and more being written about movements. And within those texts are helpful lists of characteristics of missionary movements, the universal elements found in every church-planting movement, and the catalysts for igniting movements. As we've perused the literature, rather than repeat those lists, I have put together a compilation of what we call Eight Movement Rules.[4]

1. There Are No Rules

The first rule in any movement is that rules don't rule, values do! There may be rules, expectations, or guidelines, but that isn't what makes a movement move. What motivates a movement is a common set of shared values for which the community is willing to trade their very lives. In *The Starfish and the Spider*, the authors point out that rules are someone else's idea of what you should do, and rules are something that is done to you. Values are something you believe in and hold dear. Values are the very things the community calls norms and insists we all hold to. In a movement it is values that rule.

2. The Small Rules

Jesus started this apostolic movement with a single small group. Jesus used the parable of leaven to show how small things can make a big impact. He also referred to the smallest of seeds as having massive potential for earthshaking results. In *Church 3.0*, Neil Cole champions the power of small things: "Why is small so big? Small does not cost a lot. Small is easy to reproduce. Small is more easily changed and exchanged. Small is mobile. Small is harder to stop. Small is intimate. Small is simple. Small infiltrates easier. Small is something people think they can do. Big doesn't do any of these things. We can change the world more quickly by becoming much smaller."[5]

Big can be good, but in a movement the small rules!

3. The Simple Rules

If the message is complex, it will not be easily remembered, understood, lived out, or transferred from person to person. But if the message is powerful and simple, it will be easily remembered, understood, lived out, and passed with viral mobility from one generation of followers to the next. Roland Allen writes in *Missionary Methods: St. Paul's or Ours,*

> Thus, St. Paul seems to have left his newly founded churches with a simple system of gospel teaching, two sacraments, a tradition of the main facts of the death and resurrection, and the Old Testament. There was apparently no form of service, except of course the form of the sacraments, nor any form of prayer, unless indeed he taught the Lord's Prayer.... This seems to us remarkably little. And yet it is possible that it was precisely the simplicity and brevity of the teaching which constituted its strength.... By teaching the simplest elements in the simplest form to the many, and by giving them the means by which they could for themselves gain further knowledge, by leaving them to meditate upon these few fundamental truths, and to teach one another what they

could discover, St. Paul ensured that his converts should really master the most important things.[6]

If you want your message to go viral, remember: *simple* rules!

4. The Reproducible Rules

Ignore this rule, and you will never see a movement. Integral to every movement of every kind is an infrastructure that is rapidly reproducing at every level. In *Church 3.0*, Neil Cole gives us the diagram in figure 32, which shows how reproduction in an apostolic movement will naturally occur at every level of complexity, beginning at the smallest and simplest level. It should never stop at any level but continue to fuel the whole through reproduction at each stage.

Natural Phases of Organic Church Development

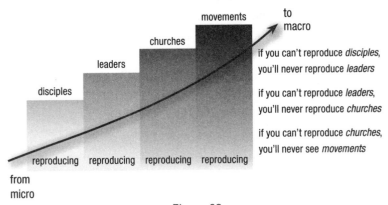

Figure 32

In his book *Church Planting Movements*, missional movement expert David Garrison makes this the first of a five-part definition for a church-planting movement: "First, a church-planting movement reproduces rapidly. Within a very short time, newly planted churches are already starting new churches that follow the same pattern of rapid reproduction.... Movements always outstrip the population growth rate as they race toward reaching the entire people group."[7]

For a movement to move, you have to let the small, simple, and reproducing rule!

5. The Apprentice Rules

Jesus knew this rule. The very first action that Jesus took when catalyzing his movement was to recruit twelve apprentices. " 'Come, follow me,' Jesus said, 'and I will make you fishers of men' " (Matt. 4:19). He was calling them into an apprenticeship and giving them instructions that they would do the same with others. Two thousand years later, the Jesus movement has reached billions and billions and continues to move forward into eternity.

In the book *Exponential: How You and Your Friends Can Start a Missional Church Movement,* my brother Jon and I champion the strategic role of apprenticeship in movements: "If a movement is to begin with you, then it begins with you being an apprentice. The core competency of any movement is apprenticeship.... This fundamental principle of reproduction is so often and so easily overlooked. A gifted communicator can attract a huge crowd; a charismatic leader can create tremendous energy and a talented writer can sell books by the millions. But if that teacher, leader or writer wants to see a missional movement they must become and surround themselves with apprentices."[8]

David Garrison calls apprenticeship "on-the-job training" and offers up the following benefits of apprenticeship:

1. It allows for exponential multiplication of training that is able to keep pace with exponential church multiplication.
2. It can be transmitted with or without written materials, which makes it accessible to nonliterate as well as literate trainees.
3. It is interpersonal and relational. Because it can take place in restaurants, public parks, or sidewalk coffee shops, it stays below the radar of government opposition.
4. The requirement to immediately pass on the teaching is reinforced in the minds and lives of those involved in the process.

Break the apprentice rule, and the penalty will be never seeing an apostolic missional movement.

6. The Network Rules

Of all the movement rules, the network rule is the one most often overlooked. When observing a movement, we are enamored by the mass of its size and intrigued by the smallness of it parts, and so we miss that what is holding it together is an infrastructure of networks. Alan does a great job of discussing network theory in *The Forgotten Ways*: "If the Apostolic Genius expresses itself in a movement ethos, it forms itself around a network structure. And once again this tends to be very different from what we've come to expect from our general concept of church. So what do these networks look like?"

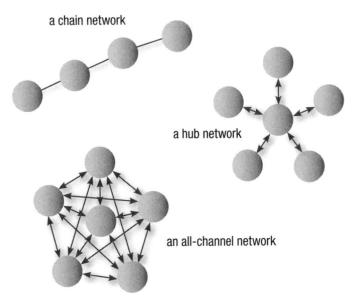

Figure 33

- *Chain network.* The most decentralized network, with each link further removed from the first and only connected to the one before and after it.
- *Hub network.* This network is more centralized, though not necessarily hierarchical, because all units connect to a central unit.
- *All-channel network.* This is the hardest network to initiate and maintain, but it's growing increasingly easy because of technological innovations that make connections more possible. Within this network, it's possible to have a variety of other networks (hub and chain) also functioning.

All these network forms can be used effectively in any organization or movement, for good (like Alcoholics Anonymous) or evil (terrorist cells). But when you couple Apostolic Genius with networked structures, you have in front of you the potential for world redemption. That rules.

7. The Sustainable Rules

Here's how we know that whatever is sustainable rules in a movement: if it isn't sustainable, it isn't reproducible, and if it isn't reproducible, you will never have a movement. Steve Addison, in his book *Movements That Change the World*, explains, "Methods must be simple enough so they can be reproduced easily, rapidly and sustainably."[9] Then he gives us the following chart of unsustainable and sustainable church-planting strategies:

Unsustainable Church-Planting Strategies	Sustainable Church-Planting Strategies
Fully fund every church-plant.	Train church planters to raise funds or become tentmakers.
Require seminary training for every church planter.	Multiply trainers in the field.
Provide a coach for every church planter.	Equip established church planters to coach the next wave of church planters.
Provide long-term subsidies for struggling church-plants.	Allow churches to take responsibility.
Parent churches take responsibility for the budgeting and administration of church-plants.	Empower church-plants to set up their own systems.
Centrally plan and coordinate where and when churches are to be planted.	Expect churches and church planters to seek God, do the research, and multiply churches where there is a need.
Start a church.	Multiply churches.
A denomination is solely responsible to identify and to recruit church planters.	Every church planter trains apprentices on their team for future church-plants.
Satellite congregations are dependent forever on the sending church.	Satellite congregations graduate quickly to interdependence and become multiplying hubs.
A movement held together by tight organizational control.	A movement held together by a common cause and relationships.

8. The Spirit Rules

The last rule goes back to the basics of mDNA: that Jesus is Lord. Our Father, who sent our Lord, sent his Spirit to guide us and to rule over us. So when the Spirit of the Lord moves, we move. When he rests, we take a Sabbath alongside him. There are times when a movement of God breaks forth that doesn't follow all that we've laid out in this book. Why? The Spirit rules.

David Garrison says that is the reason why "prayer permeates church-planting movements. Whether it's the Korean Church rising at four in the morning for a two-hour prayer time, or Spanish Gypsies 'going to the mountain' as they call their all night prayer vigils, church-planting movements are steeped in prayer."

God is on the move. God is moving within you and me and every community of faith, because our God's mission is always in motion. Movement isn't new. Movement is God at work. Movement is the way God has always worked. Movement is how Jesus' mission will be accomplished.

Alan's Response to "The Making of an Apostolic Movement"

When I think of what it takes to mobilize movements, I think it comes down to understanding, activating, shaping, and participating in the inherent potentials of the people of God. I always remind myself that every church has everything it needs to get its job done: we have the life-transforming message of the gospel, the presence and power of the Holy Spirit, the blessing of the Father, and a *communitas* of people called to be a witnessing *ecclesia* in a given place. And as we've seen, this *ecclesia*—or at least the possibility of *ecclesia*—is in everyone (seed → forest; spark → fire). The church of Jesus is perfectly designed for world transformation. We are meant to be a high-impact people-movement. When we aren't being that, then I suspect it's something we are doing that is blocking this potential.

The Professionalization of Ministry

I have little doubt that the biggest blockage to people-movement is the professionalization of the ministry of Jesus Christ. It has two effects: (1) it limits ministry to an elite group which inevitably replaces the priesthood of all believers/apprentices, and (2) it lets the people of God (the *laos*) off the hook of their God-given calling to be apprentices who are agents of the King in every sphere and domain.[10] If we are going to mobilize a movement, we have to unleash the power of God's people.

Steve Addison rightly notes that missionary movements spread through the efforts of ordinary people. The rapid spread of the gospel requires the efforts of nonprofessionals who are not dependent on external funding and are not strictly controlled. Converts must immediately begin sharing their faith and planting new churches. The role of key leaders is to model effective ministry; they recruit and deploy workers, then train them on the job.[11]

> "We need a kingdom-shaped view of the church, not a church-shaped view of the kingdom."
>
> —Reggie McNeal

As a church historian, he traces the massive influence and growth of the Methodist movement directly to the activation, training, and empowering of ordinary people; it grew from a little over 2 percent of the churchgoing population in 1776 to 34 percent in 1850. By activating the so-called laity through deliberate discipleship processes, by 1850 the Methodists had four thousand circuit riders (church planters), almost eight thousand local preachers, and over one million members.[12] Addison says, "This achievement would have been impossible without the mobilization of ordinary people—white and black, young and old, men and women—and the removal of artificial barriers to their engagement in significant leadership as class leaders, local workers, and itinerant preachers."

It had completely outgrown all the more top-heavy institutional forms and grew primarily from conversions to Christ.

But mobilization must also take into account issues of sustainability, leadership, organization, and empowerment. The resources for this are all contained within the Apostolic Genius complex as it works its way through the ethos and practices of missional movements. But in addition to activating Apostolic Genius, established churches wishing to transition to Verge church will also require significant change management skills. Leaders do well to hone their skills in this regard, because systems most often resist change. Here are some hints in that direction (excuse the tacky *P*-alliteration, but it's useful for my waning memory):

- Make sure you're operating out of the right *paradigm*. Don't assume people get it. Keep telling the alternative story.
- Have a clear *process*. If you don't follow something like the one below, develop your own, but make sure that the processing isn't left to chance.
- Be *patient*. As something of a hothead, especially in my younger years, I wish I could have understood this more back then. As far as complex systems go, what you can't achieve in one decade, you will in the next. Be patient and let process and paradigm do their work!
- *Power* is necessary for any form of social change. It's the kind of power you use that makes the difference. Follow Jesus here. Don't be naive about the nature of power. We struggle with dysfunctional forms of power entrenched in religious systems (the elemental spirits in Colossians and Galatians) and against principalities and powers (Ephesians). In addition, there are people called control freaks, and you're going to have to deal with them.
- Have the *political will* to make it work. You're going to need to make a principled decision and have the guts to stick with it. You can be sure there are going to be some people who don't like where you are going. The naysayers will come; be willing to face them.
- Have a *plan*. God never did commit us to being stupid in the way we lead. You need to think strategically and plan accordingly.
- Have some *pluck*. You are going to need to be courageous. Partly because you are innovating, and also because you're going to come up against some resistance that will threaten your sense of self among peers and members of your wider community.
- *Pray* like mad. No great movement was ever birthed and sustained without white-hot faith and lots of prayer. Leaders should model this and should be a subject of prayer very often in the community.
- Trust in God's *prevenience*. God wants your church to be an apostolic movement much more than you do. He designed us that way. Prevenience means God has prepared the way beforehand. The missional God is ahead of the curve. Look for what he is doing, make a decision to follow, and try to keep up.

As far as change processes are concerned, remember our chapter 1 discussion of the diffusion of innovation and the important role of innovators and early adopters.

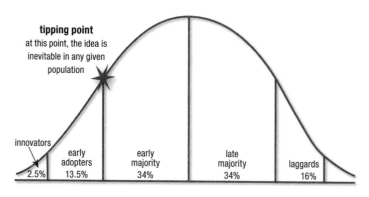

Figure 34

To briefly restate, all that is needed to create a tipping point is 16 percent of any given population—in this case, your church/organization. But here's how you might process that change: The radicals represent the 16 percent. Progressives are the early majority; the conservatives, the late majority; and reactionaries are the laggards. For change to take place, you have to reach the large majority of the population (the progressives and the conservatives equal 68 percent). The change starts from the radical edge (innovators and early adopters) and needs to diffuse through the system. The problem is that the radicals are just that: hotheads. They tend to be impatient with process and champ at the bit of systemic change.[13]

If you want a missional church, you have to have missional forms of ministry to go with it. You can't have one without the other. It's time to take Ephesians 4 much more seriously.

The trick is not to let the radicals try to convince the conservatives, because the language and urgency of the hotheads inevitably pushes the conservatives toward the more traditionalist reactionaries. The key is to get the radicals to influence the progressives, and then get the progressives to influence the conservatives. You needn't worry about the reactionaries; they will never change anyhow. Just be aware that they can be problems, especially if they're where significant money and power reside.

Remember, once you get to the tipping point, change is inevitable, but you don't want a split.

One key task of leadership is to manage influence wisely. So be subversively wise about getting X radical to talk with Y progressive, and Y progressive to talk with Z conservative. Identify each group, put names to the key people who compose them (in other words, categorize influencers in your organization), place them somewhere on the scale (hot progressive and cool progressive, and so on), and manage the process. So it will look something like figure 35.

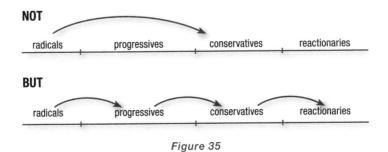

Figure 35

Finally, remember that you're made to be a Jesus movement, so *... be a movement.* That means you need to liquefy your overly solid understanding of the church. Study the nature and characteristics of movements and become one. Think like a movement, structure like a network, spread like a virus.[14] Keep the connection with the Apostolic Genius that God has coded into your movement-in-the-making, and see where the Lord will take you.

DISCUSSION QUESTIONS

Open

What was the most significant move you've ever made? It may have been an important decision, a career change, or a physical move from one address to another.

Explore

1. "The LORD had said to Abram, 'Leave your country, your people and your father's household and go to the land I will

show you. I will make you into a great nation and I will bless you; I will make your name great, and you will be a blessing'" (Gen. 12:1–2).

Do you think Abram had any idea of the impact his move would have on the future of humankind? What do you think ultimately prompted him to follow God's command and move? What inspiration do you find from Abram's story?

2. "The wind blows wherever it pleases. You hear its sound, but you cannot tell where it comes from or where it is going. So it is with everyone born of the Spirit" (John 3:8).

On page 278, Dave writes, "If you're a lover of God and a follower of Jesus, you will be moved." Which phrase best describes your current status as a follower of Jesus?

- It would take a hurricane-force wind to move me. I'm not going anywhere.
- The wind may try to move me, but I'm gonna hunker down.
- I am tired of moving with the wind and hope it's time to stay put for a while.
- I can't wait for the next gust of wind. Bring it on!

3. After reading the "blink test," would you say your church has movement momentum? If so, how is that manifesting itself? If not, what will it take to gain movement momentum?

4. What is the vivid vision of your church? How does that vision reflect movement thinking? What are the vivid values of your church? How do they reflect movement thinking?

5. Take a few minutes to go back over the Eight Movement Rules. List the rules in order from one to eight, beginning with the rule you believe your church is following most effectively and ending with the rule you believe your church is following least effectively.

Move

1. Take a few minutes to quietly reflect on whom God may want you to meet with as a result of reading this book. Schedule that meeting and pray like crazy that God will empower you

with true movementum through his Spirit to share what you've experienced with that person.

2. *On the Verge* is not simply a book; it is the product of much research, experience, and prayer. It is a handbook of sorts that we hope will be a catalyst for a movement of reproducing churches. If you read this on your own, gather a few leaders and read through it again. If you read this with others already, take a second swipe alone. The application is both individual and corporate. And we all but guarantee that what you got out of it the first time will be different from what you get the second time.

Final Thoughts

ALAN AND DAVE

New understandings of doing ministry must be created with each new generation for the church's mission to move forward.... The day of the professional minister is over. The day of the missionary pastor has come.

— KENNON CALLAHAN,
CHURCH CONSULTANT

In this book, we've attempted to point you toward a new, and yet remarkably ancient, vision of the church as apostolic movement. We have done so in the sincere belief that unless we can somehow access the potency of this way of being Jesus' people, we'll simply continue the sad decline of Christianity throughout the Western world. Part of the way we recover this way of being is by reactivating the latent missional coding of the church, namely, Apostolic Genius.

We are hopeful. Mainly because we believe that Apostolic Genius is already latent in the people of God and that it ought not to be something so utterly foreign to us that we can't recover it. We as much have to remember it as activate it, as Paul writes to Timothy: "For this reason I remind you to fan into flame the gift of God, which is in you" (2 Tim. 1:6). We are also deeply hopeful because as far as we can observe, there are real signs that the church as we know it is beginning to shift toward the verge of this apostolic future.

Appendix

Church Profiles

THE
AUSTIN
STONE

COMMUNITY CHURCH

The Austin Stone Church*

Location: Austin, Texas
Campuses and size: one campus in Austin, with 6,000 people
Established: 2002
Website: *www.austinstone.org*
Lead pastor: Matt Carter

Stories

One group from Austin Stone decided to meet at a Whole Foods store in downtown Austin every week to worship and pray. During their meeting time, they started to experience what it means to be missional in an urban area—bringing church into the common places of life and having people ask about what they were doing. They were inspired to adopt a coffee shop near the Whole Foods, and it became their go-to place whenever they had a break at work or free time. Through their time hanging out at this coffee shop, they got to know the manager and the regulars. Through the relationships they formed, they led one person to Christ. Their energy and passion spread so quickly that within two months they multiplied into five groups.

Wins

- *Experiments.* Their leaders bring a group of people together for missional imagination and ask, "What would it look like for you to incarnate the gospel in your workplace or your neighborhood?" While this process produces various degrees of success, it gives believers a place to create and take risks without the fear of failure.

---

*The profiles in this appendix were compiled by Chad Harrington.

- *Modeling.* The leaders of Austin Stone are involved in missional communities. Not only does this set the tone for the church as a whole, but also they have fresh stories with which to encourage the church.
- *Storytelling.* They have found that telling stories about people who are living missionally inspires believers more than most anything else. It gives them practical examples and ideas for mission in their own lives.

Journey to a Movement

Austin Stone got the "missional bug" four years ago. It started from a dissatisfaction with the way their small groups were functioning; they were not developing true community. Around this time, some of their leaders were reading the book of Acts every week for two months. In their reading, they came to the realization that true community comes out of mission; the community of Acts 2 came out of the people on mission in Acts 1. The leaders of Austin Stone thought back on the times in their lives when they experienced authentic community, and they realized it was when they had been a part of a sacrificial mission. As they looked for a new building, Matt Carter, the lead pastor, sensed a call from God to go to the most underresourced and at-risk community in Austin — St. John's. Soon after, a piece of property opened up in that area, and they bought it for the new campus of their church. This new building will serve as a place of worship and redemption for the city of Austin as they join the church building with a center for different nonprofits to work side by side. Their vision for the future is to create networks of churches and missional communities throughout Austin in every stratum of society. They plan on sending out one hundred people to one hundred unengaged people groups over the next two years.

Challenges

- *Idolizing mission.* They started to put missional living on the pedestal above Jesus. They were tempted to find their identity, value, and righteousness in missional imagination instead of in Jesus. It became a new type of legalism for them.
- *Developing true community.* Early on, the people were having

trouble developing community, but they found that when Jesus is the center of their lives, mission and community follow naturally.

Community Christian Church

Location: Chicago, Illinois
Campuses and size: twelve sites in Chicagoland, with 6,000 people
Established: 1989
Website: *www.communitychristian.org*
Key missional leader: Kim Hammond

Stories

A man named Mark Dwyer wanted to reach men far from God, so he decided to use golf as an avenue for developing relationships. He struck up a friendship with the managers of a local golf course and arranged a discounted rate when his group came through. This enabled him and other Christians to develop trust with those far from God and have spiritual conversations while they played golf. After the games, they hung out in the clubhouse, and a small-group dynamic developed as they enjoyed a common sport together. This has continued to grow and has reproduced to three golf courses and includes more than three hundred golfers.

A woman named Beth Kolar went out to her local gym to make it a "third place" where she could develop relationships with non-Christians. She got to know the owner's son Nate in particular, as well as other regulars, when she would come to work out at the gym. She decided to invite her new friends on her journey by asking them to join her in a fundraiser for the Leukemia & Lymphoma Society. Since the event was sponsored by Carter's, Inc., they called it "Push-Ups for Carter" and raised a few thousand dollars. It was through working together in this group project that people bonded and formed some kind of commonality besides simply working out. Then, on a climactic day, Beth shaved her head for the fundraiser, and Nate and his fiancée, Julie, were baptized into Christ. This experience impacted them as a group so much that they ended up forming a small group. Nate became Beth's apprentice leader in the small group and eventually became the leader of another group.

Wins

- *School of Theology.* Leaders teach and dialogue about mission with men and women in a classroom setting. The leaders are intentional about giving language (ways of thinking) and license (permission) for being missional.
- *Storytelling.* Leaders regularly tell stories on Sunday mornings about people from their church who are engaged in mission.
- *Modeling.* The staff of Community Christian knows that they have to model mission and lead from the front. The staff is first engaged in missional pilot projects, which are then rolled out to leaders and then to attenders of Community Christian.
- *The written word.* Community Christian provides written material to encourage independent study.
- *Integration.* They have found that integrating missional communities with existing small groups ministry creates a movement and not just a ministry.

Journey to a Movement

Started as a reproducing church, Community Christian has a history of rapidly reproducing both campuses and churches. Community has twelve campuses, and the church planting mission of NewThing has about one hundred churches and sites. The leadership of Community is building on their past success of reproducing macro and challenging their campus pastors, leaders, and people to reproduce micro. The biggest missional shift is in the small group ministry of Community Christian. While small groups have always had an outward evangelistic focus, they are now challenging all the small groups to be either a group on a mission or a group of missionaries. The group on a mission is brought together for a common mission. The group of missionaries comes together so individuals can be held accountable for being on mission. When this shift is complete, it is the hope of the leadership of Community to have the number of people who are engaged in mission equal the average weekend celebration-service attendance.

Challenges

- *Celebrating the small.* Community Christian has done well at celebrating the larger wins, such as a new campus launch and new church plants, but they want to celebrate smaller wins in the church, such as a soccer mom who is on mission as she goes about her day.

Granger Community Church

Location: Granger, Indiana
Campuses and size: three campuses in Granger and online, with 5,000 people
Established: 1986
Website: *www.gccwired.com*
Lead pastor: Mark Beeson

Stories

A man named Bob McDowell from Granger Community, having come out of both drugs and prison, was transformed through Celebrate Recovery (CR). He decided to turn his past misery into a missional ministry. For the last two and a half years, he has gone into a nearby prison to volunteer as a chaplain. He leads a CR group, and his mission is to help inmates transition back into society. He takes them into the community to work and prepare for reintegration. He recently started taking a group from the reentry facility of the prison to Granger's community center on Monroe Circle every Friday for a church service designed for inmates. His work has been so effective that the Department of Corrections invited him to bring the Friday night service into the prison each week. One-third of the entire prison showed up for their first service. Bob and others from the church have been so successful at helping inmates reengage society that the Department of Corrections wants to take their efforts to other facilities in Indiana. The leaders at Granger Community see potential for a missional movement even in the prisons of Indiana.

Wins

- *Both/and.* Granger Community values both missional innovation as well as weekend services. They plan on continuing this balance as they reach people from all arenas of life.
- *Grassroots origins.* Their primary example of missional innovation is the Monroe Circle Community Center (MC3), which started on a grassroots level (see below).
- *Equipping and releasing.* When people come to the leaders of Granger Community with ideas for mission, the leaders equip them for the project instead of making it the staff's responsibility. They have found that this empowers and energizes.
- *Missionary thinking.* Instead of seeing Granger Community merely as a church, they see themselves as missionaries.
- *Book study.* The leaders at Granger Community went through *The Forgotten Ways* with the hope that many of the ideas will trickle down to the church as a whole.

Journey to a Movement

Granger Community has an interesting story in regard to mission. They planted over 957 churches in India over the last ten years, with more than one hundred and twenty thousand people meeting on a weekly basis. But the sending church in Indiana has not grown the same way. Their heart in this shift is to bring that same missional impulse from India to their local church in Indiana. They see this shift happening through people like Jody and Sarah, two people who represent what is happening at Granger Community's Indiana location. These two women came back changed from a short-term mission trip in Chicago. They had been hosting a vacation Bible school, and as they left, the kids from the VBS asked them, "When are you coming back?" They could not really answer the question because they were not planning on coming back. The question loomed over them. In fact, it bothered them so much that they decided to do something about it in their hometown. So they went to the leaders of Granger Community, asking the church for help, but the leaders responded, "God has called *you* to do this, so *you* need to do it." They took initiative and went to Granger's housing authority. The city told them that the kids in the neighborhood needed to be mentored. Their first event of Son City Kids included only seven kids, but in eighteen months over one hundred children were coming each week for life skills. After that, Jody and Sarah were led to start a class called "Life Basics," for the kids' mothers. This grassroots movement spread to another group from the church, which turned a local food pantry on Monroe Circle into a café. Granger Community ended up partnering with Panera Bread and Starbucks to help out with food and drinks. The project has become known as the Monroe Circle Community Center (MC3). The church ended up buying the entire city block of Monroe Circle, saving it from staying in ruins or being destroyed. The city even gave them one hundred and ten thousand dollars to do it! These are the beginnings of a movement at Granger Community. What started with two women turned into a movement of two hundred to three hundred people. As the leaders at Granger Community look to the next five years, they envision one hundred thousand reproducing disciples and two thousand reproducing churches. This calls for more change in the next five years of their church than in the last twenty-five years combined.

Challenges

- *Vision casting.* As the leaders at Granger Community look at their goals for the next five years, they anticipate challenges in vision casting as they change the church.
- *Bringing it home.* Historically, Granger Community has done amazing work in other fields. Their challenge now is to bring the success they have had on the foreign mission field home to Indiana.

The Journey

Location: St. Louis, Missouri
Campuses and size: four campuses, with 3,000 people
Established: 2002
Website: *http://journeyon.net*
Lead pastor: Darrin Patrick

Stories

A member of the Journey, named Joe, owns a used-car lot and decided to start a Wednesday night gathering there. The people who come are mishmashed — some come from the neighborhood, and some work in the used-car lot. But Joe, and now a team of leaders from the Journey, are reaching out to the wide variety of people who come.

Another man from the Journey opened a thrift shop in Belleville, Illinois, a town just across the river from St. Louis. Two community groups from the Journey decided to meet in the storefront area of the shop so the groups can minister to the people who frequent the thrift shop as they come in and out. These community groups have become missional communities.

Josh Wilson and his family are moving into the neighborhood of impoverished people east of St. Louis (specifically, Forrest Park Southeast) with two other families from the church. Their house church attracted a lot of people, and they thought it would be beneficial to move there. While the church is doing good work in the schools and in the community, these three families have decided to *move* to this part of the city in order to be incarnational and on mission.

Wins

- *Imagination.* The Journey invited seventeen leaders from various ministries together in order to read, brainstorm, and dream about how they could be missional.

- *Community Loop* is a website where the leaders of community groups can go to find hundreds of service opportunities in the city.
- *Passion from the pulpit.* The missional imagination of their people comes from consistent preaching in the pulpit.
- *Equipping.* Instead of getting everyone in their church to become missional all at once, they have come alongside the passionate and proactive in order to equip them for mission. They believe that the movement will spread more naturally this way.
- *Selection and delegation.* When people at the Journey have ideas for ministry or mission, the leaders are selective about whom they support (selection), and the ones they support are encouraged to work out the mission for themselves without relying too heavily on the church leaders (delegation).
- *Discipleship.* They understand the importance of the tangible act of love, but they also understand the importance of spiritual discipleship alongside works of service. This influences the way they approach mission—a both/and approach.

Journey to a Movement

From the beginning, mission has been one of the core values in the DNA of the Journey. For them, the shift is revitalization of who they have been. They are moving closer to what has been their heart all along. This means that they are gathering leaders from the Journey to imagine new things they could do in the city of St. Louis. The energy from these meetings has influenced their small groups culture to the point that if you are in a small group, you sign up for one in your neighborhood. This gives place and specificity to their kingdom efforts. They may be moving more slowly than other more explosive groups, but it is because they are intentional about people development and training. Their growth goal is not simply numerical but developmental as well. In the future, they envision missional communities as the avenues through which God impacts their city for Christ.

Challenges

- *Time.* People in their church often repeat the line, "I don't have time." The truth, leadership has found, is that people spend too much time on entertainment and futile pursuits, time they could be using for missional engagement.
- *Defining church.* Recently the Journey has started to hear people in their church push for more programs, but they are trying to define church as missional prerogative, not institutional programs.
- *Fake community.* While people seem to be connected through social media and networks, the Journey struggles to create authentic community in which people connect on a deep, spiritual level. This is a missional imperative for them because their efforts to win people will be lost without real community.

Kensington Community Church

Location: Troy, Michigan
Campuses and size: six campuses in Orlando and Detroit, with 10,500 people
Established: 1990
Website: *www.kensingtonchurch.org*
Lead pastor: Steve Andrews

Stories

Kensington's "Field and Stream" team is made of hundreds of guys who take kids from inner-city Detroit to the country for fishing and hunting trips.

Another group from the church decided they were done putting on BBQs just for themselves, so they started cooking BBQs in the middle of Detroit for the homeless.

"Full-Throttle" is a group of people with a passion for automobiles that restores cars, raffles them off, and donates the money to inner-city schools.

The youth group is engaging the city through "Reverse" — they go into a racially segregated neighborhood in the city to serve; then they *reverse* the project by inviting the same people they served to come to the suburbs the next week so they can all serve together.

Wins

- *"Reset."* This was a churchwide study on the person of Jesus which culminated in two hundred service events. Each of the two hundred groups wrote a short proposal, and the church gave money to fund the various projects proposed.
- *Question-asking.* The leaders at Kensington have found that asking, "Where can you make the biggest impact this week?" stimulates missional imagination in their church.
- *Storytelling.* Kensington is constantly telling stories on Sunday mornings, in small groups, and through their website to inspire their people.
- *Redefinitions.* They are reorienting definitions of *church* and *small groups* in a way that helps believers see mission in both.
- *Permissional leadership.* They give permission to the visionaries in their church to be creative, innovative, and imaginative as they explore mission.
- *Mission-driven groups.* They always encourage their small groups to find outward-focused goals.

Journey to a Movement

Kensington has been on mission since they were planted in 1990. Their journey is characterized by openness to the Holy Spirit as they follow Jesus' mission. They have been overseas in India and in parts of Africa for many years now, but over the last three years, God has been moving in a new way. A group of 15 people started to engage their community and felt led to relocate — to a different state! This group of 15, along with 135 others who caught the vision, uprooted and moved from Detroit, Michigan, to Orlando, Florida, to plant Kensington's sixth campus. Meanwhile, the rest of the church is gearing up for a missional small groups launch through which they will encourage small group leaders to do a six- to twelve-week "relational serve." In the future, they envision the multiplication of these missional small groups and church campuses as they continue to follow the Holy Spirit.

Challenges

- *Discipleship.* As they seek creative and innovative forms of church and mission, they have had difficulty integrating discipleship into the rhythm of the outreach strategies already in place.
- *Leadership development.* They have wrestled with leadership development in their church. For them, this is the tension between training and releasing.

Mosaic Church of Central Arkansas

Location: Little Rock, Arkansas
Campuses and size: four campuses in Little Rock, Arkansas, and Durham, North Carolina, with 700 people
Established: 2001
Website: *www.mosaicchurch.net*
Lead pastor: Mark DeYmaz

Stories

Cesar Ortega, a leader at Mosaic, suggested that the church stock a small closet with food and clothing to serve the homeless members of the church. The idea spread, and within twelve months the church had provided free assistance to 250 people. Now, after six years, more than 12,000 people benefit from this ministry every year, and the ministry also offers HIV testing, immigration counseling, job training, and other services.

Mark DeYmaz encouraged Eric Gilmore to chase his dream of

providing transitional housing and life coaching for young people who were aging out of the foster care system. The result is an organization called Immerse Arkansas, which provides residency, case management, and wraparound services to these unique young adults (ages eighteen to twenty-four) by coaching them into maturity, responsibility, and purpose.

As a church, Mosaic purchased an abandoned trailer in an impoverished trailer park. This gave the church an opportunity to identify and meet many of the physical, material, social, and spiritual needs of that community. In time, the neighborhood was revitalized from the inside out, and many residents embraced the name and message of Christ by faith.

Wins

- *Economic development.* Mosaic took an abandoned Walmart, renovated it, and used it for worship services. This helped the owner to provide additional rental space for businesses and to recreate community activity, jobs, and tax revenue.
- *Homeless connections.* Mosaic purchased the necessary materials to create an opportunity for the working homeless living in a residential facility to join their worship service through an internet campus. Members of the church host the weekly worship time, build relationships, and serve the families living in this unique space.
- *Community engagement.* They launched Vine and Village, a 501(c)(3) community development corporation, which helps improve the quality of life for people living in and around Little Rock's university district.
- *Strategic focus.* By reviewing its developmental strategy in the summer of 2010, Mosaic redefined the scope of its missional engagement to four areas: compassion, children, women, and freedom.

Journey to a Movement

Mosaic is a multiethnic and economically diverse church established by men and women seeking to know God and to make him known through the pursuit of both unity and diversity for the sake of the gospel. Their missional commitment has been present from the very beginning as both cross-cultural and incarnational engagement in an everyday reality in an environment where diverse individuals are learning to walk, work, and worship God together as one in Christ.

Even though they have been missional for many years, the church experienced a renewed sense of purpose and understanding as they reconsidered what *missional* means. After teaching through a series called *Missio Dei,* the church began to describe themselves as multiethnic *and* missional, which incorporates both membership and purpose into their identity. In addition, Mosaic relaunched their life groups as missional communities to advance definable mission through these small group settings.

Mosaic believes that a healthy church is intrinsically missional and will embrace greater diversity over time. This is evident in their expression of compassion, mercy, and justice not only to those outside the church but also to those seeking unity inside the church. In the future, the church will continue to influence and assist existing denominations, networks, and individuals seeking to plant, grow, and develop healthy local churches.

Challenges

- *Sacrifice.* They have witnessed the struggle to embrace suffering over comfort. This is true even in a church of ethnic and economic diversity.
- *Understanding privilege.* It is important that some first recognize a privileged past in order to move beyond the colonial-type mentality of helping "those people."
- *Trust.* As they seek to be missional and multiethnic, they have found that trust is built more slowly over time when they engage others different from themselves.
- *Humility.* It is difficult for some to believe that their way is just *one way* to do something at any given moment and not always the *best way.*
- *Economics.* A healthy multiethnic church is economically diverse. This has made the church more dependent on nonmembers to supplement the annual budget.

Mountain Lake Church

Location: Cumming, Georgia
Campuses and size: one campus in Cumming, with 2,000 people
Established: 2000
Website: *www.mountainlakechurch.org*
Lead pastor: Shawn Lovejoy

Stories

Colin is a construction worker from Mountain Lake, and he founded a nonprofit called *trashwater.com* to bring clean water to those in need. This idea started when he was preaching the gospel in Cairo, Egypt, and saw Egyptians drinking dirty water. He did not realize the magnitude of the problem until he saw two Egyptians go to the hospital from drinking bad water. The whole experience affected him and his team so much that when they came back to the States, they did research on the global water crisis and decided to take action. This led to starting a nonprofit for bringing filtration systems to the people of Cairo, and now it has spread beyond Egypt to Honduras and Nicaragua.

Wins

- *Vision casting.* They have done a five-week sermon series called *Mountain Lake 2.0*, in which they cast a vision for who they want to become in the next few years.
- *Qualifications.* They make the standard for leadership low at the *entry point* because they believe in qualifying the unqualified. If someone wants to serve, they plug him or her in as quickly as possible.
- *Adoption.* Every life group is a little church-plant that adopts a people group. They actually register with a local agency designed for that purpose.

Journey to a Movement

Mountain Lake is starting over. They were planted in the year 2000, and now they are moving toward becoming a new kind of church, "Mountain Lake 2.0." This revitalization started a few years ago when the leaders became discontent with the way things were going in their church. They were successful at growing to around 2,000 people and baptized exactly 1,068 in only eight years (even in the Bible Belt!), yet they are discontent with spiritual depth in their church. So they are getting ready for the second decade of their church by completely revamping their "growth group" ministries, launching two churches in a neighboring county, and strengthening missional partnerships around the world. Closer to home, they are changing the way they think about church. They think of Mountain Lake not as an island but as a kingdom force for reaching the entire city of Cumming. In the future, they see a network of campuses and churches that all share missional DNA and have 90 percent of their members in biblical community.

Challenges

- *Old wineskins.* They had to let go of a few popular leaders who were not ready to make the shift, and hired new staff members who were ready for the change.
- *Resistance.* After the church made some significant leadership changes, some people in the church are complaining and leaving.
- *Community.* They have done well at getting people plugged into one of their "growth groups" *quickly,* but they want to move toward growing disciples in "life groups" *deeply.*

RiverTree Christian Church

Location: Massillon, Ohio
Campuses and size: three campuses around Massillon, with 2,500 people
Established: 1964
Website: *www.rivertreechristian.com*
Lead pastor: Greg Nettle

Stories

Tom is an older man at RiverTree and a pharmicist by trade. He felt God draw him to start a missional community in his neighborhood. Throughout his life, he has made the habit of helping people in the community in seemingly random ways, like mowing a deserted property. He loves to fix things up for people; it's his heart. One day he went to the city council to find out what he could do to help the area. He said, "The church should be part of helping the town, and I want to know how we can be a part of that." Through a series of events, he was able to help an older lady by repairing the gutters of her house, and now there is a missional community of twelve people helping Tom out with community projects in their area.

Wins

- *Curb time.* The leaders at RiverTree make time to sit down and talk with people one-on-one in order to help make the transition to being more missional.
- *Vision casting.* In their sermons and teaching, they are constantly casting a vision about where their church is going. The lead pastor, Greg Nettle, is always talking about movement.
- *Permission giving.* They equip and encourage people to pursue their missional passions, without keeping them on a leash.
- *Modeling.* The leadership is becoming more and more missional. They are showing the people of the church how it is

done—not just *in front of* them but *with* them.

- *Funding.* They have created a memorandum of understanding through which they allocate funds for each missional community for projects and events that require money.

Journey to a Movement

RiverTree is a church-plant from the 1960s, and their journey started with discontent—the way they were doing church was not really growing the kingdom. As they studied Scripture and evaluated their progress toward Jesus' mission, they asked themselves whether they were being true to their understanding of the kingdom movement. After networking with other churches, they met with nine people from their church who were interested in missional communities. At first they hesitated to release these leaders, because they did not know what these communities would look like. But four of them were champing at the bit, so they went ahead and unleashed them. In the future, they envision a more chaotic and organic kind of growth—not necessarily a growth dependent on smooth marketing but a growth based on real life-change and kingdom work. While the future is unclear for them, they want to be a sending hub where believers are discipled and sent out.

Challenges

- *Letting Go.* They struggle to let go as they transition into becoming a movement.
- *Identity.* While they know who they are, they find it challenging to know who they are becoming.
- *Small Groups.* They don't want their "Thrive Groups" to be prayer and brownie clubs. They want people to be on mission—disciples making disciples.
- *Visioneering.* The biggest challenge for them is transferring vision to the church. They are ready to pull the trigger as leaders, but the rest of the church is not quite ready for it.

 **ROCK**HARBOR

Rock Harbor

Location: Costa Mesa, California
Campuses and size: three campuses in the Greater Los Angeles area, with 5,500 people
Established: 1997
Website: *http://rockharbor.org*
Lead pastor: Todd Proctor

Stories

One of Rock Harbor's missional communities decided to fast from regular meals for a month and eat only rice and beans. Their goal was to raise money for their community. This group of forty people saved all the money that would have gone toward regular meals during that month, and after the month was over, they put together the money they had saved. The Holy Spirit led them to a significant need in the community, and they gave the money away. When the recipients asked why, they responded, "We didn't know about this need when we started, but we knew God would reveal a need. You're the need." In an affluent area like Orange County, this was completely unexpected. Not only were those who had a need changed, but also one of the kids from the missional community was changed. He got so fired up that he and some of his schoolmates raised even more money for a need at their school. He caught the vision.

Wins

- *Rhythm.* Every context for missional communities is different, so they are thinking of development in terms of rhythms — they encourage people to pray and discern, engage in mission, assess and ask, "Is this sustainable and reproducible?"
- *Replication.* This is a huge value for them, to the point that they train their leaders in twos, with the expectation that they will branch at some point.
- *Firstfruits.* Ten percent of their church's budget goes to mis-

sional communities. But if the communities receive this money, they match the amount from their own pockets.

- *Movement language.* Their lead pastor always uses movement language about vision, direction, and mission in order to create a shift that will last.
- *"Story patio."* They post pictures and stories of missional successes on a patio outside their church.
- *Storytelling.* They gather people together to imagine and catalyze missional ideas as a group.

Journey to a Movement

Having begun in 1997, Rock Harbor was not always missional. They have always been volunteer driven. So this shift toward a missional movement was not a "big left turn," one of their pastors said; rather it was a redirection of the overwhelming volunteer attitude in the church. A major shift for Rock Harbor happened when their "church on wheels," which had been meeting in a senior center, was not able to meet in that place. They decided that instead of *going to* church, they were going to *be* the church. This gave them a glimpse of what they could be as a church. Their next shift happened under the mantra "Give yourself away," which to them was a posture of everyday service in their hearts and lives. Perhaps the most pivotal shift in their journey as a church was when they had the opportunity to buy a large building across the street to expand their Sunday seating capacity. They bought it and turned it into a training center instead of more seating. This set their future trajectory away from being attractional and toward being missional. The only growth they have made room for are missional communities and new campuses. The future for Rock Harbor includes hundreds of missional communities out of which new campuses and new churches will be born.

Challenges

- *Buy-in.* During the summer months of 2010, they asked all their small groups to oscillate between simply meeting together and serving the community. The challenge was that only half of their small groups had bought into doing missional projects.
- *Modeling.* Their leaders have realized that this change is so sig-

nificant that it is not just a collective change; it is a personal change. They are making an effort to change themselves as well as the church.

• *Initiative.* Believers at Rock Harbor are used to approaching the church staff for action in the church. This continues to be a challenge, but the church has found success in empowering the passionate to live out their own ideas.

• *Patience.* Although they have some missional communities in place, they have pushed their major promotion back a year so they can have a healthier shift.

Seacoast Church

Location: Mt. Pleasant, South Carolina
Campuses and size: twelve campuses in North Carolina, South Carolina, and Georgia, with 12,000 people
Established: 1988
Website: *www.seacoast.org*
Lead pastor: Greg Surratt

Stories

Seacoast has several people who have adopted a city block in Charleston, South Carolina, to care for residents as they build relationships and help with needs that arise. They are crossing racial barriers to be a reconciling force in a segregated city. The group of people from Seacoast that is involved with this part of the city is made up of predominantly white suburbanites, and they are spending time in a black urban neighborhood in Charleston—the seventh most dangerous city in the United States. The police stopped by to tell the church that since they started coming to the area, crime has dropped 25 percent. Through their involvement in the city, they have had the opportunity to help one little boy who needed surgery for a cleft palate. The church paid for everything: the surgery, the transportation, and the follow-up care. Seacoast is bringing reconciliation and peace to one of the most segregated and violent places in the country.

Wins

- *Storytelling.* On Sunday mornings, the staff at Seacoast intentionally give examples of and use new language for mission.
- *Education.* They spend time educating their leaders and their coaches.
- *Grassroots.* They are not trying to make every small group a missional community cart blanche; instead they want to awaken people and encourage them in what God is already doing in their hearts.

Journey to a Movement

Seacoast began as a church-plant in 1988, but the idea of missional movement is a more recent one for them. It began when Geoff Surratt and his wife, Sherry, attended two church-planting conferences in Europe through Leadership Network. It was through conversations with European leaders that they realized how important the work of missional communities could be in the States. At the time, they did not know many people in the States who were thinking about missional communities. Their missional ideas really took off when the church went through Saddleback Church's "40 Days of Community," in which Seacoast encouraged all their small groups to have an outward-focused community project. This made a radical shift in their small group DNA. Instead of being just small groups, they became small groups with a mission. Then four years ago, Seacoast did something as a collective whole — they created the Dream Center in North Charleston, which became the biggest free medical clinic in the city. They are not just about medicine at the Dream Center, though; they also share the gospel as they meet physical needs. Their small groups and church as a whole are focusing more and more on mission. It has become so important to them that they are reorganizing their church structure around missional communities. In the future, they envision the twelve existing campuses of Seacoast becoming networks of churches which are made of missional communities.

Challenges

- *Communication.* Just like with any shift in a church, communicating the meaning and implications of being missional has been a struggle for them as they try to redefine themselves.
- *Contextualization.* They have been wrestling through mission and discipleship in their context. In regard to mission, they are asking the question, what does missional mean in Charleston? And then, how does discipleship work through our mission here?

Soma Communities

Location: Tacoma, Washington
Campuses and size: two campuses with around 1300 in the movement
Established: 2003
Website: *www.somacommunities.org*
Lead pastor: Jeff Vanderstelt

Stories

Jeff, a pastor at Soma Communities, formed a missional community reaching out to his neighbors. Through BBQs and parties, he and his wife struck up a relationship with another couple from the area. Over a period of months building relationships and throwing parties with neighbors, Jeff invited a couple to serve with their missional community. They were helping restore a widow's home. The yard was overgrown with blackberry bushes, to the point where no one could even walk through it. Working on this project bonded everyone together, and their friendship grew deeper. They ended up going on vacation together on the coast soon after, and when they were eating one night, the couple told them, "We see a light in your life. Tell us more about what you believe." Through a series of events, Jeff and his wife told them the whole redemptive story of God, from Genesis to

Revelation. Eventually this couple joined the church and placed faith in Jesus. Now the husband is helping lead a missional community and has invited some of his friends as well.

Nicky, the elderly widow from the same story, ended up becoming a Christian through their work on her home. After they cleaned her house up, they opened their home to her, sharing a meal with her at least once a week. She kept so much clutter in her house that while they cleaned up her house, she lived out of her van. When the van broke down, Jeff and his family let her use their van for a while, and eventually their missional community paid to have her van fixed. She came over to their house crying one night because of troubles with a man. Jeff was able to tell her about the love of the man Jesus, and through a series of events, she became a Christian. What started as a small group of people helping a widow became a growing missional community.

A musician/songwriter from Soma created a songwriters' forum where a few songwriters trained up people from their city to write and record music. The songwriters' group practiced writing songs together, wrote songs independently, and even showcased their music together. Over time, the group began to develop relationships with a variety of people. They decided to put on a ten-week writing forum called "The Story of God," where they wrote songs based on ten major stories from Genesis to Revelation. As they critiqued and crafted their songs, the group shared the gospel with people in the pub who were listening. What started as a writers' club turned into a thriving community. The songwriters' group has to turn people away because they have too many people who want to be a part of it.

Wins

- *Coaching.* Every missional community leader has a coach. Each year, the coaches develop a plan for the leader, each member, and the group as a whole for how they can engage in mission.
- *Training.* They train their leaders like they would train missionaries. All training at Soma is done "in ministry on mission and in community."
- *Apprenticing.* One of the two core commitments of missional communities at Soma is that when they begin a group, they

establish the apprentice who will eventually branch off to form a new community.

- *Focus in mission.* The second core commitment for Soma groups is that they commit to reach a specific people group. Every missional community has an unreached people group they are reaching.
- *Bottom-up planting.* Their church-planting strategy is that new church-plants emerge from missional communities and not the other way around.
- *Commissioning.* When a group branches, the new community is commissioned for a new people group.

Journey to a Movement

Soma has been on a mission since they were planted seven years ago, but they are still growing and changing. From the beginning, they have been a church of missional communities, starting with just four, and now they have thirty missional communities from Tacoma, Seattle, Boise, and San Diego. Their vision is that missional communities would continue to be the primary life force of the church and that out of these groups, "new expressions of the church" would emerge and gain some form of independence. The shift they are making now is to be a more apostolic movement in which every believer is a church planter and every church is a church-planting church. In the next five years, they want to have missional communities in every major city on the West Coast. Then, in twenty to thirty years, they envision these types of missional communities in every major city in North America.

Challenges

- *Contextualization.* Soma has a threefold template for ministry—the gospel, the people of God, and the everyday rhythms of life. These are the focus of training and mission. The challenge for their communities is working out each of these in their specific contexts as they target certain people groups.
- *Priesthood of believers.* In their efforts toward being a missional movement, they have wrestled with the question, what would it look like if every member of the body of Christ actually was a minister of the gospel?

Westridge Church

Location: Dallas, Georgia
Campuses and size: two campuses in the Atlanta, Georgia, area, with 4,400 people
Established: 1997
Website: *www.westridge.com*
Lead pastor: Brian Bloye

Stories

A twelve-year-old middle school student at Westridge realized that not all kids her age are as fortunate as she is. She went to an affluent school and realized that some do not have backpacks and school materials. So, with the help of her family, she started a nonprofit called Fresh Hope, which raises money for backpacks and school supplies for underresourced kids in the community.

A construction worker at Westridge who had done very well in his business left his job to pursue a missional building project — a community center called Warehouse of Hope. This building serves as a food and clothing pantry for the community to fulfill medical, counseling, and legal needs. The church sends volunteers to this site every week. The people who come pay only eight dollars for sixty dollars' worth of food and get counseling and clothes as well.

Wins

- *Engage Atlanta.* This is a nonprofit designed to break down denominational walls through ecumenical service projects involving various churches from different backgrounds.
- *Catch and release.* The leaders at Westridge are a missional catalyst for their people (catch) and encourage them as they make their ideas a reality (release).
- *Vision casting.* In his sermons on Sunday mornings, Brian always talks about being others-focused.
- *Last Saturday.* The last Saturday of every month, Westridge

sends their people out for three- to five-hour relational-tangible projects in the community. They call this Last Saturday.

- *Storytelling.* The leaders facilitate story-sharing meetings where people will share stories of their missional projects.

Journey to a Movement

Their journey toward a movement is best represented by their annual community projects. They have been a church since 1997, but it was not until four years ago that this movement was awakened in their hearts. They have been involved in mission globally, but it started to become widespread in their campuses when they rallied their people to do an extreme home makeover. The needs of the community were greater than just those of one house, so they decided to do dozens of small projects instead of one large one. The next year, they not only extended the amount of projects to 250 but also included eight other churches in their efforts. Just last year, they had ten thousand people from different churches help with 500 projects, and now they are looking at more than eighty churches working on 875 projects this year! In just four years, they have seen amazing growth and spontaneous projects emerge from their people. As they look forward to the next five years, they want to have five venues, an online campus, and continued growth in community projects.

Challenges

- *Technology.* Westridge wants to utilize this ever-changing tool as they reach the world around them, but their imagination in this area of advancement is still in the early stages.
- *Alignment.* They have found that it takes time to get the missional flywheel moving. It takes patience, consistency, and time.

Notes

Chapter 1: On the Verge of the Future

1. Verge Network hosted its first conference in 2010. It was an instant success. Coming out of a very effective megachurch, Verge Network is the movemental arm which seeks to develop missional church planting across Austin and beyond *(www. vergenetwork.org)*.

2. Everett M. Rogers, *Diffusion of Innovations* (1962; Free Press, 1995) and Malcolm Gladwell, *The Tipping Point: How Little Things Can Make a Big Difference* (Back Bay, 2002).

3. See our list of resources at the back of the book for books on this topic.

4. We did test this idea out with two of *the* foremost researchers in America (we can't give names, because they're simply venturing opinion, but you all know them); they said—averaged out across America—we can be relatively certain the numbers are at least fifty-fifty. That is, what we are currently doing might have appeal to up to 50 percent of the population but not beyond that.

5. We have to face this: The combination of resources, timing, leadership ability, and talent and charisma that come together to make a successful megachurch simply doesn't happen for most churches. In fact, research by Leadership Network, the peak body servicing megachurches in America, indicates there are twelve hundred churches greater than two thousand in the U.S. This segment has grown significantly over the last ten years. But when you consider that there are around four hundred thousand churches in the U.S., with the average attendance of eighty, *then* one gains the real perspective. The *overwhelming* majority of churches won't be able to produce a successful megachurch. And it's not that they haven't tried; they have read the books, attended the conferences, and so on. Forty years of church-growth theory and practice in America has not *fundamentally* altered the decline.

6. W. Chan Kim and Renée Mauborgne, *Blue Ocean Strategy: How to Create Uncontested Market Space and Make the Competition Irrelevant* (Harvard Business, 2005). I am grateful to Mike Breen for referring me to this book.

7. Interview with Rob Wegner, used with permission.

8. Rex Miller, *The Millennium Matrix: Reclaiming the Past, Reframing the Future of the Church* (Jossey-Bass, 2004).

9. See resources at the back of the book for details.

10. Dwight Friesen, *Thy Kingdom Connected* (Baker, 2009) and Neil Cole, *Church 3.0* (Jossey-Bass, 2010).

11. We adopted this metaphor from Ron Gladden at Mission Catalyst Network. *www.missioncatalyst.org/article.php?id=197.*

12. Ori Brafman and Rod Beckstrom, *The Starfish and the Spider: The Unstoppable Power of Leaderless Organizations* (Penguin, 2008).

13. Jim Collins, "Building Companies to Last," *www.jimcollins.com/article_topics/articles/building-companies.html.*

14. "Apostolic Genius" is a term Alan coined that encompasses the genetic code of apostolic movement, or mDNA, and involves six critical elements to be explained later in the book.

15. Dee Hock, *The Birth of the Chaordic Age* (Berrett-Koehler, 1999).

16. M. Mitchell Waldrop, "Dee Hock on Organizations," *Fast Company* 5 (October/November 1996), 84. Online article at *www.fastcompany.com/online/05/dee3.html*.

17. Michael Fullan, *The Six Secrets of Change: What the Best Leaders Do to Help Their Organizations Survive and Thrive* (Jossey-Bass, 2007).

Chapter 2: The Silver Imagination

1. Gordon McKenzie, *Orbiting the Giant Hairball: A Corporate Fool's Guide to Surviving with Grace* (Viking, 1998).

2. Max De Pree, "What Is Leadership?" in Gill Robinson Hickman, *Leading Organizations: Perspectives for a New Era* (Sage, 1998), 130.

3. An organizational paradigm can be defined as "a world view, a frame of reference, or a set of assumptions, usually implicit, about what sorts of things make up the world, how they act, how they hang together, and how they may be known. This world view is composed of three interrelated components: (1) a way of looking at the world which creates an image of the subject matter about the world's phenomena and constructs a system of beliefs; (2) a way of doing things that provides the methods and instruments needed to apply fundamental beliefs to internal and external realities; and (3) an interaction among human agents to support both the belief system and the normative behavior, including social networks that support the adoption and practice of a particular paradigm." Hasan Simsek, "Organizational Change As Paradigm Shift: Analysis of the Change Process in a Large, Public University," *Journal of Higher Education* 65, no. 6 (November–December 1994): 670.

4. Gary E. Schwartz, *The G.O.D. Experiments: How Science Is Discovering God in Everything* (Atria, 2006), 197.

5. Russell H. Granger, *The 7 Triggers to Yes: The New Science behind Influencing People's Decisions* (McGraw-Hill, 2008), 216.

6. Walter Isaacson, *Einstein: His Life and Universe* (Simon & Schuster, 2007), 7.

7. From one of Geoff Maddock's (and Sherry's) monthly newsletters.

8. The next few paragraphs draw heavily from ideas developed in Alan Hirsch, *The Forgotten Ways: Reactivating the Missional Church* (Brazos, 2007).

9. Thomas Kuhn, *The Structure of Scientific Revolutions* (Phoenix, 1962). Kuhn specifically explored how paradigms play themselves out in the advance of scientific knowledge. He noted that because science, in her best moments (just like the church), is always searching for greater understanding and truth, the desire for deep knowledge and understanding drives it, and so imaginative leaps in learning bring about changes in paradigm.

10. Science is so committed to the search for answers based on verifiable truth that there have been a number of significant clearly discernable paradigm shifts in its history. Most notable have been the shift from the pre-Copernican to the Copernican, and from the Newtonian to the Einsteinian, and from relativity to quantum physics, and so on. As Lewis Mumford notes, "Every (transition) ... has rested on a new metaphysical and ideological base, or rather upon deeper stirrings

and intuitions whose rationalized expressions take the form of a new picture of the cosmos and of (humanity)." Quoted in Bill Easum, *Leadership on the Other Side* (Abingdon, 2000), 31.

11. David Bosch, *Transforming Mission: Paradigm Shifts in the Theology of Mission* (Orbis, 1992), chap. 5.

12. Bill Easum, *Unfreezing Moves: Following Jesus into the Mission Field* (Abingdon, 2001), 31.

13. Do an exercise: go to Google images, type in "Escher drawing," and then study the diagrams. They force you to see things from different directions. These are great examples of how paradigms frame and filter our perceptions.

14. Quoted in Corita Kent and Jan Steward, *Learning by Heart: Teaching to Free the Creative Spirit* (Allworth, 2008), 12.

15. Richard Ogle, *Smart World: Breakthrough Creativity and the New Science of Ideas* (Harvard Business School, 2007), 63–65.

16. Garrett Green, *Imagining God: Theology and the Religious Imagination* (Eerdmans, 1989), 109–11.

17. Bill Easum, *Leadership on the Other Side: No Rules, Just Clues* (Abingdon, 2000), 39.

18. Thomas Kuhn, *The Structure of Scientific Revolutions* (Phoenix, 1962).

19. Ogle, *Smart World*.

20. David Kord Murray, *Borrowing Brilliance: The Six Steps to Business Innovation by Building on the Ideas of Others* (Gotham: 2009), 111–12.

21. William James, *The Principles of Psychology* (Cosimo, 1890), 110.

22. Again, we quote our friend Rob Wegner here in his profound feedback he gave on the text: "There's a lot about 'remembering' in the Bible. In the Old Testament, God would call His people to build altars out of stones so they would remember. He instructed them to tie the law on a string and bind it around the fingers, put it on their doorposts. Remember, remember, remember ... And in the Bible, remembering is more than just recalling information. In the Bible, when you remember something, if you do it right, what was real once before becomes present, becomes real once again. When you consider the constant injunction in the Bible, especially in Deuteronomy, to remember, this injunction from Isaiah stands out like a diamond against black velvet." The injunction: "Forget the former things; do not dwell on the past. See, I am doing a new thing! Now it springs up; do you not perceive it? I am making a way in the desert and streams in the wasteland" (Isa. 43:18–19).

23. Alan Hirsch and Michael Frost, *ReJesus: A Wild Messiah for a Missional Church* (Hendrickson, 2009).

24. For a thoroughgoing study on how principalities and powers relate to organizational life in the New Testament and today, see Walter Wink's *The Powers That Be: Theology for a New Millennium* (Galilee Trade, 1999).

25. Alan Hirsch and Lance Ford, *Right Here, Right Now: Everyday Mission for Everyday People* (Baker, 2011).

26. *Newsweek* (July 19, 2010), 50.

Chapter 3: Mission to the Mind and Heart

1. Nicholas Ind, *Living the Brand: How to Transform Every Member of Your Organization into a Brand Champion* (Kogan-Page, 2001), 30.

2. Lars Kolind, *The Second Cycle: Winning the War against Bureacracy* (Wharton School, 2006) and Gareth Morgan, *Imaginization: New Mindsets for Seeing, Organizing, and Managing* (Barret-Koehler, 1993).

3. See the chapter "Refocusing the Family" in my book *Untamed: Reactivating a Missional Form of Discipleship* (Baker, 2010).

4. In *Untamed,* my wife, Deb, and I constantly remind the reader of the difference between holiness and moralism and the temptations to confuse the two. This is a major problem in societies where Christianity has been the predominant religion for so long.

5. Clotaire Rapaille, *The Culture Code: An Ingenious Way to Understand Why People around the World Live and Buy the Way They Do* (Broadway, 1996).

6. Alan Hirsch and Michael Frost, *The Shaping of Things to Come: Innovation and Mission for the 21st Century Church* (Hendrickson, 2003), chap. 11.

7. See my forthcoming book with Michael Frost, which is a theology of adventure and risk and explores the implications of these for church, mission, leadership, discipleship, and spirituality: *The Faith of Leap: Embracing a Theology of Adventure, Risk, and Courage* (Baker, 2011).

8. Daniel H. Pink, *A Whole New Mind: Why Right-Brainers Will Rule the Future* (Riverhead, 2005).

9. This involves seeing the big picture, crossing conceptual boundaries, and the ability to take seemingly unrelated pieces and form and articulate the big picture. Pink, *A Whole New Mind*, 130.

10. Alan Hirsch, *The Forgotten Ways: Reactivating the Missional Church* (Brazos, 2007), 160–62, 117.

11. Hirsch and Frost, *The Shaping of Things to Come*, 124–26.

12. Rodney Stark, *The Rise of Christianity: How the Obscure, Marginal Jesus Movement Became the Dominant Religious Force in a Few Centuries* (Princeton Univ. Press, 1996) has a whole chapter on how women played a role in the mission of the church. See also Stark's *Cities of God: The Real Story of How Christianity Became an Urban Movement and Conquered Rome* (HarperOne, 2006) for how women and slaves played significant roles in the movement.

13. Jon Zens, *What's with Paul and Women?* (Ecclessia Press, 2010) provides a scripturally rooted and missionally sensitive exploration of the dignity, giftedness, and role of women in church life.

14. Hirsch, *The Forgotten Ways*, 151, 248–49.

15. Frank Trippett, "Slogan Power! Slogan Power!" *Time* (February 12, 1979), *http://bit.ly/5JNXzV.*

16. Ibid.

17. This outright rejection of ideas because they are new is called the Semmelweis Reflex and is a human phenomenon. See *http://bit.ly/1dsOS1.*

18. Chip Heath and Dan Heath, *Made to Stick: Why Some Ideas Survive and Others Die* (Random House, 2007).

19. Ibid., 16.

20. Ibid., 116.

21. Ibid., 17.

22. Ibid.

23. Ibid.

24. Ibid., 17–18.

25. Everett M. Rogers, *Diffusion of Innovations* (1962; Free Press, 1995).

26. For instance, Ed Stetzer and David Putnam suggest this: "One of the most important considerations in breaking the [missional] code is to break from our own preferences. Simply put, being missional doesn't mean doing things the way we like them. It means to take the gospel into the context where we have been called.... You cannot be missional and pick what you like at the same time." *Breaking the Missional Code: Your Church Can Become a Missionary in Your Community* (Broadman & Holman, 2006), 50.

27. Neil Postman, *Teaching As a Subversive Activity* (Delta, 1969), 136.

28. Peter Drucker, *The Five Most Important Questions You Will Ever Ask about Your Organization* (Jossey-Bass, 2008), 54.

Part 2: Introduction to the "Shift" Section

1. See his online essay "Living a Transformed Life Adequate to Our Calling," *http://bit.ly/9Blogm*.

2. In the complex systems of the existing church, lasting and deep change must come from the mouth of the river, the paradigm level. Even so, this is not to say that the process is a one-way street. Again, we must think systems, with their two-way flows. The best way to look at this process is as so: paradigm ↔ethos ↔practice. Each element or layer is always dynamically interacting with the others. Renewal takes place along these lines.

3. It must be stated here that in making this massive claim, I do not believe that this is the product of my supposedly smart intellect. I feel that I have been a custodian of something given to me to pass on. I really feel this has been a revelation to me. I do not claim any authority in that; I simply state it as I have experienced it. Also, *The Forgotten Ways* thesis has been out there for five years now, and no one has been able to fault its claims as yet. And while it needs more study, it seems to apply.

4. This is a big claim, but we stand by it. To be sure, in *The Forgotten Ways* Alan is suggesting that while distinct movements in history might have more than six elements present, they never have less than the six described here. As such, the six elements of mDNA represent the irreducible *phenomenology* of all apostolic movements in every time and place. Once again we suggest that leadership wishing to apply the Verge church process should seriously engage the ideas laid out in *The Forgotten Ways* and *The Forgotten Ways Handbook*. Furthermore, all of Alan's books are in some ways elaborations and developments of the key ideas of *The Forgotten Ways*. Dave's book *Exponential* is a further elaboration of the ideas of movements.

5. In *The Forgotten Ways*, Alan elaborates on this idea of latent potentials and partly draws it out from the logical implications of the fact that a young believer, scattered by persecution, can start a church and a church can start a movement. In other words, it must have all been present in potential in the smallest part, in this case the fleeing believer. As a seed contains the full potential of a forest, and the spark contains the full potential of a forest fire, so even the smallest unit of *ecclesia* carries the potential for the whole movement.

6. This is the chief metaphor of Ori Brafman and Rod A. Beckstrom's book *The*

Starfish and the Spider: The Unstoppable Power of Leaderless Organizations (Portfolio, 2006).

7. Rob Wegner recently told me of Satheya Salin, a man he met on a trip to India not long ago. This man was first to bring the gospel to an unreached people group called the Paliyar. They live at the top of the mountain in the jungle, harvesting honey and fungus from trees to survive. Satheya, the church planter who brought the good news to them, is a day laborer who carries wood for a living. He has a fifth-grade education. From the viewpoint of the world, he is among the most insignificant people on the planet. He is poor, uneducated, and noninfluential. Yet, in light of eternity, he is among the most significant people on the planet. In terms of what really matters, what is more important than ushering a new people group into the kingdom? The Paliyar are spread out in villages all over that mountain range. Satheya is giving the rest of his life to plant churches in each village. So he works sixty hours a week hauling wood, but the rest of the time he is the pastor of the Paliyar people. I could talk for an hour straight about him. If Satheya Salin can do it, anyone can do it.

8. Does this mean that all the churches that result from spontaneous expansion are mature? Of course not! But are most of the churches in the dominant expression of church in the West mature? We don't think so! So maturity is another matter, and immaturity is not limited to people-movements.

9. In many ways, it is a radicalizing process, because it takes us to the roots (Latin, *radix*) of apostolic movements.

Chapter 4: Apostolic Genius

1. Read *The Starfish and the Spider*, for instance. Also Dee Hock, *One from Many: VISA and the Rise of Chaordic Organization* (Berrett Koehler, 2005).

2. Alan Hirsch, *The Forgotten Ways: Reactivating the Missional Church* (Brazos, 2007), and Alan Hirsch and Darryn Altcass, *The Forgotten Ways Handbook: A Practical Guide for Developing Missional Churches* (Brazos, 2010).

3. This emphasis on Christology (the phenomenon of Jesus) doesn't obscure the reality of the Trinity but rather gives it a distinct shape. We are introduced into the Trinitarian life of God exactly as we have received it—through the lens of the life and ministry of Jesus. It means that our focus as *Christ*-ians, our very identity, is directly related to our understanding and experience of Christ. It is the second person of the Trinity who is the Mediator between God and man; no one can come to the Father except by means of him. And the Spirit is given to the church to lead us into a true understanding of God in Christ.

4. This concept is more thoroughly discussed in Alan Hirsch and Michael Frost, *ReJesus: A Wild Messiah for a Missional Church* (Hendrickson, 2009).

5. Hirsch, *The Forgotten Ways*, 114–16.

6. Find at *www.weare3DM.com*.

7. Also behind this theology lies a "formula": Christology determines missiology, which in turn determines ecclesiology. Another way of saying this is that God in Christ sets the agenda (mission) for the church, and the mission in turn determines and shapes the cultural forms of *ecclesia*. This will be very important in the Verge process because it helps us understand how mission prompts innovation in cultural expressions of church. Hirsch, *The Forgotten Ways*, 142–44.

8. Find at *www.apest.org*.

9. Apostolic environment is such an important issue, I've developed a new book with Mike Breen and Tim Catchim on the topic. I feel strongly that key leadership in any church that wants to move toward the kind of apostolic movement described herein can't afford to miss this. *The Permanent Revolution: Apostolic Imagination and Practice in the 21st Century Church* (Jossey Bass, 2011) — to be published in late 2011. See also Hirsch, *The Forgotten Ways*, chap. 6.

10. Some underground movements in China have around three million adherents, and they do it without centralized headquarters, vast payrolls, buildings, etc. History proves time and again that these kinds of movements are somewhat unstoppable because they are highly committed, can reproduce rapidly, are hard to eradicate, and tend to bypass the need for centralized structures. In short, they simply spread from person to person.

11. Find at *www.somacommunities.org*.

12. Vineyard Central is the epitome of a church that is morphing with its mission. It was a conventional congregation in Cincinnati until the church building was condemned by the city. Instead of getting another building, the pastor made an unconventional move and had the congregants stand in the sanctuary based on zip codes during their final Sunday gathering. He then said, "Look around you. This is now your church." And a network of house churches was born. Since then, they weaned themselves off virtually all administrative costs, live in several monastic-style community houses, and own an old Catholic church building that they use as an art space, periodic homeless shelter, and place for monthly larger gatherings. See *www. vineyardcentral.com/about*.

13. Again, this is a massive issue in itself. Mike Frost and I have teamed up again to produce a book right on topic; it's tentatively titled *The Faith of Leap: Embracing a Theology of Adventure, Risk, and Courage* (Baker, 2011).

14. Further reading to defamiliarize yourself with these terms, respectively, would be Leonard Sweet and Frank Viola's *Jesus Manifesto* (Nelson, 2010) and Dallas Willard's *The Renovation of the Heart* (NavPress, 2002).

15. In our book *Exponential*, Jon Ferguson and I give a full chapter explaining what it means to apprentice with Jesus and to enter into a life-on-life apprenticeship with someone else.

16. From a February 12, 2002, Department of Defense news briefing, as recorded by *Salon* at *www.slate.com/id/2081042*.

Chapter 5: Verge Vibe

1. *Third place* is a term referring to a social environment separate from the home and the workplace. Community planners, entrepreneurs, and sociologists have popularized the term over the last two decades.

2. If most people can't easily discern the decidedly intangible contours of the paradigm, they certainly can intuit the feel of a culture and understand some of the ideas that come together to create ethos. Even though ethos is still somewhat conceptual, it is more concrete than the paradigm level, and so more people can access this. We are all well-attuned to cultural vibe.

3. Ernest Becker, *The Denial of Death* (Free Press, 1973), 1–11.

4. We all do this to some degree or another, and when branding is left to some

indistinct, unconscious process, even more damage can be done than if we were out there being manipulative spin doctors. Branding should be about responsibility and integrity, not manipulation.

5. Michael Stewart has done much to champion the missional movement through Verge. A great grassroots activist, he has guided much of Austin Stone's learnings over the last few years. In my opinion, the whole leadership team is one of the best expressions of a Verge church ethos around today. *http://vergenetwork.org*.

6. A powerful recent book on how Jesus' life and ministry breaks down the dualisms of the false sacred-secular dichotomy and presents a nondualistic spiritual approach of embodying the kingdom is Richard Rohr's *The Naked Now* (Crossroad, 2009).

7. See Alan Hirsch and Debra Hirsch, *Untamed: Reactivating a Missional Form of Discipleship* (Baker, 2010), 146–57 for an elaboration of this idea.

8. We suggest getting your people to do an APEST test *(www.apest.org)* and then helping develop their gifts appropriately.

9. Warren Bennis and Patricia Ward Biederman, *Organizing Genius* (Purseus: 1997), 24, 95.

10. Hirsch, *The Forgotten Ways*, 233–36.

11. John P. Kotter, *A Sense of Urgency* (Harvard Business Press, 2008).

12. Will Mancini, *Church Unique: How Missional Leaders Cast Vision, Capture Culture and Create Movement* (Jossey-Bass, 2008). The particular contribution of this book is that it provides both a systematic process and a helpful model to summarize your ethos in a clear, concise, yet comprehensive way.

Chapter 6: Embodying Movement-Programming Practices

1. Alan Hirsch and Darryn Altcass, *The Forgotten Ways Handbook: A Practical Guide for Developing Missional Churches* (Brazos, 2010).

2. Is what we are saying here undermining the Verge process we have articulated in these last few chapters? No. Because however we might think of them, our practices don't rise in a vacuum; they are outward and visible expressions of what we think are important. They are formulated out of what we believe and are given their true meaning and significance from the way we perceive the world and our place within it. In other words, our practices are both expressions of our paradigms and embodiments of our ethos. Rather than thinking of this as being in conflict with the Verge process, think of it as simply reinforcing and supporting it.

3. Max Dimont calls these rhythms and practices "ritual markers" and maintains that these are the primary reasons for the longevity and survival of the Jewish people over time and through dispersion. *Jews, God and History*, 2nd ed. (Penguin, 1994).

4. Find at *www.smallboatbigsea.org/bells*.

5. Find at *www.3dministries.com*.

6. Find at *www.missionorder.org*.

7. Find at *http://bit.ly/9aHxeB*.

8. This is a place where sacramental churches can transform their age-old catechumenate process into real missional dynamite by making it the first stage of a lifetime apprenticeship to Jesus. The traditional Easter baptism can then become ordination and commissioning!

9. Neil Cole is undoubtedly the best articulator of organic church as a movement in our day. See *Church 3.0* (Jossey-Bass, 2010); *Search & Rescue* (Baker, 2008), chap. 5; *Organic Leadership* (Baker, 2010), chap. 18; *Organic Church* (Jossey-Bass, 2005), chap. 8.

10. Find at *www.rivertreechristian.com*.

11. Alan Hirsch, *The Forgotten Ways: Reactivating the Missional Church* (Brazos, 2007), 235.

12. TEMPT stands for Together we follow, Engagement with Scripture, Mission, Passion for Jesus, and Transformation. See how they worked in practice in chapter one of *The Forgotten Ways*.

13. Keith Ferrazzi and Tahl Raz, *Never Eat Alone: And Other Secrets to Success, One Relationship at a Time* (Broadway Business, 2005).

Chapter 7: Innovate or Die

1. Find at *http://rookery4.aviary.com/storagev12/2216500/2216992_4b81_625x 1000.jpg*.

2. Find at *www.wired.com/wired/archive/15.05/st_badideas.html*.

3. Find at *www.strangenewproducts.com/2005/08/lawngrips-shoes-for-lawn-mowing .html*.

4. Find at *http://the99percent.com/videos/5995/scott-belsky-creativity-x-organization -impact*.

5. Find at *www.bigelowhomes.com/downloads/NBOTY_article.pdf*.

6. Find at *www.wbur.org/npr/126229305*.

7. This is from Theodore M. Hesburgh in his book *God, Country, Notre Dame* (University of Notre Dame Press, 2000).

8. Peter Drucker, *Innovation and Entrepreneurship: Practice and Principle*, 34.

9. Hugh Halter and Matt Smay, *AND: The Gathered and Scattered Church* (Zondervan, 2010).

10. Find at *http://missio.us*.

11. Find at *http://compassionbydesign.org*.

12. Find at *http://www.instituteforcommunity.org/Pages/Community%20Life.aspx*.

13. Find at *www.bryanhouse.org*.

14. Drucker, *Innovation and Entrepreneurship*.

15. Find at *www.time.com/time/specials/packages/completelist/0,29569,1898670,00 .html*.

16. Find at *www.time.com/time/specials/packages/article/0,28804,1898670 _1898671_1898679,00.html*.

17. Find at *www.foodfightforhunger.com*.

18. Erwin McManus, *The Barbarian Way: Unleash the Untamed Faith Within* (Nelson, 2005), 50–52.

19. Alan Hirsch, *The Forgotten Ways: Reactivating the Missional Church* (Brazos, 2007), 151, 232–33, 273.

20. Ibid., 261.

21. See, for instance, *http://bit.ly/bBtOgi*.

22. Steve Addison, *Movements That Change the World* (Missional, 2009), 106–7.

23. Find at *http://bit.ly/aBVcdF*.

Chapter 8: Out-of-the-Box Innovation

1. This is well documented and accepted. See, for instance, Marshall McLuhan, *The Guttenberg Galaxy: The Making of Typographic Man* (Univ. of Toronto Press, 2002) and Rex Miller, *The Millennium Matrix* (Jossey-Bass, 2004), chap. 2.

2. Marshall McLuhan, *Understanding Media: The Extensions of Man* (Routledge, 2005).

3. See, for instance, Richard Ogle, *Smart World: Breakthrough Creativity and the New Science of Ideas* (Harvard Business School Press, 2007).

4. Ogle, *Smart World*, chap. 2.

5. Ibid.

6. James C. Collins and Jerry I. Porras, *Built to Last* (Century, 1996).

7. Alan Hirsch and Michael Frost, *The Shaping of Things to Come: Innovation and Mission for the 21st Century Church* (Hendrickson, 2003).

8. For some rules of brainstorming, see *http://bit.ly/11DKXI*.

9. Take the test to determine what thinking type you are: *http://bit.ly/crbT9*.

Chapter 9: Gaining Missional Momentum

1. Dave Olson, *American Church in Crisis*.

2. A good example of sacramental church practiced missionally is the Anglican Church in North America and their goal of planting hundreds of missional sacramental churches in the next decade. See Todd Hunter, *Giving Church Another Chance* (InterVarsity, 2010).

3. Richard Bolles, *What Color Is Your Parachute?*

4. The mPULSE assessment can be taken at *www.theforgottenways.org/mpulse*.

5. *www.divinebacknine.com*.

6. Find at *www.theforgottenways.org/mpulse* to take your group's mPulse.

7. Peter Senge, *The Fifth Discipline: The Art and Practice of the Learning Organization* (Random House, 2006), part 1.

8. NCD is church-growth theory that helped us to factor systems-thinking into church development *(www.ncd-international.org)*. Barrel used with permission. While being a great tool to help churches with quality-type approaches to church health, it is not a tool that helps engender movement. By and large, it assumes the prevailing, more institutional form of church.

9. The mPULSE assessment is very reasonably priced at thirty-five dollars per test. We have tried to make it this way because it should be used regularly (say, annually) to assess and readjust strategy.

Chapter 10: The Making of an Apostolic Movement

1. David Garrison, *Church Planting Movements: How God Is Redeeming a Lost World* (Wigtake Resources, 2003).

2. Roland Allen, *The Spontaneous Expansion of the Church: And the Causes That Hinder It* (World Dominion, 1927).

3. Neil Cole, *Church 3.0* (Jossey-Bass, 2010).

4. The works used to create this list are: Ori Brafman and Rod A. Beckstrom, *The Starfish and the Spider: The Unstoppable Power of Leaderless Organizations* (Portfolio, 2006); Cole, *Church 3.0*; Roland Allen, *Missionary Methods: St. Paul's or Ours?* (Eerdmans, 1962); Garrison, *Church Planting Movements*; Dave Ferguson and Jon

Ferguson, *Exponential: How You and Your Friends Can Start a Missional Church Movement* (Zondervan, 2010); Alan Hirsch, *The Forgotten Ways: Reactivating the Missional Church* (Brazos, 2007); Steve Addison, *Movements That Change the World* (Missional, 2009).

5. Cole, *Church 3.0.*

6. Roland Allen, *Missionary Methods: St. Paul's or Ours*, 90.

7. Garrison, *Church Planting Movements*, 21–22.

8. Ferguson and Ferguson, *Exponential.*

9. Addison, *Movements That Change the World.*

10. For a penetrating analysis of the reasons for rise of movements and their decline, see Roger Fink and Rodney Stark, *The Churching of America: 1776–2005* (Rutgers Univ. Press, 2005).

11. Addison, *Movements That Change the World*, 74, 88, 97.

12. Ibid., 92. This made them by far the largest religious body in the nation. There was only one national institution that was more extensive: the U.S. government. What is startling is that this growth curve was slowed and eventually reversed through one major cause—the requirement that the circuit riders get degrees and master Hebrew, Latin, and Greek in seminaries.

13. I am grateful to Peter Corney for introducing this change management interpretation of Rogers' theories to me.

14. Hirsch, *The Forgotten Ways*, chapter on organic systems. See also suggested resources at the back of the book.

Resources for Verging the Church

Here are some of the key resources available for developing missional forms of church. They are arranged as key training systems, online tools for assessment and strategy, and books cataloged by category.

Training Systems

3D Ministries is an interdenominational and innovative church-movement that has planted hundreds of churches as they learn how to engage the European and American post-Christian culture *(www.3dministries.com)*.

Forge Mission Training Network International, or Forge, (U.S., Canada, Australia) is a training center that exists to birth and nurture the missional church. They provide training, internships, resources, and consulting for church leaders *(www.forge.org.au, www.forgecanada. ca, www.forgeamerica.org)*.

Future Travelers is a two-year learning cohort initially composed of twelve megachurches (representing more than eighty thousand people) committed to seriously factoring missional movements into their current equation of church.

Missio exists to inspire and apprentice the church's missional spirit — one leader, one church, and one organization at a time. Codirectors Hugh Halter and Matt Smay and their team provide training and resources to church leaders *(www.missio.us)*.

NewThing (www.newthing.org) is an international movement of reproducing churches and networks relentlessly committed to the mission of helping people find their way back to God.

Shapevine is a ministry of *Leadership Journal* and *Christianity Today* that focuses on providing people with missional resources, training, and networking opportunities *(www.shapevine.com)*.

Together in Mission (TIM) is a British training system led by pioneering missiologist Martin Robinson *(http://togetherinmission.co.uk/)*. It offers degrees from the University of Wales and does the training in local church contexts.

GCM Collective, led by Jeff Vanderstelt and Caesar Kalinowski. Learning from the experience of Soma, one of the Future Traveler churches *(www.gcmcollective.com).*

Tools for Change

APEST. This is a highly regarded tool to help people access and operate in their fivefold ministry vocation. This can be done individually and (even better) in teams, using 360-degree feedback that the test provides *(www.theforgottenways.org/apest* or *www.apest.org).*

mPULSE. This is a test designed to help churches and organizations diagnose and strategize using the concept of Apostolic Genius as the central core. It is designed with Verge churches in mind. It can be taken as small as cell group level as well as systemwide *(www.theforgottenways.org/mpulse).*

Key Books for Verge Churches

More from Alan Hirsch

Hirsch, Alan. *The Forgotten Ways: Reactivating the Missional Church.* Brazos, 2007.

Hirsch, Alan, and Darryn Altcass. *The Forgotten Ways Handbook: A Practical Guide for Developing Missional Churches.* Baker, 2009.

Hirsch, Alan, and Tim Catchim. *The Permanent Revolution: Apostolic Imagination and Practice for the 21st Century Church.* Jossey-Bass, 2011.

Hirsch, Alan, and Lance Ford. *Right Here, Right Now: Everyday Mission for Everyday People.* Baker, 2011.

Hirsch, Alan, and Michael Frost. *The Faith of Leap: Embracing a Theology of Risk, Adventure, and Courage.* Baker, 2011.

———. *ReJesus: A Wild Messiah for a Missional Church.* Hendrickson, 2009.

———. *The Shaping of Things to Come: Innovation and Mission for the 21st-Century Church.* Hendrickson, 2003.

Hirsch, Alan, and Debra Hirsch. *Untamed: Reactivating a Missional Form of Discipleship.* Baker, 2010.

More from Dave Ferguson

Ferguson, Dave, and Jon Ferguson. *Exponential: How You and Your Friends Can Start a Missional Church Movement.* Zondervan, 2010.

Ferguson, Dave, Jon Ferguson, and Eric Bramlet. *The Big Idea: Focus the Message, Multiply the Impact.* Zondervan, 2007.

From Neil Cole

While Cole is something of a purist in relation to distinctly organic forms and perspectives, his writings are nonetheless excellent examples of apostolic movement thinking and are highly accessible. We recommend:

Cole, Neil. *Church 3.0: Upgrades for the Future of the Church.* Jossey-Bass, 2010.

———. *Organic Church: Growing Faith Where Life Happens.* Jossey-Bass, 2005.

From Ed Stetzer

Stetzer writes largely from a church-planting perspective. Two of his most helpful books are written collaboratively:

Stetzer, Ed, and Warren Bird. *Viral Churches.* Jossey-Bass, 2010.

Stetzer, Ed, and Thom S. Rainer. *Transformational Church.* Broadman & Holman, 2010.

From Steve Addison

Steve Addison has been a consultant and researcher on church planting movements. He lives in Australia and leads Church Resource Ministry there.

Addison, Steve. *Movements That Change the World.* Missional, 2009.

Other Relevant Books

People-Movements

Allen, Roland. *The Spontaneous Expansion of the Church: And the Causes That Hinder It.* World Dominion, 1927.

Anderson, Allan. *Spreading Fires: The Missionary Nature of Early Pentecostalism.* Orbis, 2007.

Cahill, Thomas. *How the Irish Saved Civilization: The Untold Story of Ireland's Heroic Role from the Fall of Rome to the Rise of Medieval Europe.* Doubleday, 1995.

Finke, Roger. "Innovative Returns to Tradition: Using Core Teachings as the Foundation for Innovative Accomodation." *Journal for the Scientific Study of Religion* 43:1, (2004): 19–34.

Finke, Roger, and Rodney Stark. *The Churching of America, 1776–1990: Winners and Losers in Our Religious Economy.* Rutgers Univ., 1992.

———. "How the Upstart Sects Won America 1776–1850." *Journal for the Scientific Study of Religion* 28:1 (1989): 27–44.

Resources for Verging the Church **345**

Garrison, David. *Church Planting Movements: How God Is Redeeming a Lost World.* Wigtake Resources, 2003.

Gerlach, Luther P., and Virgina H. Hine. "Five Factors Crucial to the Growth and Spread of a Modern Religious Movement." *Journal for the Scientific Study of Religion* 7 (1968): 23–40.

———. *People, Power, Change: Movements of Social Transformation.* Bobbs-Merrill, 1970. Out of print.

Gladwell, Malcolm. *The Tipping Point: How Little Things Can Make a Big Difference.* Little, Brown and Co., 2000.

Godin, Seth. *Tribes: We Need You to Lead Us.* Penguin, 2008.

Heath, Chip, and Dan Heath. *Made to Stick.* Random House, 2007.

Heitzenrater, Richard P. *Wesley and the People Called Methodists.* Abingdon, 1994.

Hock, Dee. *One from Many: VISA and the Rise of Chaordic Organization.* Berrett-Koehler, 2005.

Hutton, J. E. *A History of the Moravian Church.* 2nd ed. Moravian Publication Office, 1909.

Kelley, Dean M. *Why Conservative Churches Are Growing: A Study in Sociology of Religion.* HarperCollins, 1972. Out of print.

Lewis, Arthur James. *Zinzendorf, the Ecumenical Pioneer: A Study in the Moravian Contribution to Christian Mission and Unity.* Westminster, 1962. Out of print.

Logan, Robert E. *Be Fruitful and Multiply.* Churchsmart Resources, 2006.

Moore, Ralph. *How to Multiply Your Church: The Most Effective Way to Grow.* Regal, 2009.

Pollock, John Charles. *A Cambridge Movement.* John Murray, 1953. Out of print.

Roberts, Bob. *The Multiplying Church: The New Math for Starting New Churches.* Zondervan, 2008.

Snyder, Howard A. *Signs of the Spirit: How God Reshapes the Church.* Wipf & Stock, 1997.

Stark, Rodney. *Cities of God: The Real Story of How Christianity Became an Urban Movement and Conquered Rome.* HarperSanFrancisco, 2006.

———. *The Rise of Christianity: A Sociologist Reconsiders History.* Princeton Univ., 1996.

Timmis, Steve, ed. *Multiplying Churches: Reaching Today's Communities through Church Planting.* Christian Focus, 2000.

Visser 'T Hooft, Willem Adolph. *The Renewal of the Church: The Dale Lectures delivered at Mansfield College, Oxford, October 1955.* SCM, 1956. Out of print.

Missional Church

Allen, Roland. *Missionary Methods: St. Paul's or Ours?* Eerdmans, 1962.

Bergquist, Linda, and Allen Carr. *Church Turned Inside Out: A Guide for Designers, Refiners, and Re-aligners.* Jossey-Bass, 2010.

Breen, Mike, and Alex Absalom. *Launching Missional Communities: A Field Guide.* Weare3dm, 2011.

Gibbons, Dave. *The Monkey and the Fish: Liquid Leadership for a Third-Culture Church.* Zondervan, 2009.

Guder, Darrel. *Missional Church: A Vision for the Sending of the Church in North America.* Eerdmans, 1998.

Hull, John. *Mission-Shaped Church: A Theological Response.* SCM, 2006.

Mancini, Will. *Church Unique: How Missional Leaders Cast Vision, Capture Culture, and Create Movement.* Jossey-Bass, 2008.

McNeal, Reggie. *Missional Renaissance: Changing the Scorecard for the Church.* Jossey-Bass, 2009.

Minatrea, Milfred. *Shaped by God's Heart: The Passion and Practices of Missional Churches.* Jossey-Bass, 2004.

Stetzer, Ed. *Planting Missional Churches.* Broadman & Holman, 2006.

Winter, Ralph. "The Two Structures of God's Redemptive Mission." In Ralph D. Winter, *Perspectives on the World Christian Movement: A Reader.* William Carey Library, 1999.

Incarnational Mission

Barker, Ashley, and John Hayes. *Sub-merge: Living Deep in a Shallow World.* Go Alliance, 2002.

Guder, Darrel. *The Incarnation and the Church's Witness.* Wipf & Stock, 2004.

Halter, Hugh. *The Tangible Kingdom: Creating Incarnational Community: The Posture and Practices of Ancient Church Now.* Jossey-Bass, 2008.

Halter, Hugh, and Matt Smay. *AND: The Gathered and Scattered Church.* Zondervan, 2010.

Missional Discipleship

Breen, Mike. *The Passionate Church.* NexGen, 2005.

———. *A Passionate Life.* NexGen, 2005.

Cole, Neil. *Search & Rescue.* Baker, 2008.

Frost, Michael. *Exiles: Living Missionally in a Post-Christian Culture.* Hendrickson, 2006.

Gupta, Paul R., and Sherwood G. Lingenfelter. *Breaking Tradition to Accomplish Vision: Training Leaders for a Church-Planting Movement: A Case from India.* BMH, 2006.

Hirsch, Alan, and Debra Hirsch. *Untamed: Reactivating a Missional Form of Discipleship.* Baker, 2010.

Nouwen, Henri. *The Return of the Prodigal Son.* Doubleday, 1994.

Willard, Dallas. *The Divine Conspiracy: Rediscovering Our Hidden Life in God.* HarperSanFrancisco, 1998.

————. *The Great Omission: Rediscovering Jesus' Essential Teachings on Discipleship.* HarperSanFrancisco, 2006.

Missional Leadership and Ministry

Cole, Neil. *Organic Leadership: Leading Naturally Right Where You Are.* Baker, 2010.

Creps, Earl. *Off-Road Disciplines: Spiritual Adventures of Missional Leaders.* Jossey-Bass, 2006.

Goleman, Daniel. *Primal Leadership: Learning to Lead with Emotional Intelligence.* Harvard Business School, 2004.

Roxburgh, Alan. *The Missional Leader: Equipping Your Church to Reach a Changing World.* Jossey-Bass, 2006.

Multiethnic church

Anderson, David. *Multicultural Ministry: Finding Your Church's Unique Rhythm.* Zondervan, 2004.

DeYmaz, Mark. *Building a Healthy Multi-ethnic Church: Mandate, Commitments and Practices of a Diverse Congregation.* Jossey-Bass, 2007.

DeYmaz, Mark, and Harry Li. *Ethnic Blends: Mixing Diversity into Your Local Church.* Zondervan, 2010.

DeYoung, Curtiss Paul, Michael Emerson, George Yancey, and Karen Chai Kim, *United By Faith: The Multiracial Church and the Answer to the Problem of Race in America.* Oxford Univ., 2004.

Emerson, Michael, and Christian Smith. *Divided by Faith: Evangelical Religion and the Problem of Race in America.* Oxford Univ., 2001.

Rah, Soong Chan. *Many Colors: Cultural Intelligence for a Changing Church.* Moody, 2010.

Yancey, George. *One Body, One Spirit: Principles of Successful Multiracial Churches.* InterVarsity, 2003.

Leadership, Organizations, and Change

Adizes, Ichak. *Corporate Lifecycles: How and Why Corporations Grow and Die and What to Do About It.* 4th ed. Prentice Hall, 1998. Out of print.

————. *Managing Corporate Lifecycles.* Prentice Hall, 1999.

Arbuckle, Gerald A. *Refounding the Church: Dissent for Leadership.* Orbis, 1993.

Barker, Joel Arthur. *Paradigms: The Business of Discovering the Future.* HarperBusiness, 1993.

Brafman, Ori, and Rod A. Beckstrom. *The Starfish and the Spider: The Unstoppable Power of Leaderless Organizations*. Portfolio, 2006.

Collins, James. *Good to Great: Why Some Companies Make the Leap . . . and Others Don't*. HarperCollins, 2001.

————. *Good to Great and the Social Sectors: A Monograph to Accompany Good to Great*. Random House, 2006.

Collins, James, and Jerry I. Porras. *Built to Last: Successful Habits of Visionary Companies*. Century, 1994.

Godin, Seth. *Tribes: We Need You to Lead Us*. Penguin, 2008.

Heifetz, Ronald. *Leadership on the Line: Staying Alive through the Dangers of Leading*. Harvard Business School Press, 2002.

————. *Leadership without Easy Answers*. Harvard Univ. Press, 1994.

————. *The Practice of Adaptive Leadership*. Harvard Business Press, 2009.

Kotter, John P. *Leading Change*. Harvard Business School Press, 1996.

Morgan, Gareth. *Images of Organization*. Sage, 2006.

————. *Imaginization: New Mindsets for Seeing, Organizing and Managing*. Sage, 1997.

Pascale, Richard et al. *Surfing the Edge of Chaos: The Laws of Nature and the New Laws of Business*. Three Rivers Press, 2001.

Global Issues

Jenkins, Philip. *The Next Christendom: The Coming of Global Christianity*. Oxford Univ. Press, 2002.

Nouwen, Henri. *In the Name of Jesus: Reflections on Christian Leadership*. Crossroad, 1989.

Roberts, Bob. *Glocalization: How Followers of Jesus Engage a Flat World*. Zondervan, 2007.

Sachs, Jeffrey. *The End of Poverty: Economic Possibilities for Our Time*. Penguin, 2005.

Volf, Miroslav. *Exclusion and Embrace: A Theological Exploration of Identity, Otherness, and Reconciliation*. Abingdon, 1996.

Zarkaria, Fareed. *The Post-American World*. W.W. Norton & Co., 2009.

Early Church

The gospel of Luke, and the book of Acts.

Cole, Neil. *Journeys to Significance: Charting a Leadership Course from the Life of Paul*. Jossey-Bass, 2011.

Schnabel, Eckhard J. *Early Christian Mission: Jesus and the Twelve*, vol. 1. IVP Academic, 2004.

————. *Early Christian Mission: Paul and the Early Church*, vol. 2. IVP Academic, 2004.

————. *Paul the Missionary: Realities, Strategies and Methods*. IVP Academic, 2008.